CONTEMPORARY COMMUNITY HEALTH SERIES

THE SOCIOLOGY OF PHYSICAL
DISABILITY AND REHABILITATION

THE SOCIOLOGY
OF PHYSICAL

University of Pittsburgh Press

DISABILITY AND REHABILITATION

Gary L. Albrecht

EDITOR

To Maryann, Jeff, Stephanie, and Dave

Copyright © 1976, University of Pittsburgh Press
All rights reserved
Feffer and Simons, Inc., London
Manufactured in the United States of America
Paperback reprint 1982

Library of Congress Cataloging in Publication Data

Main entry under title:

The Sociology of physical disability and rehabilitation.

(Contemporary community health series)
Includes bibliographies and index.
1. Physically handicapped—Rehabilitation—United States—Addresses, essays, lectures. 2. Physically handicapped—United States—Addresses, essays, lectures. I. Albrecht, Gary L. II. Series.
HV3023.A3S62   362.4   75–33544
ISBN 0–8229–3312–8
ISBN 0–8229–5341–2 (pbk.)

Contents

Preface *ix*

Acknowledgments *xiii*

1 Socialization and the Disability Process
  Gary L. Albrecht *3*

2 Disabled Persons' Self-Definitions and Their
  Implications for Rehabilitation
  Constantina Safilios-Rothschild *39*

3 Societal Reaction Theory and Disability
  Walter R. Gove *57*

4 A Behavioral Perspective on Rehabilitation
  Wilbert E. Fordyce *73*

5 Coping and Adaptive Behaviors of the Disabled
  Israel Goldiamond *97*

6 Conceptual Model of Family as a Group: Family
  Response to Disability
  Betty E. Cogswell *139*

7 Disability and Stratification Processes
  Karl L. Alexander *169*

8 The Political Sociology of Rehabilitation
  Elliott A. Krause *201*

9 The Disabled and the Rehabilitation System
  Marvin B. Sussman *223*

10   Some Notes on Rehabilitation and Models for
     Interdisciplinary Collaboration
     Rodney M. Coe   247
11   Social Policy and the Management of Human Resources
     Gary L. Albrecht   257

Contributors   289
Name Index   291
Subject Index   298

Preface

This book brings current behavioral science thinking to the field of physical disability and rehabilitation. The contributions were written specifically for the book by knowledgeable behavioral scientists who are applying their present understanding of the theory and application of social science research to the study of physical disability and rehabilitation. The presentations have been enriched by considerable discussion of each paper by academic colleagues and health practitioners. Therefore, the tenor and thrust of the papers embody reactions to many viewpoints, and in some respects are the result of a vital interchange between academics of different persuasions and experienced health professionals. The book both presents current thinking and reflects the vitality of the field.

There is genuine consensus on some issues, while others provoked heated controversy. For this reason, the reader may find himself agreeing with an author at one point and disagreeing at another. This state of affairs reflects the development of the field. Some facts are commonly accepted, while other issues are open to exploration, argument, and tentative explanation. Although most authors agree that the primary focus of attention should be actual patient care and behavior, there are numerous approaches to the study of this behavior. Both the behaviorist and the macrosociological perspectives on understanding individual response to disability are represented in the volume. The effect of expectations and labeling upon patient behavior; the learning of adaptive responses; the amount of patient involvement in the rehabilitation process; the effect of environment on patient performance; the interplay of policies, programs and politics; and the translation of behavioral science knowledge into management objectives, cost accountability, and diffusion of information are some of the major issues discussed.

The book is not an aggregation of papers written for other sources or an integrated text that attempts to produce compromises from divergent viewpoints and conflicting data. It does raise the major issues that behavioral scientists see in the field of physical disability and rehabilitation, and, it is hoped, will stimulate the reader to serious thought and reflection.

Considerable research and theory in the social sciences has been developed on the basis of institutional records and behavioral observations in mental health facilities. While mental illness is a major concern of the medical profession, the volume and severity of problems associated with heart attack, stroke, cancer and traumatic injury warrant equal, if not more, attention. Even though there are psychosomatic aspects to any medical problem, a large number of individuals who present serious symptoms to the examining physician do have observable physical conditions that require treatment. Therefore, it seems appropriate that social scientists apply their knowledge to and test their theories on individuals with observable physical problems, that is, individuals who experience either short-lived or chronic physical disabilities and who undergo rehabilitation.

In the first chapter, Albrecht describes the extent and the impact of physical disability in the United States. He examines rehabilitation as a socialization process in which the established interactional patterns between the individual, others, institutions, and society are dramatically affected by disability. Safilios-Rothschild raises the problems that an individual confronts in being labeled physically disabled or handicapped. She indicates that, in many respects, the effects of labeling seem detrimental to the individual in need. On the other hand, Gove points out that, if a person is not labeled, he is not likely to receive rehabilitation help. The label identifies the person in need and justifies his entry into the system designed to assist him. Fordyce discusses ways in which the treatment effectiveness of the rehabilitation system can be improved by the use of behavioral techniques. He also explores how these techniques can be applied in family, community, and societal settings. The behavioral perspective is also taken by Goldiamond, who describes and analyzes his own accident, hospitalization, disability, and rehabilitation experiences. He describes how he used behavioral techniques to achieve his rehabilitation goals.

Cogswell shifts emphasis away from the individual and onto the family as a unit of analysis. Using artistic as well as scientific sources, she develops a conceptual approach for observing families which are coping with a disabled member. The family is also considered by Alexander, who attempts to incorporate disability into structural models developed in the status achievement literature. First he studies some of the interacting variables that contribute to the etiology of and susceptibility to disability. Then he treats disability as a variable that affects class and status changes. Krause also looks at the etiology of disability, emphasizing class susceptibility. He focuses on the institutional and bureaucratic practices that cause and perpetuate disability for the lower and working classes. Krause argues that vested political and economic interest groups actually encourage unhealthy and unsafe environments and obstruct improvements in the rehabilitation system. Sussman shares Krause's interest in the effects of the political and economic climate on the rehabilitation system. He analyzes the relationships between the government, rehabilitation agencies, and the client-consumer.

The interdisciplinary character of rehabilitation is underscored by Coe. He contends that new models for the delivery of rehabilitation services are needed if the patient is to receive the integrated complement of treatments necessary for rehabilitation. Coe argues that these new models require interdisciplinary cooperation and training experiences extending over the traditional boundaries between professions and institutions. Albrecht concludes the book with a chapter showing the effect of social policies on rehabilitation.

These chapters provide the reader with an insight into the sociology of physical disability and rehabilitation. The book offers the reader an overview of a field. At the same time, it is an invitation for further investigations in a field of research and treatment that is both fertile and topical.

GARY L. ALBRECHT
Northwestern University

Acknowledgments

This book is the result of the ideas and energies of many people. A verbal and written dialogue developed between the authors and readers of sequential versions of the manuscript. The book is the result of that dialogue.

While the editor and the authors bear final responsibility for the product, Ronald Andersen, Pauline Bart, Howard Becker, Rue Bucker, Ronald Crawford, Fred Davis, David Featherman, Geoffrey Gibson, Howard Kelman, Bernard Kutner, Theodor Litman, Harold Lyon, Richard O'Toole, Stephan Richardson, Paul Roman, Julius Roth, Ethel Shanas, G. E. Ned Sharples, Richard T. Smith, Carole Tokarczyk, Charles Tucker, Albert Wesson, Robert Wilson, Robert Winch, Rachelle Zalman, and Irving Zola responded in detail to parts of the manuscript. Byron B. Hamilton supported the project from the beginning and improved the quality of the results by carefully questioning unsupported arguments.

The book was made possible by support from the American Sociological Association and from DHEW-SRS Medical Rehabilitation Research and Training Center Number 20 (Grant No. 16-P56 80/5-07). Henry B. Betts and Don A. Olson of Northwestern University and the Rehabilitation Institute of Chicago and Richard H. Kessler of Northwestern University encouraged the development of the book and helped to overcome obstacles in its development. Rochelle Coonley and Alice Kapuscinski typed numerous versions of the manuscript. Frederick A. Hetzel, the

Director of the University of Pittsburgh Press, offered the consistent support that moved the book into print.

Numerous disabled persons applied the reality test to the theory and research presented in the book. Without these people the book would have no meaning.

THE SOCIOLOGY OF PHYSICAL
DISABILITY AND REHABILITATION

CHAPTER 1

Socialization and the Disability Process

Gary L. Albrecht

The Impact of Physical Disability on the Socialization Process

While most people anticipate that they will be injured or even suffer from a disease at some point in their lives, few individuals foresee that they will ever be disabled. Pain and discomfort are expected with injury and disease, but the implications of chronic incapacitation are seldom anticipated, let alone understood. Individuals realize that injury and disease might require medical treatment, perhaps even surgery, followed by short-term rest and recuperation, but they also expect that they will soon be able to resume their former levels of activity. The fact is that a large percentage of Americans experience sustained disability for which they are not prepared.

One of the anomalies of modern medicine is that patients, families, and medical staff are not prepared to accept the consequences of injury and disease conditions found in industrialized countries. Because of medical advances, victims of serious accidents, coronary infarctions, cancer, and respiratory diseases now live for years beyond the time of the trauma or the onset of the disease (Glazier, 1973). Yet most people expect these individuals to die within a short time and are not prepared for the prolonged years of life in altered conditions (Morison, 1973; White, 1973). In some senses, the patients are treated as living dead. The patients and those around them are not socially and psychologically ready to cope with the chronic medical conditions. There is a demonstrated capacity in modern medical practice to prolong life, but there is difficulty in adjusting to this technological change. The extension of life implies learning to live with the chronic condition. Disability is most often physical and requires a complete reorientation of roles by the individual and his family and friends. Disability has a substantial impact on both attitudes and behavior.

Disability has different meanings and different consequences from illness or disease (Safilios-Rothschild, 1970). An individual can have a variety of illnesses and diseases but not be disabled. Both injuries and diseases are classified by diagnostic categories, which for purposes of examining behavior and its consequences are not as useful as operational measures of level of physical function (Haber, 1971). For this reason, increasing attention is being given to the functional limitations resulting from pathological conditions (Haber, 1973). Disability refers to limitations in the kind and amount of individual physical and mental function. Since many of the studies of disability have been sponsored by the Social Security Administration, much of the empirical research on disability has been operationalized in terms of work limitations (Haber, 1968).

There is some dispute over the incidence and prevalence of disability in the United States. The discrepancies in the results of various surveys are probably caused by measurement and sampling errors and by differences in data-collection instruments, identification procedures, and target populations. While National Health Interview Surveys are based on the entire noninstitutionalized U.S. population and are aimed at assessing the health of the country, the Social Security Survey is directed at identifying disability and its consequences in noninstitutionalized members of the labor force aged eighteen to sixty-four. Although the statistics presented by these surveys vary considerably across time and between studies, the data consistently show that large numbers of American adults are physically limited for long periods of time in their everyday activities.

The U.S. National Health Interview Survey conducted from July 1, 1957, to June 30, 1961, indicated that 7.3 percent of the noninstitutionalized U.S. population was seriously limited in such major activities as working, keeping house, or going to school and 10.4 percent was seriously limited if recreational, social and civic activities were included (U.S. Department of Health, Education, and Welfare, 1963). In 1971, Health Survey results showed that approximately 12.3 percent of the U.S. population reported some degree of functional disability, more than 8 percent was limited in a major activity, and 10.5 percent had had at least one hospital stay during the preceding year. According to the 1966 Social Security Survey, 17.2 percent of the noninstitutionalized population aged eighteen to sixty-four was disabled six months or longer. Of these 17.9 million disabled persons, only 7.2 percent had mental disabilities (Haber, 1971:472).

Each of the studies shows a strong relationship between disability and age. While less than 3 percent of the persons under seventeen years of age in the 1971 Health Interview Survey reported some limitation, 44 percent of the persons sixty-five years and over reported activity limitation by one or more chronic conditions (U.S. Department of Health, Education, and Welfare, 1973). The same data show that disabilities are likely to be more limiting and last for longer periods of time as a person grows older. Other studies suggest that disability is disproportionately found among older, male, nonwhite, lower- and working-class populations (Nagi, 1969).

While these statistics are sobering, they do not reflect the institutionalized population in the United States, nor do they usually include disability caused by alcoholism and mental retardation. It is likely that every family in the United States will be affected at one time or another by some form of chronic physical disability.

The Consequences of Physical Disability Throughout Life

Conventional adolescent and adult socialization includes the anticipated processes of education, learning a career, courtship and marriage, becoming a parent, developing a set of social relationships, participating in recreational activities, maturation and aging, and dying. Yet many individuals experience and learn to cope with the less expected processes of divorce, having children prematurely leave home and move far away, the deaths of close friends and relatives, losing a job, financial crises, widow-hood, and sickness and disability. Physical disability has a major impact on all of these components of the socialization process because it affects every activity from getting married to finding and keeping a job.[1]

One of the major overwhelming consequences of physical limi-tation is the lack of physical mobility. This lack of mobility pre-vents or greatly impedes the individual from actively participating in the important roles in his life. Limited mobility forces far-reaching role adjustments. If a person cannot drive a car, easily climb stairs, and step over sidewalk curbs, he is not likely to participate in many activities. Architectural barriers present an excellent example of how individual characteristics combine with environment to influence performance. There are numerous disabled individuals who are employable but who are unable to go to and return from work.

A recent follow-up study of four hundred accident-disabled persons revealed that inaccessibility of transportation and lack of physical mobility were outstanding problems in posthospitaliza-tion adjustment (DiAngelo et al., 1973). A Carnegie-Mellon re-port (1968) shows that 82 percent of all persons over sixty-five are chronically handicapped. It is estimated that fewer than 50 per-cent of urban residents over sixty-five do not drive and do not have cars (Altshuler, 1968). The costs to modify cars and insure a disabled driver are considerable, even if a disabled person can drive. As the median income of families with employable hand-icapped adults was below $4,000 as reported in a 1968 study, it is to be expected that 63 percent of the respondents did not drive (U.S. Department of Health, Education, and Welfare, 1968). Age, financial resources, and physical limitations prevent most disabled persons from driving a car.

Public transportation is no solution to the mobility problems of the disabled, for it does not run close enough to most residences to be of use to the handicapped. Most riders live up to 1,500 feet from the route which they use (Peterson, 1968; Wynn and Levin-son, 1967). The disabled cannot travel long distances to reach public transportation. Many cannot negotiate the curbs, stairs, turnstyles, and high steps necessary to get on city buses and trains. Furthermore, they have serious difficulty traveling in large rush hour crowds when the transportation system is operating most efficiently. Thus the disabled are restricted both from driving and from using public transportation.

Architectural and mobility barriers seriously affect the patterns of social interaction of the physically disabled person and subsequently his self-image. Ludwig and Collette (1970) point out that the social isolation and economic and personal dependency that frequently result from disability also influence the person's mental health status. The severely disabled often experience a childlike dependency (Meyer, 1964). The disruptive consequences of this dependency have far-reaching effects on self-esteem and self-concept. After the onset of trauma or disease, the disabled person has to reconstruct his new self-identity through social interaction. The person is forced to ask the question of the symbolic interactionists: "Who am I?" (Kuhn and McPartland, 1954). This reconstruction process of self-identity and meaning for the disabled person is difficult because he has a new set of data, resources, and expectations with which to work.

The disabled individual's redefinition of roles takes place through social interaction with his family, friends, coworkers, other disabled persons, and members of the medical staff. The important difficulty for him is that his disability affects his interaction with others. Therefore he cannot rely on old patterns and role expectations. The disabled person must reconstruct many of his social relationships with others as he rebuilds his roles and self-identity.

Research on the social responses of both humans and animals to physically defective infants reveals much about the interaction between the able-bodied and the disabled in a social context. Turnbull (1972) describes a human society, the Ik of East Africa, where human responsibility degenerated under crowded, stressful conditions so that adult members did not care for their young, old, and disabled. There are other reported studies of social organization breaking down under conditions of extreme crowding. Nevertheless a general feature of human and primate society seems to be that the social organization of the society functions to maintain the welfare of the individuals in it. In a series of field and laboratory studies, Berkson has demonstrated that visually impaired monkeys are not killed by their own group even in crowded conditions (1970, 1973). When food and water are available and predators are not present, the disabled monkeys seem to function quite well in their social group. Defective infants are provided compensatory care during the first year of life by both the mother and the other members of the group (Rumbaugh, 1965). As the disabled monkey grows older, members of the group adapt their individual and group behavior to compensate for his behavioral deficits (Berkson, 1973). These animal studies suggest that social groups and disabled individuals mutually adapt their behaviors after the onset of disability to form new roles and patterns of social interaction. Individuals and the group exhibit helping and adaptive behaviors in response to the manifest disability of one of the members.

Similar adaptive processes are observed among human groups. In fact, the more clearly defined and visible the disability, the greater the facility with which the disabled individual and the group adjust to each other (Davis, 1964). Although disabled individuals are maintained in the society, drastic changes in roles and interaction patterns occur. Goffman has argued that the physically disabled are stigmatized and set apart from the able-bodied (1963). In this context, the disabled frequently feel shame and confusion as they try to manage their "spoiled identities" and redefine their roles.

In a set of experiments, Farina (1966, 1968) demonstrates that the reaction of the able-bodied to the disabled is less severe in a punishment paradigm in cases where the physical disability is both serious and visible than in situations where it is moderate and less visible. These findings are strongly supported in a large study by Zahn (1973) that showed that the more severely impaired are likely to have better interpersonal relationships with the able-bodied than the less seriously impaired. A disabled person's ability to work and hold a job was positively associated with interpersonal relations among nonfamily members in Zahn's study. However, individuals who were not able to work had better relationships with their spouses and other family members. Communication impediments disrupted interpersonal relationships. Zahn found that those who were sexually impaired had better relationships with their spouses than did those who did not suffer sexual dysfunction. In general, Zahn's data show that ambiguity regarding the degree of impairment has the most negative impact on interpersonal relationships. The severely disabled are more easily perceived as having decreased ability, and clear expectations can be formed and new roles developed. When a disabled person has an ambiguous status, where he is defined as being neither sick nor well, expectations are confused, goals are unclear, and roles are contradictory. Social interaction under these circumstances results in dissatisfaction for all of the participating parties.

In actual face-to-face interaction, the able-bodied tend to keep more physical distance between themselves and the disabled, tend to terminate interaction sooner, and tend to feel less comfortable than they do in interaction with other able-bodied persons (Kleck, 1966, 1969; Kleck, Ono, and Hastorf, 1966). The able-bodied person displays less variability in verbal output, exhibits less smiling behavior, shows less eye contact, and demonstrates greater motor inhibition with the disabled than he does with other able-bodied persons (Comer and Piliavin, 1972). All of these behaviors limit the types and variability of social interaction for the physically disabled and provide them with fewer opportunities for trying out new roles and behavior.

With these constraints on social interaction, it is not surprising that the behavior of physically disabled persons tends to be more restrained and stereotyped than the behavioral output of the able-bodied. In this instance, people are a product of their social-interaction environment. The behaviors and expectations of others mold the behaviors and expectations of self.

The impact of disability on the family can have catastrophic consequences for both the individual and the family. Immediately at the onset of traumatic injury and after chronic disease has taken its toll, the resources of the family are seriously diminished. A study of married, low-income males who became disabled to some degree between 1958 and 1965 showed that disability produced an average per family income loss of $2,104, which for this group was more than a 40 percent loss (Murphy and Johnson, 1973). A comparison of predisability income and income four years after discharge from rehabilitation for four hundred accident-disabled persons, revealed a similar 40 percent loss in family income (DiAngelo, et al., 1973). Income loss because of disability often strikes families who can ill afford a large income loss because they did not have high predisability incomes and are now faced with endless medical and drug bills. Because most insurance policies are deductible or have upper limits, the family that has to support a severely and chronically disabled member is often financially ruined.

The burdens of financial pressures and the physical dependency of a family member place stress on the family's social relationships. There is a lack of consensus on the effect that a disability has upon marriage. Some evidence suggests that divorce is not higher among families with disabled members than it is among other families (DiAngelo, et al., 1973), while other data indicate that disability is associated with high divorce rates (Safilios-Rothschild, 1970; Nagi and Clark, 1964). Disabled husband-fathers seem to place more stress on the family than do disabled children or wife-mothers (Deutsch and Goldston, 1960).

Regardless of the disabled person's position in the family, many families react to the behavioral demands made by the disability crisis by manifesting rejection of the disabled family member, exhibiting emotional difficulties in responding to the crisis, and overprotecting the disabled person (McMichael, 1971:144). The most serious strain is placed on the family when the expectations and role definitions of the members are ambiguous and unrealistic (Fink, Skipper, and Hallenbeck, 1968). Familial adjustment to disability is affected largely by the financial resources and the active, realistic involvement of the disabled member and his family in the resocialization process. Families do help the disabled person adjust to his new condition, but they can also impede learning by refusal to become involved or by their ambiguous or unrealistic expectations for the disabled member (Litman, 1972:200-201). Disability affects not only the socialization of the individual with the injury or disease but all of the persons of importance in his life and those with whom he interacts socially.

American Values and Normative Structures

The values and norms of a society direct and influence the socialization process. The onset of crises such as physical disability must be interpreted in the light of societal norms if individual and group responses are to be understood. Values and norms do not determine behavior and produce the "oversocialized conception of man" (Wrong, 1961), but they do exert powerful influences on human social interaction and the entire socialization process. While the exact relationships are not known, research has shown that attitudes, values, norms, and behavior mutually influence one another (Bem, 1970; Rokeach, 1968; Triandis and Davis, 1965). As measurements and research designs are improved, the relationships between attitudes, values, behavior, and the socialization process emerge.

Bandura, Blanchard, and Ritter (1969) were able to demonstrate relationships over time between affect, attitudes, and behavior of snake-phobic subjects. In the process of modifying snake-phobic behavior, they discovered that direct contact with snakes produced more behavioral, attitudinal, and affective change than did modeling or other desensitization techniques. Furthermore, the authors indicated that behavior seemed to have a stronger influence on attitudes than did attitudes on behavior In a large-scale field experiment Warner and DeFleur (1969) showed that social constraint and social distance served as mediating influences between verbal attitudes toward blacks and overt acts of acceptance or rejection of blacks. In another field experiment, Brannon et al. (1973) were able to demonstrate a high correspondence between attitudes toward open housing and overt behavior supporting open housing. These studies point out that, although the precise relations are not yet fully delineated, there are strong mutual influences between values, attitudes, and overt behavior.

The physically disabled person undertakes resocialization within the context of his own and his family's and friends' values, attitudes, and behavior as well as those of the larger society. The dominant values in a society are important considerations in a study of adaptation to physical disability. There is a surprising agreement on what are the dominant values in American culture and society. American society is highly competitive, with a strong emphasis upon achievement and success (Williams, 1960). Achievement and success are measured in terms of income, occupation, prestige, power, and a general high standard of living. Education is valued as a means of attaining these desired goals. With success measured in terms of material possessions, the automobile and television set are special symbols in American society. Americans spend more of their disposable income on transportation and communication than any Europeans (Katona, Strumpel, and Zahn, 1971:171).

Achievement, reflected in the possession of material goods, has a moral connotation. Americans believe that they have a right to be physically comfortable after working hard. The "good life" and material possessions are the reward for a virtuous life of hard work (Williams, 1972). Americans place a high value on democracy and freedom of expression; they believe that any American can achieve if he works hard. The result of this value set is that Americans are more optimistic about the future than are citizens of most other countries. In a recent cross-national study, 43 percent of all American heads of household anticipated being better off four years in the future than they were at the time of the study, and one-third reported that they were better off than they had been four years before (Katona, Strumpel, and Zahn, 1971). The French, the Germans, and the British are not nearly so optimistic.

Americans also feel that they should be actively involved in the world. They value productivity, independence, physical health, youth, and beauty, to which they apply a moral sanction. The good person is judged to have health, youth, beauty, and independence and to be productive. A recent study by Dion, Berscheid, and Walster (1972) reconfirms the existence of the stereotype, "What is beautiful is good." Physically attractive persons were judged to be more socially desirable, to hold more prestigious jobs, to have happier marriages, and to have better prospects for happy social and professional lives than those less physically attractive. Lack of achievement, poor health, and failure connote deficiencies in virtue and morality. Americans are repelled by poverty, uncleanliness, illness, physical limitations, pain, and physical suffering. They place high values on marriage, children, and sexual performance. Recently there has even been an increased emphasis upon leisure and recreational activities (Kimmel, 1974).

These expectations in the American value system operate according to a social clock. A study by Neugarten, Moore, and Lowe (1965) on a sample of middle-aged American adults indicates a consensus that most people should finish school and go to work at between twenty and twenty-two years of age, most men should settle on a career before they are twenty-six, both men and women should marry before they reach their late twenties, most men should hold their top jobs when they are between forty-five and fifty, parents should become grandparents before they are fifty, and most persons should be ready for retirement when they reach the sixty to sixty-five age bracket. These age-specific norms have a major impact on the socialization process. Individuals feel pressure from others and from social institutions when they violate these norms.

Effects of the Disability on Values and Norms

The onset of physical disability is accompanied by a complex series of shocks to the individual and to everyone around him.

The disability is usually the result of some trauma or disease. The first effects are often physical pain, limitation of mobility, disorientation, confusion, uncertainty, and a disruption of roles and patterns of social interaction (Schoenberg et al., 1970). Initial concern is frequently with the question of survival: Will I live or will I die? After this emotional shock has subsided, the difficult process of redefining the situation continues. Who am I now? What can I do? What will I be able to do? What do others expect of me now? Why did this happen to me? These are the questions that the disabled person confronts. Those around the disabled person pass through a similar series of shocks and questions. Their initial concern is with survival, but as time passes they question and reexamine the effect that his disability will have on their lives. The series of shocks set off by the onset of a disability seriously disrupts the lives of everyone who has continuing social relationships with the disabled person. Established role sets and socialization processes are interrupted and torn asunder. At this point the entire redefinition of the situation, reconstruction of roles and social interaction patterns, and reestablishment of the socialization process take place in relation to American values and normative structures.

At best, the onset of disability arouses unresolved ambiguity. Who is to blame? Why did this happen? What can we do? Questions surrounding the sick role and deviancy are also brought to the forefront. The task is to resolve the ambiguity and assign meaning to this very stressful and disruptive series of events.

Ambiguity wreaks havoc on the socialization process and on role performance because no one knows what to expect and therefore individuals do not know how to act. Ambiguity and uncertainty produce stress, which in turn inhibits behavioral responses (Monat et al., 1972). After onset, the disabled individual and his family and friends need help, but repeated research has shown that it is difficult to get help when the situation is ambiguous (Clark and Word, 1972). For these reasons, adjustment to disability is an excellent example of the problems in ambiguity resolution.

When an individual suffers a traumatic injury or is discovered to have a disease, the physician is the person designated in American society to inform the individual and the family. In our present medical system, this communication of information is usually limited at first to the essential medical facts. Yet the questions that disturb the person and his family revolve around the consequences of the injury or disease. The patient and his family do not know whether the person is disabled, the extent and consequences of the disability, how long the disability might last, or what adjustments they will have to make to cope with the disability. A typical case in point involves traumatic injury. When an individual suffers severe trauma, he frequently loses control over bowel and bladder function. If the individual is a male, he might experience not only incontinence but also impotence. Physicians frequently tell patients that temporary incontinence and impotence often occur after a traumatic injury and that full functional return is expected after some time in the majority of the cases. At this point the injured person is cast in a very ambiguous position. Is he sick and disabled or is he well? How long does he have to wait for functional return? Will he ever get functional return? *How* long is long enough? Is this a typical case, or will the individual get only partial return or no return at all? The individual is rendered inactive and confused. His role sets and socialization processes are disrupted. He is cast in the position of comparing information that he receives from the medical staff with expectations of others, the behavior of his own body, and the American values of physical independence and sexual potency.

When the injured person is lying in his hospital bed experiencing pain and confusion, the act of getting up to go to the bathroom, of attempting to be continent, is very threatening. The person is risking failure, defeat, and humiliation. As time progresses, the situation becomes more intolerable because the individual experiences social pressures to perform. People around him encourage him to try to be continent, and societal norms place high value on active body control and cleanliness. His incontinent behavior is what is expected of babies and very dependent invalids. A further complication is the assignation of causality, which is reminiscent of the dilemma posed in Malinowski's *Magic, Science and Religion* (1948). If the patient attempts to become continent and fails, is his failure due to physiological and neurological causes or is it due to his psychological problems and lack of effort?

In-depth interviews with males who had suffered serious spinal cord injuries have raised these issues in regard to sexual potency (Albrecht and Coonley, 1973). After the men had survived the immediate effects of the trauma and realized that they were going to live, they began to wonder about the long-term effects of their injury. There was concern about returning home, about being able to walk and perform everyday personal-care activities, and about being able to go back to work. However, one of their major concerns was with being able to resume an active sex life. Most of the men interviewed had experienced impotence after the serious injury. The fear of failure was very apparent in all of these men. How does a man judge whether he will ever be able to have sexual intercourse again? They realized that an erection is necessary for intercourse but were reluctant to attempt to stimulate themselves because they might not succeed.

A few individuals expressed great relief when an erection occurred while they were urinating or while a catheter was being inserted. Their ambiguity about their ability to have an erection was resolved. Other men reported that they had never attempted to get an erection, have sexual intercourse, or engage in any other sexual activity after their injury because they were sick, seriously impaired physically, and could not be expected to perform sexually. However, their physicians reported that most of them should be able to participate in some forms of sexual activity, and some of them should even be able to have intercourse.

This reaction to impotence experienced after trauma seems to be an excellent example of the use of illness to legitimate failure (Cole and Lejeune, 1972). The male who attempts to stimulate himself sexually and fails is in a difficult situation. Is his failure caused by problems with his body or with his head? Furthermore, the patient is not the only one to raise the question. A man's "understanding" wife may repeatedly encourage him to try. His doctor and other medical staff members may tell him that he should be able to perform. When he fails, he is not only humiliated but confused about the cause of his failure.

Clear definitions of physical capabilities and lucid expectations are not always easy to achieve. For instance, some spinal-cord-injured males can have both reflexogenic and psychogenic erections (Bors and Comarr, 1960). The reflexogenic erection cannot be produced by a psychological stimulus. In contrast, a psychogenic erection is one which leads a man to feel that he is experiencing an erection when in reality there is no physical response. The individual realizes that he does not have control over his own body and that his internal communication system is not reliable. These facts are very unsettling to the person involved. While these examples are taken from the area of sexual performance, the same problems hold true for educational, occupational, civic, social, and familial performance.

These performance problems also raise the issues of playing the sick role and defining deviant behavior. When an individual is severely injured or is told that he has a serious disease, he might know that he will be disabled, but he may not know for how long. Furthermore, he has to define his adjustment to the disability in terms of American values and norms in terms of his own values and past behavioral patterns. In American society health, physical beauty, independence, and activity are highly valued. If the disabled person accepts the sick role, he accepts dependency, the help of others, reduced expectations and performance, and, to some degree, the fact that he is responsible and to blame for his disabled condition (Kassebaum and Baumann, 1965).

Because American values reward independence, activity, achievement, and success as measured by material comforts and physical health, the behavior required of sick persons is antithetical to the behavior valued by the larger society. Not only that, the individual who suffers illness and deprivation is judged to be in some ways responsible for the course of events and therefore to have earned his present-status. This value set and the moral judgments based upon it often produce feelings of guilt and embarrassment in the disabled individual and his family (Kubler-Ross, 1969).

Taking on the sick role is a difficult process for most Americans because it contradicts many of their values. The transition from being healthy to being sick is painful, but it is just as stressful to move from the sick role back to being healthy. One of the ambiguous circumstances surrounding disability involves the time dimension of the disability. Frequently patients do not know how long they are going to be incapacitated. Therefore they do not know whether or not to take on the sick role. If a person is told his disability will last but for a few months, he would just begin to adapt to the sick role when he would have to readapt to being healthy again. On the other hand, if an individual thinks that he is to be permanently disabled, immediate adaptation to the sick role might facilitate his rehabilitation. Uncertainty concerning the length of time that the disability will functionally limit the individual often further complicates adjustment to disability and learning of adaptive behavior. A patient might well ask, "Why should I learn to use crutches, if I won't need them in two months?"

The onset of disability also forces a redefinition of deviant behavior, values, and norms. In a rather short time span, the disabled person discovers that he is no longer able to conform to the values and norms of American society which he probably assimilated during his continuing socialization. With his new set of data and information, he finds out that what was "normal" for him yesterday is not "normal" for him now. He may no longer be healthy, independent, active, physically attractive to others, capable of long work hours, and sexually potent. His income has been drastically cut, he probably has huge medical bills, and he has to learn entire new sets of adaptive behaviors. How does this individual now define himself? If he cannot measure up to the values of society, what worth does he have to himself and others? Now that his life condition has changed, is he still normal or is he a freak and a deviant? The entire question of self-identity and deviancy is faced in the resocialization process.

The disabled person redefines deviancy and values in terms of his resources, his own and others' expectations, and his reference group. What was "normal" for him yesterday is impossible or inappropriate for him today. An individual's success at adaptation to this new condition is largely dependent upon his flexibility and ability to adjust to new norms, expectations, and resources. For instance, a man who is physiologically impotent may decide that he will never again attempt to engage in sexual activity. He is fearful of failure and accepts incapacitation as a reason for not attempting to perform sexually.[2] This person will be viewed as a failure and a deviant by the larger society because he has not even attempted to be sexually active, whereas the person himself may feel that his adaptation was the only proper solution because of his medical condition.

Many researchers and clinicians have assumed that the successful, or "best," outcome of socialization in the disability process is frequent sexual intercourse with a member of the opposite sex (Zubin and Money, 1973; Lieberman, 1971). If this activity is not feasible, then positive value is placed on oral sex, masturbation, and the use of sexual prosthetics. Some disabled individuals achieve the professionals' criteria for sexual performance, but many others do not share the same values and criteria for adjustment or the physical ability to achieve them. Whose value set is going to predominate? A disabled person may have been socialized to believe that oral sex, masturbation, and the use of prosthetics are somewhat deviant. The professionals tell him that, given his present set of circumstances, this is not so. His sexual partner is giving him cues either to abstain or to become sexually active again. His disabled peer group provides a variety of adjustment patterns. His final pattern of adjustment and definition of deviancy will be determined by which set of expectations he accepts and attempts to meet. The same type of issues are present in the disabled person's decision to go back to work, choice of a place to live, and restructuring of networks of social relationships.

Through this process of adjusting expectations, norms, and values to the disabled person's condition, the values and normative structure of the larger society are called into question. The well-adjusted disabled individual is the person who has "normalized" his new patterns of interactions and role behaviors (Davis, 1964). Regardless of the ideal values and norms of the larger society, the individual has taken on those patterns of behavior and values which he finds rewarding and which fit with his new self-definition and the expectations of those around him. In this fashion, he redefines norms in the light of new information and his resources and he views himself as acting normatively and consistently within this new framework. The readjustment of values and normative structures by the physically disabled is an excellent example of the cultural relativity of norms. The disabled person finds himself in a new cultural setting after he has suffered the consequences of injury or disease.

Rehabilitation as a Socialization Process

The disabled person goes through a learning process to acquire new attitudinal and behavioral patterns that help him to adjust to his new life condition. This is frequently described by the term "rehabilitation," which process has unfortunate connotations of patient passivity and dependency. In actual fact, the participant in the rehabilitation process is actively engaged in a socialization process that permits him to become increasingly independent of those around him. Rehabilitation is like other socialization processes except that it is not anticipated, the individual must readjust to a new set of resources, old patterns of social interaction are changed, and the cultural norms that guide the socialization process are modified to fit the new circumstances.

Socialization is very much affected by the characteristics of the specific disability. There are disabilities that result from acute conditions and those which are the result of degenerative disease processes. Disabilities that are produced by an acute episode are usually not anticipated, come as a sudden shock to the individual, and may or may not last throughout his life. On the other hand, disabilities that are associated with degenerative disease usually develop over a period of time, allowing the individual and his family time to adjust gradually to the disability. Chronic disabilities usually become more severe with time and last the lifetime of the individual. Some disabilities result from birth defects or disease conditions, such as some forms of cancer and heart disease, that are hereditary or seem to run in families (Mozden, 1965; Spodick, 1965). When these disease symptoms appear in an individual from a family that has previously experienced such a disease and its consequent disabilities, the disabled and his family are more prepared to deal with the situation.

Various types of disability have different degrees of visibility. Serious facial burns may be highly visible and elicit dramatic responses from others, and yet not be very disabling in terms of physical function. Oral and orthodontic problems may be very disabling for eating and speaking and yet have little effect on social interaction, self-concept, engagement, and marriage (Rutzen, 1973). In these instances there is a distinct difference between the visibility of the disability and its social and psychological consequences. Both of these aspects of disability have a lasting impact on the socialization process.

Physical disabilities are related to specific injury and disease conditions and types of treatment. The type of disability and the type of treatment have an influence on the socialization process of the disabled person. For instance, individuals with kidney failure must continually undergo renal dialysis to remain alive. These people are literally tied to a machine which allows them to live. But the machine, unlike a pacemaker, cannot be carried on the body or kept at home. Furthermore, renal dialysis is very expensive, and there are more people who want dialysis than there are machines. The individual with kidney failure must go to the hospital or clinic on a very strict schedule to spend hours statically dependent for his very life blood on an expensive machine.

The person who is disabled by a coronary infarction is told to alter his diet, begin a carefully controlled exercise program, stop smoking, and avoid stress on the job. Spinal-cord-injured individuals are usually bound to a wheelchair for the remainder of their lives and are therefore limited by the ubiquitous architectural barriers found throughout America. The cancer victim is bound to surgery, massive drug doses that have strong side effects, and radiation therapy. In addition, the cancer victim is stigmatized by society as being condemned to death regardless of what his actual life expectancy might be. Since the constraints differ from one disability to another, the demands made upon the persons involved vary somewhat from one situation to another.

The social class of the disabled individual and his family has marked effects on disability incidence and rehabilitation outcome. Studies indicate that serious disability is more likely to be found among members of the working classes than among white-collar workers (DiAngelo et al., 1973; Nagi, 1969). This pattern is understandable in terms of the types of work and living situations that produce serious accidents and chronic diseases (Page and O'Brien, 1973).

In a study of four hundred accident-disabled individuals who received similar rehabilitation services, DiAngelo et al. (1973) discovered that only 25 percent of the working-class disabled were employed four years after the disability onset and the majority of these had menial jobs. On the other hand, 40 percent of those who had had professional, technical, or managerial positions before they became disabled had similar positions four years later. These results reflect social class differences in resources, expectations, exposure to risk, and job demands, which have significant effects on an individual's adjustment to his disability.

The manner in which a disabled person adjusts to his new circumstances is also influenced by his age and particular stage in the life cycle. A child or young adult who is seriously disabled must rely on his parents for assistance, or his only recourse will be an institution. An adult who is married and has job skills has a much better chance of living an integrated family life and going back to work than does an unmarried adolescent. An elderly person is much less likely to be rewarded for undergoing strenuous physical therapy than is a young married woman who has a husband and children waiting for her at home.

In examining socialization in the disability process many researchers have adopted a developmental stage model. Cohn (1961) suggests that there are five stages of adapting to physical disability: shock, expectancy of recovery, mourning, defense, and adjustment. Fink (1967) claims that an individual responding to a personal crisis passes through the phases of shock, defensive retreat, acknowledgment, and adaptation. In a study on paraplegic adaptation, Cogswell (1967) concludes that the resocialized individual moves sequentially through the processes of abandoning the old role, identifying with the new role, overemphasizing the new role for mastery, and integrating the new role into his total constellation of roles. Finally, Kubler-Ross (1969) presents a five-stage adjustment to death and dying that is applicable to physical disability: denial and isolation, anger, bargaining, depression, and acceptance.

Of these models, that of Kubler-Ross has the most flexibility because she recognizes that the stages "will last for different periods of time and will replace each other or exist at times side by side" (1969:138). Yet all of these developmental models at least partially assume that (1) an individual must move sequentially through all of the stages to become fully socialized; (2) there is but one path through the stages; (3) an individual can be placed clearly in one stage by operational criteria; (4) there is an acceptable time frame for each stage and the entire process; and (5) movement through the system is one-way, that is, the system is recursive. While these developmental models can be helpful in the study of the post-disability socialization process, they can be deceptively misleading by making the process seem simpler than it actually is.

Although the developmental perspective of the disability process is useful and informative, the behavioral model of man which emphasizes the continuous reciprocal process of socialization of the individual and those around him within the context of their environments has additional advantages. Rather than stressing the stages through which the disabled person must pass if he is to become rehabilitated, the behavioral approach focuses upon problem-specific behaviors. The behavioral approach does not imply that there is but óne path to resocialization and rehabilitation success, that individuals can be positioned in specific developmental stages, that the same goals and norms are shared by all disabled persons and their therapists, that movement in the process is unidirectional, and that there are established time norms for moving through each stage of a developmental sequence. A behavioral model of man is based on the establishment of behavior, the maintenance of behavior, the extinction of behavior, and the modification of behavior by means of behavioral principles (Kunkel and Nagasawa, 1973).

Within the behavioral framework, socialization after the onset of disability can be conceptualized in terms of identifying the problems that need to be solved and learning the adaptive behaviors necessary to solve these problems. This behavioral problem-solving approach is undertaken with a view toward the accomplishment of some set of goals. These goals are typically negotiated between the patient, therapist, family, and social organizations such as insurance companies, employers, and government agencies. For most disabled individuals, independence and maximum physical function are the goals of the rehabilitation process. These goals are determined by and interpreted in the light of the individual's resources, his own and others' expectations, and his environment.

McHugh (1966) argues that social disintegration is a prerequisite for resocialization. While this might not be completely true, the onset of disability does in fact disrupt and destroy social relationships. The disabled person and those around him have a monumental reconstruction job before them. Disability brings on an entirely different set of problems that is new to most persons. Values and goals have to be changed and new behaviors learned if the problems introduced by physical disability are to be solved. The success of the socialization process is contingent upon the changing of values and goals, the identification of specific problems, an accurate assessment of resources, and the modification of behavior.

This complex process is facilitated by the reciprocal nature of the socialization process, which involves a set of interdependent individuals and institutions; people are already used to behavioral and value changes because of the changing expectations and demands made upon them throughout the socialization process; every individual is reinforced by a variety of rewards; individuals receive immediate feedback from all social contacts and the environment; and disabled persons learn by observation and vicarious reinforcement. When a disabled person is going through the socialization process following the onset of physical disability, he spends considerable time with other disabled individuals. The social interaction with this peer group and the behavioral modeling that takes place within treatment environments enhance the learning required to alter goals and values and solve the new set of behavioral problems necessary to achieve these goals (Bruch et al., 1973).

Vance (1973) has correctly observed that disability occurs within a social context. While an individual may experience a physical disability, he must function within both a social and physical environment. There is a definite interaction and interdependency between the organism and the environment. Poverty, cultural deprivation, lack of education, and a depressed job market do influence the impact of physical disability on the disabled person, those who are close to him, and society. But the relationship is reciprocal. The disabled person also serves positive functions in society by forcing redefinitions of normality and deviant behavior, creating jobs for others, working at monotonous and low-salaried jobs that others do not want, guaranteeing the status of those who are not disabled, serving as a political interest group to force changes in the American health care system and health insurance industry, forcing architectural changes that make cities more tolerable places in which to live, and redefining and questioning the values and normative structures of the larger society (Gans, 1972).

There is some question about the most appropriate unit of

analysis in studies on the physically disabled. Most research on disability has dealt with the individual as the primary unit of analysis (McDaniel, 1969). Yet physical disability can be conceived of as an attribute of the entire family or of the society (Byrd, Taft, and Kuvlesky, 1972; Hrubec, 1959). Disability dramatically affects the interaction patterns of the family and its entire system of generation and allocation of resources. However, disability also influences the larger society. Whole industries, which not only provide health care, drugs and prosthetics, and physical, speech, and occupational therapy, but pay the bills, are built up around the problems of the disabled. For these reasons, there is an evident need for more disability research which uses the family and larger society as well as the individual as units of analysis. What is good for an industry may not be good for the individual or the family.

Who Is in Control of the Socialization Process?

Much of what transpires in the rehabilitation of physically disabled persons is immediately influenced by the socialization agents who exercise control over the process. Individuals, groups, and institutions serve as agents of social control by shaping the behavior of the physically disabled individual and those around him. The direction of effects in the socialization process is reciprocal. While primary attention is frequently given to the power exercised over the physically disabled by individuals, groups, and institutions, these agents of social control are also socialized by the seemingly dependent client-consumer. Adaptation and behavioral change in the socialization process are in many regards mutual. Families, treatment agencies, and government bureaucracies modify their behavior to meet the expectations and demands of the consumer. The client-consumer is often cast in the dependent role, whereas in fact he is usually an active and/or reactive party in the socialization process. He modifies the behaviors of those around him while they are attempting to modify his behaviors.

Families, others close to the disabled person, and professionals in social service agencies are able to shape the behavior of the physically disabled person through the use of a powerful combination of rewards, coercion, authority, expertise, and social pressure (French and Raven, 1968). In this context, the physically disabled person is most often perceived as passive, malleable, powerless, and without much direction (Bem, 1972; Dean, 1961).

However, the disabled person, the consumer of services, does himself exert power over the agents of social control. If there were no disabled persons, many large agencies would lose their reason for existence. There are large industries built up around the problems of the physically disabled. One method of exerting influence on the agencies and bureaucracies that control these industries is to develop alternative treatments, to draw public attention to the "ripping off" of the poor and the handicapped, to withhold payment until the treatment measures up to the consumer's expectations, to appeal to disabled politicians and public figures for new legislation, to organize and form vocal and visible political lobbies, and to demand an active role in the treatment process. The disabled person might well cry out, "Whose body is this?" If he is the one with the physical disability, why should he not be the most important member of the treatment team?

Since both the patient and the agents of social control do have and exercise power in the socialization process, diagnosis and treatment of physical disability can be better understood as a negotiation process than as a one-sided disbursement of treatment from the socialization agent to the patient. Frequently the goals of the disabled person, his family, medical professionals, insurance companies, and other bureaucracies are not complementary. These basic conflicts about diagnosis and treatment are resolved through bargaining between all of the parties with a vested interest in the disabled individual. No one party has sufficient control over the disabled person and his situation to allow a unilateral exercise of power. The parties are mutually interdependent. The conflicts and mutual interdependence most often result in negotiated settlements that are agreeable to all of the interest groups (Apfelbaum, 1974). These characteristics of the socialization process of the physically disabled are what make the contracts of the behavioral shapers so effective in the treatment of specific problems and the modification of identified behaviors (Bandura, 1969). If the terms of the behavioral contract are clearly defined and agreed upon, the attainment of the goals will benefit each contracting party. Each will reap rewards by fulfilling the terms of the contract and will establish a firmer foundation upon which to engage in further negotiation.

The negotiation of the disabled person's diagnosis and treatment takes the internal and external control of the socialization process into account. The traditional analysis of agents of social control focuses upon the external control of reinforcement. The family and others close to the disabled individual, the medical profession, government, and agencies are viewed as manipulating and controlling the socialization of the physically disabled. Within the conceptual framework of the negotiation process, these agents do exercise social control, but not in the absolute manner sometimes attributed to them.

There is considerable literature which indicates that the disabled individual also exercises internal control over his rehabilitation process (Safilios-Rothschild, 1970; McDaniel, 1969). The research following upon Rotter's (1954, 1966) social learning theory indicates that "the effects of external reinforcement on behavior in various task settings are systematically influenced by the individual's expectations about the extent to which the occurrence of reinforcement will be determined by his own behavior" (McLaughlin, 1971:265). The socialization of the physically disabled is, then, a negotiated process which is controlled by both the external agents of social control and the disabled person himself. Under these conditions any long-range successful treatment requires that both diagnosis and treatment be unmistakably agreed upon by all of the interest groups in the socialization process.

The Confluence of Theory and Application:
Problems for Future Research

Effective dialogue between social science researchers and practitioners in the rehabilitation field is lacking. Physical medicine and rehabilitation is one of the newest and least prestigious medical specialties. Internal medicine and surgery still head the list of the most respected medical specialties. This differential between physical medicine and rehabilitation and internal medicine and surgery is an excellent example of prestige, reputation, knowledge, and research lagging behind need. The overwhelming problems of medical practice in industrial countries are with chronic illness and disease and with the health care delivery systems (Glazier, 1973). Yet there is more knowledge and prestige attached to those professionals and areas that concern themselves with acute care. While the resources of the medical profession are in the area of acute care, practiced on a one-to-one basis in hospitals, the needs are in the areas of chronic illness and disease, rehabilitation, prevention, and community medicine practiced outside of the hospital setting in the community, work, and home environment.

Many of the medical advances of previous decades were the result of breakthroughs in basic health sciences. The problems confronting medicine today such as prevention of hypertension, periodic cancer screening, population control, genetic counseling, dental care, pollution control, elimination of smoking, eradication of venereal disease, and utilization of health care facilities are more social in nature and are not going to be fully solved by research results from the laboratory. Effective solutions to these problems require the utilization of behavioral science knowledge.

In the absence of strong research evidence, much of the practice of rehabilitation medicine has been based on subjective clinical observations by medical professionals accumulated within the walls of a hospital. Yet the disabled person is hopefully being prepared to function in a noninstitutional setting. Therefore it would seem that the training of specialists and the practice of rehabilitation medicine should take place outside of institutional walls. If many of the problems of the disabled person are social, then the solutions must take this into account. Conversely, the behavioral scientist researcher will not be able to communicate well with medical professionals or disabled persons unless he enters their worlds.

Rehabilitation problems are social learning and cultural problems, but they are also based on a complex set of medical complications and physical deficits. The ultimate test of theory is the explanation and prediction of behavior. The behavioral scientist must observe the actual behavior of the physically disabled under varying conditions and for long periods of time before he can make predictions and explanations. Research based on official records explains what was reported, but it may not be an accurate indication of the actual behavior. The problems of the physically disabled span many disciplines. Therefore, the solutions will require the cooperation and knowledge of a broad range of professionals and practitioners.

The fruitful areas for research in rehabilitation are almost unlimited. There are problems of measurement and problem definition. What is physical disability, and how is it related to illness and disease? There is still divergent evidence about the prevalence and incidence of disability. The manner in which the disabled person defines his situation through social interaction with those in his environment is not well understood. The impact of insurance companies on the rehabilitation process is just beginning to be investigated. Whose side are they on? What are their interests? Are the goals of the insurance industry the same as the goals of the disabled person? The interaction of control agents is now being investigated. The entire process of identity transformation and redefinition of deviant behavior for the disabled is also open for investigation. The manner in which diagnosis and treatment are defined and negotiated is not well described or understood. The study of the risk-taking behavior of the disabled has not been fully explored. The full use of behavior-shaping principles has not been applied through the use of behavioral contracts. The relationships between disability and acts of self-destruction are just beginning to be explored. The financial impact of disability on the family is known, but little is known about the social and psychological cost to the family and the community. Much could be learned about the effects of values and normative structures on behavior by an examination of the influence that the onset of physical disability has on norm changes.

There is accumulated evidence that most Americans will feel the effects of physical disability during their lifetimes. Yet because of the American values which have been internalized by many persons, physical disability is unanticipated. Persons with disabilities are hidden and avoided. Discussions about disability and its consequences are perceived as being unpleasant and distasteful. While the immediate causes of disability are primarily physical, the effects have far-reaching social repercussions. The study of socialization in the disability process suggests that rehabilitation is a social learning process governed by the same principles as other socialization processes. Careful study of the socialization process, then, has many applications in the rehabilitation field, and the study of physical disability promises to contribute to a better understanding of human socialization.

NOTES

1. In general "disability process" is used by the various authors to refer to those experiences which directly lead up to and result from the disabling event or diagnosis. The term emphasizes the fact that disability can be conceptualized and understood in terms of socialization over time.

2. While this example deals with the well-documented problem of male impotence resulting from traumatic injury or disease, women who have undergone hysterectomies and mastectomies have similar experiences in redefining their sex roles and sexual expression.

BIBLIOGRAPHY

Albrecht, G. L., and Coonley, R.
    1973. Sexual resocialization of the physically disabled: Constraints of time
           and resources on the adult socialization process. Paper presented at
           the American Sociological Association meetings, New York City.
Altshuler, A. A.
    1968. *The Role of Transit in Metropolitan Life.* Washington, D.C.: Barton-
           Aschman Associates.
Apfelbaum, E.
    1974. On conflicts and bargaining. In *Advances in Experimental Social
           Psychology,* vol. 7, edited by L. Berkowitz, pp. 103–156. New York:
           Academic Press.
Bandura, A.
    1969. *Principles of Behavior Modification.* New York: Holt, Rinehart and
           Winston.
Bandura, A.; Blanchard, E. B.; and Ritter, B.
    1969. Relative efficacy of desensitization and modeling approaches for
           inducing behavioral, affective and attitudinal changes. *Journal of
           Personality and Social Psychology,* 13:173–199.
Bem, D. J.
    1970. *Beliefs, Attitudes and Human Affairs.* Belmont, Calif.: Brooks/Cole.
    1972. Self-perception theory. In *Advances in Experimental Social Psychology,*
           vol. 6, edited by L. Berkowitz, pp. 1–62. New York: Academic Press.
Berkson, G.
    1970. Defective infants in a feral group. *Folia Primatologia,* 12:284–289.
    1973. Social responses to abnormal infant monkeys. *American Journal of
           Physical Anthropology,* 38:583–586.
Bors, E., and Comarr, A. A.
    1960. Neurological disturbances of sexual function with special reference
           to 529 patients with spinal cord injury. *Urological Survey,* 10:191–222.
Brannon, R.; Cyphers, G.; Hesse, S.; Hesselbart, S.; Keane, R.; Schuman, H.;
    Viccaro, T.; and Wright, D.
    1973. Attitude and action: A field experiment joined to a general popula-
           tion survey. *American Sociological Review,* 38:625–636.
Brim, O. G., Jr.; Freeman, H. E.; Levine, S.; and Scotch, N. A., eds.
    1970. *The Dying Patient.* New York: Russell Sage Foundation.
Bruch, M. A.; Kunce, J. T.; Thelen, M. H.; and Akamatsu, T. J.
    1973. *Modeling, Behavior Change, and Rehabilitation.* Columbia, Mo.: Univer-
           sity of Missouri, Regional Rehabilitation Research Institute.
Byrd, F. M.; Taft, E. A.; and Kuvlesky, W. P.
    1972. Black families under stress: A metropolitan-nonmetropolitan com-

parison of human disability in a southern area. Paper presented at the annual meeting of the Rural Sociological Society, Baton Rouge, La.

Carnegie-Mellon Report
  1968. *Latent Demand for Urban Transportation.* Pittsburgh: Transportation Research Institute.

Clark, R. D., III, and Word, L. E.
  1972. Why don't bystanders help? Because of ambiguity? *Journal of Personality and Social Psychology,* 24:392–400.

Cogswell, B. E.
  1967. Rehabilitation of the paraplegic: Processes of socialization. *Sociological Inquiry,* 37:11–26.

Cohn, N.
  1961. Understanding the process of adjustment to disability. *Journal of Rehabilitation,* 27:16–18.

Cole, S., and Lejeune, R.
  1972. Illness and the legitimation of failure. *American Sociological Review,* 37:347–356.

Comer, R. J., and Piliavin, J. A.
  1972. The effects of physical deviance upon face-to-face interaction. *Journal of Personality and Social Psychology,* 23:33–39.

Davis, F.
  1964. Deviance disavowal: The management of strained identity by the visibly handicapped. In *The Other Side,* edited by H. S. Becker, pp. 119–137. New York: Free Press.

Dean, D. G.
  1961. Alienation: Its meaning and measurement. *American Sociological Review,* 26:753–759.

Deutsch, C. P., and Goldston, J. A.
  1960. Family factors in home adjustment of the severely disabled. *Marriage and Family Living,* 22:312–316.

DiAngelo, E.; Hamilton, B. B.; Swarts, P. S.; and Betts, H. B.
  1973. Rehabilitation follow-up of the accident disabled. Unpublished manuscript. Chicago: Rehabilitation Institute of Chicago.

Dion, K.; Berscheid, E.; and Walster, E.
  1972. What is beautiful is good. *Journal of Personality and Social Psychology,* 24:285–290.

Farina, A.; Holland, C. H.; and Ring, K.
  1966. Role of stigma and set in interpersonal interaction. *Journal of Abnormal Psychology,* 71:421–428.

Farina, A.; Sherman, J.; and Allen, J. G.
  1968. Role of physical abnormalities in interpersonal perception and behavior. *Journal of Abnormal Psychology,* 73:590–593.

Fink, S. L.
  1967. Crisis and motivation: A theoretical model. *Archives of Physical Medicine and Rehabilitation,* 48:592–597.
Fink, S. L.; Skipper, J. K., Jr.; and Hallenbeck, P. N.
  1968. Physical disability and problems in marriage. *Journal of Marriage and the Family,* 30:64–73.
French, J. R. P., Jr., and Raven, B.
  1968. The bases of social power. In *Group Dynamics: Research and Theory,* edited by D. Cartwright and A. Zander, pp. 259–269. New York: Harper and Row.
Gans, H. J.
  1972. The positive functions of poverty. *American Journal of Sociology,* 78:275–289.
Glaser, B. G., and Strauss, A. L.
  1968. *Time for Dying.* Chicago: Aldine.
Glazier, W. H.
  1973. The task of medicine. *Scientific American,* 228:13–17.
Goffman, E.
  1963. *Stigma: Notes on the Management of Spoiled Identity.* Englewood Cliffs, N.J.: Prentice-Hall.
Haber, L. D.
  1968. Disability, work, and income maintenance. Report No. 2 of the 1966 Social Security Survey of the Disabled. Social Security Administration. Washington, D.C.: U.S. Department of Health, Education and Welfare.
  1971. Disabling effects of chronic disease and impairment. *Journal of Chronic Diseases,* 24:469–488.
  1973. Disabling effects of chronic disease and impairment II. Functional capacity limitations. *Journal of Chronic Diseases,* 26:127–152.
Hrubec, Z.
  1959. The association of health and social welfare problems in individuals and their families. *The Milbank Memorial Fund Quarterly,* 37:251–276.
Jaco, E. G., ed.
  1972. *Patients, Physicians and Illness.* Second edition. New York: Free Press.
Kassebaum, G. G., and Baumann, B. O.
  1965. Dimensions of the sick role in chronic illness. *Journal of Health and Human Behavior,* 6:16–27.
Katona, G.; Strumpel, B.; and Zahn, E.
  1971. *Aspirations and Affluence: Comparative Studies in the United States and Western Europe.* New York: McGraw-Hill.
Kimmel, D. C.
  1974. *Adulthood and Aging.* New York: John Wiley.

Kleck, R.
  1966.   Emotional arousal in interactions with stigmatized persons. *Psychological Reports*, 19:1226.
  1969.   Physical stigma and task-oriented interactions. *Human Relations*, 22:53–60.
Kleck, R.; Ono, H.; and Hastorf, A. H.
  1966.   The effects of physical deviance upon face-to-face interaction. *Human Relations*, 19:425–436.
Kubler-Ross, E.
  1969.   *On Death and Dying.* New York: Macmillan.
Kuhn, M. H., and McPartland, T. S.
  1954.   An empirical investigation of self attitudes. *American Sociological Review*, 19:68–76.
Kunkel, J. H., and Nagasawa, R. H.
  1973.   A behavioral model of man: Propositions and implications. *American Sociological Review*, 38:530–543.
Lieberman, B., ed.
  1971.   *Human Sexual Behavior.* New York: John Wiley.
Litman, T. J.
  1972.   Physical rehabilitation: A social-psychological approach. In *Patients, Physicians and Illness*, edited by E. G. Jaco, pp. 186–203. Second edition. New York: Free Press.
Ludwig, E. G.; and Collette, J.
  1970.   Dependency, social isolation and mental health in a disabled population. *Social Psychiatry*, 5:92–95.
Malinowski, B.
  1948.   *Magic, Science and Religion.* New York: Doubleday.
McDaniel, J. W.
  1960.   *Physical Disability and Human Behavior.* New York: Pergamon Press.
McHugh, P.
  1966.   Social disintegration as a requisite of re-socialization. *Social Forces*, 44:355–363.
McLaughlin, B.
  1971.   *Learning and Social Behavior.* New York: Free Press.
McMichael, J. K.
  1971.   *Handicap: A Study of Physically Handicapped Children and Their Families.* Pittsburgh: University of Pittsburgh Press.
Mechanic, D.
  1968.   *Medical Sociology: A Selective View.* New York: Free Press.
Meyer, R.
  1964.   Dependency as an asset in the rehabilitation process. *Rehabilitation Literature*, 25:290–298.

Monat, A.; Averill, J. R.; and Lazarus, R. S.
    1972.   Anticipating stress and coping reactions under various conditions of uncertainty. *Journal of Personality and Social Psychology,* 24:237–253.
Morison, R. S.
    1973.   Dying. *Scientific American,* 229:54–62.
Mozden, P. J.
    1965.   Neoplasms. In *An Orientation to Chronic Disease and Disability,* edited by J. S. Meyers, pp. 323–361. New York: Macmillan.
Murphy, E., and Johnson, W. G.
    1973.   The effects of disability on the family. Syracuse University: mimeo.
Nagi, S. Z.
    1969.   *Disability and Rehabilitation.* Columbus: Ohio State University Press.
Nagi, S. Z., and Clark, D. L.
    1964.   Factors in marital adjustment after disability. *Journal of Marriage and the Family,* 26:215–216.
Neugarten, B. L.; Moore, J. W.; and Lowe, J. C.
    1965.   Age norms, age constraints and adult socialization. *American Journal of Sociology,* 70:710–717.
Page, J. A., and O'Brien, M.
    1973.   *Ralph Nader's Study Group Report on Disease and Injury on the Job.* New York: Grossman Publishers.
Peterson, S. G.
    1968.   Walking distances to bus stops in Washington, D.C. residential areas. *Traffic Engineering,* 26:28–34.
Rokeach, M.
    1968.   *Beliefs, Attitudes and Values.* San Francisco: Jossey Bass.
Rotter, J. B.
    1954.   *Social Learning and Clinical Psychology.* Englewood Cliffs, N.J.: Prentice-Hall.
    1966.   Generalized expectancies for internal versus external control of reinforcement. *Psychological Monograph,* 80 (Whole No. 609).
Rumbaugh, D. M.
    1965.   Maternal care in relation to infant behavior in the squirrel monkey. *Psychological Reports,* 16:171–176.
Rutzen, S. R.
    1973.   The social importance of orthodontic rehabilitation: Report of a five year follow-up study. *Journal of Health and Social Behavior,* 14:233–240.
Safilios-Rothschild, C.
    1970.   *The Sociology and Social Psychology of Disability and Rehabilitation.* New York: Random House.
Scheff, T. J.
    1966.   *Being Mentally Ill: A Sociological Theory.* Chicago: Aldine.

Schoenberg, B., Carr, A., Peretz, D., and Kutscher, A. H.
    1970. *Loss and Grief: Psychological Management in Medical Practice.* New York: Columbia University Press.
Spodick, D. H.
    1965. Diseases of the heart and peripheral blood vessels. In *An Orientation to Chronic Disease and Disability,* edited by J. S. Meyers, pp. 25–58. New York: Macmillan.
Triandis, H., and Davis, E.
    1965. Race and belief as determinants of behavioral intentions. *Journal of Personality and Social Psychology,* 2:715–725.
Turnbull, C.
    1972. *The Mountain People.* New York: Simon and Schuster.
U.S., Department of Health, Education and Welfare
    1968. *Employment, transportation and the handicapped.* Washington, D.C.: Mimeo.
U.S., Department of Health, Education and Welfare, National Center for Health Statistics
    1963. *Selected Health Characteristics by Occupation.* Series 10, No. 21. Washington, D.C.: Department of Health, Education and Welfare.
    1973. *Current Estimates from the Health Interview Survey United States—1971.* Rockville, Md.: National Center for Health Statistics.
Vance, E. T.
    1973. Social disability. *American Psychologist,* 28 (June):498–511.
Warner, L. G., and DeFleur, M. L.
    1969. Attitude as an interactional concept: Social constraint and social distance as intervening variables between attitudes and action. *American Sociological Review,* 34:153–169.
White, K. L.
    1973. Life and death and medicine. *Scientific American,* 229:23–33.
Wicker, A. W.
    1969. Attitudes versus actions: The relationship of verbal and overt behavioral responses to attitude objects. *Journal of Social Issues,* 25:41–78.
Williams, R., Jr.
    1960. *American Society.* New York: Alfred A. Knopf.
Williams, T. R.
    1972. *Introduction to Socialization.* St. Louis: C. V. Mosby.
Wrong, D. H.
    1961. The over-socialized conception of man in modern sociology. *American Sociological Review,* 26:183–193.
Wynn, F. H., and Levinson, H. S.
    1967. Some considerations in appraising bus transit potentials. *Highway Research Record,* 197:17.

Zahn, M. A.
  1973. Incapacity, impotence and invisible impairment: Their effects upon interpersonal relations. *Journal of Health and Social Behavior*, 14:115–123.
Zubin, J., and Money, J.
  1973. *Contemporary Sexual Behavior*. Baltimore: The Johns Hopkins University Press.

CHAPTER 2

Disabled Persons' Self-Definitions and Their Implications for Rehabilitation

Constantina Safilios-Rothschild

The Disabled as a Minority Group

Disabled people can be conceptualized as a disadvantaged or minority group because they have a great deal in common with the old, blacks, women, the poor, and other minorities in that they are treated and reacted to as a category of people. They also share with other minority groups the fact that up to now there has been very little direct information concerning their self-definitions. The main reason for this similarity is the popular notion that disability, physical or mental (as well as old age, poverty, the female gender, or blackness of skin color), entails biological inferiority. Therefore, the disabled person is often considered to be less intelligent, less able to make the "right" decisions, less "realistic," less logical, and less able to determine his own life than a nondisabled person.

There is an acknowledged paucity of direct information concerning the feelings, wishes, and self-definitions of underprivileged minority groups. Yet, without gathering sufficient direct information from their target populations, professionals assume the authority to decide the fate of underprivileged persons. Furthermore, a professional in one specific area often makes important decisions about individuals in areas in which he may have no greater legitimate knowledge and expertise (and

This paper profited considerably from the comments of Bernard Kutner and Julius Roth.

often less) than those about whom he makes the decisions (Orzack, 1969; Haug and Sussman, 1969).

In the case of the disabled, just as is true for all other underprivileged groups, different professionals connected with rehabilitation define the self-concepts, goals, and inner motivations of disabled persons and determine their "real" wishes and potential. They often do so either without asking the individuals about their problems, preferred solutions, and alternatives or by openly disregarding all information received from the disabled persons themselves about desirable goals and solutions (Safilios-Rothschild, 1970:141–152 and 216–249).

When the disabled formulate innovative plans, solutions, and alternatives, such plans are usually labeled "unrealistic" by the rehabilitation experts regardless of their degree of functionality for the disabled person, especially when the plans and alternatives do not conform to the stereotyped role of the disabled and the stereotyped sex-appropriate roles. In fact, as Julius Roth has pointed out, "what is commonly considered realistic by professional experts is that [social] construction which helps to enhance their own rewards and their control over other people."[1] Therefore, the goals and solutions arrived at by the experts often serve to keep the disabled within the constraints of the inferior and dependent role reserved for the disabled as a category and to discourage any significant deviations from it.

When professionals deal with individuals in this way, the disabled persons' endorsement of the official, desirable "line," in other words the "acceptance" of their disability, deprives them of their most important right to self-determination and seriously reduces their options in all life sectors. Of course, some options may be curtailed by virtue of the disability. But even then the extent of *necessary* disability-related curtailment cannot always be clearly established because there is considerable functional variation among similarly disabled persons. Hence, acceptance of the disability may imply acceptance of a different set of functional limitations even among people with the same disability. Furthermore, if disabled people are not treated as a minority group, functional limitations usually curtail only a few options, and a considerable range of options still remains. A serious overall curtailment of options occurs when professionals adhere to a stereotyped role for the disabled, which, like sex-appropriate roles, offers a single "appropriate" model of thinking and behaving for the disabled person and precludes a whole range of "inappropriate" options, regardless of the individual's abilities, talents, and inclinations. Thus the disabled are said to accept their disability when they accept not only their strictly functional limitations but also the stereotyped "appropriate" role that implies their being different from the nondisabled and thereby deviant. The individual's assumption of the disabled role implies that he is willing to accept any job, even one inferior to his level of ability, to associate mainly with other disabled persons, and to maintain the status quo.

A disabled social scientist has reacted to the restrictive disabled role as follows: "The lingering notion [persists] that [the disableds'] range of interests and awareness is extremely limited. . . . We hear, for example, references to the 'role' or the 'place' of disabled persons in society, as though there were only one role for them to play, or one place for them to be" (Race, 1972*a*).[2]

Even in the occupational life sector in which disabled persons have been permitted and encouraged to participate actively, they are in fact allowed only a few restricted options characterized by low prestige, pay, and advancement possibilities. Only these few occupational options are officially sponsored and available to the disabled when they accept the institutional definition of themselves, despite the fact that in many, if not most, cases their disability does not objectively disqualify them from a vast array of jobs and occupations. Even in the case of the mentally retarded, many more occupations than necessary are barred (Truzzi, 1968; Orzack, 1969).

One very important and striking similarity between the rationales used to explain the restrictive nature of the feminine role and of the disabled role is the fact that, in both cases, a wide range of options are precluded "for the sake of" the individuals in question, in order to protect them. Thus, women often are not permitted to be competitive or aggressive or to achieve successful or powerful positions because their innate sweet, "feminine" personalities could not withstand the stress and strain that accompany high achievement and power (Safilios-Rothschild, 1974). Similarly, the disabled are cut off from most prestigious and well-paying jobs, as well as from a wide range of interpersonal relations with nondisabled persons, because they are considered to be physically fragile and mentally incapable of functioning at the appropriate level. They, too, are protected from unbearable stress and strain and unquestionable failure. Disability, like female gender, becomes all-important and all-permeating, overshadowing other abilities, talents, and characteristics. The disabled and women are judged solely on the basis of their disability or their female gender and, as a result, are automatically categorized as second-class citizens with very limited chances for self-determination (Kerr, 1970; Wolff, 1972).

There is, however, an important difference between the non-congenitally disabled on the one hand and women and blacks on the other, a difference with considerable conceptual and practical implications. Those who become disabled when they are teen-agers or adults have experienced at least for some years the majority status of nondisabled persons.[3] They have been socialized into the majority status of an able-bodied person and into the prejudiced attitudes toward the disabled. Since the success of rehabilitation has been equated with the "acceptance of the disability," that is, with the relinquishing of majority status rights, rehabilitation entails a highly stressful resocialization process into an "inferior" status. Only the congenitally disabled share with women and blacks the fact that they are socialized into a minority status from infancy.[4]

Minority group socialization of a large number of disabled explains the great emphasis placed on "acceptance" of the disability, that is, on relinquishing the self-determination and choice of alternatives that are rights of the able-bodied majority. While it is very difficult to give up important majority rights, there are strong negative sanctions against deviant behavior. The physically disabled individual is considered deviant by the "experts" if he expresses unwillingness to give up the rights of the able-bodied. Most often, the sanction is severe and clear-cut: no access to rehabilitation facilities, at least those supported by means of societal subsidies, until the disabled role is accepted (Safilios-Rothschild, 1970).

It must be further pointed out that the possession of several minority statuses usually has a compound effect. Disabled poor, blacks and women, particularly disabled lower-class women, have been most often barred from vocational rehabilitation programs as "bad rehabilitation risks" (Safilios-Rothschild, 1970:216–249). Even if they are accepted, they tend to have few rights and few choices and to be totally controlled by the rehabilitation professionals (Roth and Eddy, 1967).

In contrast, it seems that high social status is an overriding characteristic whose desirability can outweigh the undesirability of several other characteristics including disability. In fact, high-status disabled people are most often able to retain their majority status rights and to become rehabilitated on their own terms. This deviance is possible either because they are tolerated as a function of their high status and prestige or because they can reject altogether the institutional societal rehabilitation system and buy whatever rehabilitation services they deem desirable and compatible with their needs (Scott, 1970; Krause, 1972). In addition, in some cases disabled persons of high social status (for example, disabled physicians or nurses) possess pertinent knowledge that enables them to exert considerable control over their fate.

The Disabled as a Social Movement

Until now, the disabled, like other minorities during stages of oppression, have had low self-esteem and "have been reticent to speak out on behalf of their own . . . cause" (Race, 1972*a*). This can be explained on the basis of several convergent conditions:

1. The stereotyped beliefs about the limited mental and physical capacities of the disabled and the inferior status assigned to them have had a considerably negative effect on the self-confidence and self-esteem of the disabled. This result is partly due to internalization of stereotyped beliefs by the disabled and partly due to widespread sets of social-structural barriers. The disabled, unable to generate sufficient self-esteem and self-confidence, could not effectively question, demand and protest (Race, 1972*b*).

2. There has been a hostile and unaccepting atmosphere for the disabled, in which their words, wishes, and plans have been scrutinized, questioned, doubted, and finally rejected as inappropriate and unrealistic. In order to stand up for their rights, needs, preferences, and potentials under these conditions, the disabled had to possess special interpersonal skills as well as a high degree of self-confidence and a clear definition of their own goals. Many, if not most, of the disabled did not possess such skills and confidence.

3. Disabled persons often have unclear, fluctuating, and occasionally contradictory self-definitions and goals, partly because of their experience of the disability. Furthermore, most disabled persons are subject to alienating conditions from the time that they incur the disabling illness or accident, especially if their disability is compensable. They are exposed to the often contradictory advice, plans, and goals imposed upon them by a variety of professionals, societal agents, as well as by family members and significant others with very different interests and motivations. Under such conflictful circumstances, some of the disabled may in fact become alienated in all senses of the term, submitting to the dictates of the most powerful expert as a function of their feelings of meaninglessness and powerlessness in the situation.

4. The very few "token" cases of exceptionally intelligent and talented disabled persons who were allowed to succeed in the "majority world" have had to play the "majority game" as well as or even better than the majority group members. That is, they

had to adhere, at least verbally and officially, to the stereotyped disabled role and were flattered to believe that their "extraordinary" achievement was the result of special, unusual skills, abilities, and conditions that could not be generalized to all disabled persons. Thus, the few successful disabled people were psychologically and structurally isolated and alienated from the larger body of disabled persons so that they never became representatives and spokesmen for the disabled (Safilios-Rothschild, 1974).

During the last few years, however, disabled persons with high social status and educational attainments not only have refused the stereotyped disabled role and minority status but also have successfully set and realized their own conditions and expectations. They have verbalized and written protests against and critical analyses of the status quo of rehabilitation.[5] This development is significant because it satisfies one of the important conditions for the creation of a social movement of the disabled: the willingness of the elite members among the disabled to identify with the mass of the disabled, to protest against undesirable aspects of their common experiences, and to fight along with all the disabled against discriminatory practices in order to broaden the range of options available to them. The growth of this leadership, the occurrence of public hearings on rehabilitation held by informed parties,[6] sporadic protest marches and demonstrations like the six-mile march and Capitol rally demanding "civil rights for the handicapped" (Martin, 1972), and a two-week hunger strike by a protesting disabled woman in Paris,[7] all are promising signs of a developing social movement.

The time may be ripe for the disabled to generate a social movement patterned after the at least partially successful examples of the Black Movement and the Women's Movement. Of course, as it has been pointed out elsewhere, the disabled represent an unusually fragmentary group in which some persons with nonvisible disabilities are prejudiced against those with visible disabilities (Safilios-Rothschild, 1970:173–176). It could be predicted, therefore, that the visibly disabled persons will most probably lead the social movement of the disabled, to be gradually followed by all other disabled as awareness is raised. The movement should gain more members and momentum as successes occur and it becomes clear that all categories of disabled can benefit from joining an organized protest movement.

The Nature of the Self-Definitions
and Their Implications for Rehabilitation

The new awareness among disabled persons, especially among the well-educated, high-status disabled, has produced some eloquent biographical statements. For example, a social scientist disabled since early adolescence has critically analyzed his experience and described his self-definition as follows:

Unfortunately, those people whose task was to rehabilitate me had also made certain assumptions about me and the world I was to inhabit after I left the home [rehabilitation facility]. The assumption about me was simple: I should be grateful for whatever existence I could scrape together. After all, there had been a time when my life itself had been forfeit and, compared to many of my peers in the ward, I was relatively functional. About the world, the assumption was equally simple—although here, perhaps, less forgivable. Society existed. Whatever it meted out to the cripple, the cripple accepted. The way of the world was not to be challenged. . . .
    Once [the disabled] has accepted being pigeonholed by society, he finds that he is safe as long as he is willing to live within the boundaries of his categorization. . . . He is expected to behave in such-and-such a way; he is expected to react in the following manner to the following stimulus. . . . He reacts as he is expected to react because he does not really accept the idea that he can react in any other way. Once he accepts, however unconsciously, the images of self that his society presents to him, then the guidelines for his behavior are clearcut and consistent. (Kriegel, 1969)

The following self-definition of a disabled professional nurse also speaks quite eloquently, this time with the voice of protest:

After much thought I began to understand why I felt insulted and angry at the request to "accept your disability." Acceptance implies the result of a choice with the option to refuse. We are not injured or diseased and handicapped by choice, Why should we be made to feel obligated to accept?

Searching, learning, and trying for the new and better come through dissatisfaction with what is, not acceptance. For lack of a better word, I use cope as a more positive term. It denotes a continuous struggle with some hope of a success on a long list titled "I can do."

In coping, my self-set goals are often higher than those that others would set for me. I often achieve my goals because I cannot accept the restriction of those standardized and imposed ones. But it seems strange to me that, when I succeed, I am commended for "accepting my disability so well." Accept my disability? Never. (Jones, 1972)

What are the implications of these self-definitions for rehabilitation, that is, what changes would have to be brought about in order to satisfy the disabled persons' conditions and requirements? The main issue pointed out by the disabled and by some rehabilitation practitioners is the need to diminish the social distance between experts and nonexperts and thereby to decrease the degree of control exerted by the former over the latter (Leviton, 1972). The existing social distance is legitimized by a model specifying that the expert has all the pertinent and valid information while the nonexpert has none. Hence, the decision of the expert can be legitimately imposed upon the nonexpert client without any challenge or scrutiny on the part of the client and his significant others.

In order to diminish the social distance between expert and nonexpert, the model must be changed to assume only a difference of degree and type of knowledge between the expert and nonexpert. Thus, the nonexperts would be legitimized to contribute their knowledge of their own idiosyncratic reactions, preferences, and choices as supplementary to the scientific expertise. Even in the technical-medical expertise area, the nonexperts might be able to contribute valuable "tips" that they have discovered through continuous trial and error and that might or might not have a broader application (Leviton, 1972).

This basic change in the model of the rehabilitation expert–disabled client relationship touches the core power-control issue in which much professional interest is invested. The decreased social distance between experts and nonexperts and the legitimation of nonexpert knowledge would facilitate the sharing of power and control between experts and clients. Because of this, the resistance on the part of the professionals is great, although, as a recent study indicates, at least some of them, particularly those in new and less powerful rehabilitation professions, are amenable to the idea of this new model (Leviton, 1972). Most probably, both the professional experts and the clients need special training and reorientation in order to function adequately within such a radically different role model. Indeed, the foregoing model of the rehabilitation expert–disabled client relationship entails a number of specific changes in the rehabilitation process and interaction that must be examined in detail.

First, rehabilitation would have to be redefined from a treatment process to a teaching experience in which the rehabilitation practitioners are showing the disabled ways to cope with and control their disability and to utilize available rehabilitation resources and personnel, whenever such aid is needed. This change would be significant in that it would tend to diminish the social distance between the expert and the client through the transmission of knowledge relevant to the client's condition, treatment, and exercise of control. Furthermore, it would also help alter the rehabilitation definition and focus from aiding the disabled to become as functional as possible in a rehabilitation setting to teaching the disabled to actively cope with their disability throughout life. Two assumptions underlie this new focus: (1) The peak of rehabilitation may be reached at any time in any setting, and it is largely up to the individual to bring about the greatest rehabilitation accomplishment of which he is capable. (2) A large part of rehabilitation will take place outside institutional rehabilitation settings and facilities, and the rehabilitation practitioners will be available as consultants and resources at the disabled person's home and work settings throughout life.[8]

The new rehabilitation model assumes a completely different rehabilitation practitioner–disabled client relationship in which the professional acts as a teacher and consultant rather than as an authority figure who orders and controls the disabled. Thus, disabled individuals would enjoy a much greater degree of self-determination and be free to explore different alternative solutions and styles until they could find the one that suited them best. Only through such a radically different rehabilitation model can the disabled escape being cast in the "sick role" and being penalized for being autonomous, independent, active, and inquisitive instead of dependent and submissive to professional authority (Ludwig and Adams, 1968).

This active patient involvement would facilitate a second major change in the rehabilitation process. The expert no longer would dictate but would assist the client in structuring a series of alternative goals and plans from which he could select those most suitable to his particular set of needs. This process would use the professional as a consultant rather than as the ultimate authority on goal-setting. The right of self-determination and the ability to choose among a wide range of options would be facilitated and guaranteed to the client in a rehabilitation process that did not oblige the disabled to adhere to a packaged deal concocted by the rehabilitation experts as the condition for rehabilitation.

Regardless of whether rehabilitation occurs in the home or in the institution, training the disabled would involve explanations of the disability, estimates of anticipated pain and discomfort, and adequate information about alternative types of treatment, exercises, medications and their side effects, treatment costs, and coping mechanisms. It would be essential to offer disabled persons several alternatives that specifically addressed the individual problems of low-income persons, persons with low tolerance of pain, uneducated persons, highly educated and sophisticated persons, and those extremely preoccupied with the status of their health.

This structuring of treatment alternatives for each disabled individual would be expected to stimulate bioengineers to develop new equipment and techniques to meet individual needs (Safilios-Rothschild and Yehia, 1972). Rehabilitation practitioners would have to keep up to date with the available technological innovations that could help the disabled avail themselves of more options. Requiring that all possible therapies and equipment be presented to all persons with the same type of disability might encourage and stimulate evaluation research on differential treatment effectiveness.

A third important change in the concept of rehabilitation would involve the self-definitions of disabled persons. The question raised is, How are the disabled different from the nondisabled? Many of the distinctions are based on artificial societal barriers. Breaking down these barriers would facilitate and enrich the lives of the nondisabled as well as the disabled. A striking example is the required abolition of architectural barriers from all buildings (residential, educational, recreational, and commercial), cities, and roads—from the entire environment. The institutionalization of barrier-free cities, buildings, roads, and inside and outside environments would make life easier for and many more options accessible to not only the disabled but also pregnant women, infants, persons pushing baby carriages or pulling grocery carts, old people, and individuals with broken legs (Martin and Psomopoulos, 1972). The tearing down of social and architectural barriers would, then, improve the mobility potential of considerable numbers of nondisabled people while increasing the mobility potential of the disabled themselves. Certainly, many individuals experience mobility limitations for a short time after an operation or for an entire life stage, such as old age. Much more careful and extensive analysis is needed of the different sets of conditions and changes that could broaden the disabled person's options in different life sectors while having a similar effect for at least some, if not all, categories of nondisabled people. Such changes would implement the equalization of options open to disabled and nondisabled people and would also help "normalize" the disabled vis-à-vis the nondisabled.

Finally, the most crucial change in rehabilitation increasingly demanded by the disabled is not only their more active involvement in rehabilitation decision-making but their actual control of the decision-making process. This latter change would involve a significant shift of power from the hands of the professionals to the consumers themselves. This is greatly resisted by the professionals, who frequently attribute negative and dangerous revolutionary overtones to the desire for such a shift. The reluctance of the rehabilitation professionals, as of all professionals, to relinquish their extensive power and control over the lives of their clients cannot be easily broken. Especially difficult to achieve is the lessening of the absolute control enjoyed by rehabilitation professionals over the specific sector of life in which they are experts, such as the control enjoyed by vocational counselors over disabled persons' work plans or that of social workers and psychologists over their family and life styles.[9] However, one can legitimately question, as some disabled persons have, whether the professionals' expertise entitles them to go beyond the consultant role into determining the "appropriate" alternative for the disabled individual and imposing it regardless of the individual's wishes.

The question of whether the increasing control of rehabilitation decision-making by the disabled will improve the technical quality of rehabilitation is at this point irrelevant since it is not this consideration that makes such control necessary and desirable (Thursz, 1969). There is, however, considerable evidence that whenever disabled persons have a say in, or even better, determine their own rehabilitation goals and plans, they are highly motivated and reach the peak of their potential (Safilios-Rothschild, 1970). Furthermore, as Julius Roth states, the existing criteria and measures for the evaluation of rehabilitation services may be quite inappropriate and may frequently have served as "mechanisms for controlling the clientele, rather than simply being measurements of the worth of the services or the success of the outcome." Roth further states that, when the clients control the services, they do not need an expert to make an evaluation study since they can judge the quality of the service through direct experience. Roth does see that the need for evaluation might emerge, but he thinks that this should be a decision of the controlling clients.[10]

It may be argued that a good evaluation study is always necessary to ensure that all different options for physician-client models are possible and coexist to satisfy the variety of needs and preferences of the different types of health-care clients. Otherwise, the danger exists that one particular group of clients will seize control and impose its own set of preferences, needs, and wishes on all clients.

Disabled persons' noncontrolling involvement and participation in rehabilitation have been attempted by means of milieu therapy, different models of patient government, and ward advisory boards. Advisory boards made up of disabled people, the consumers, can be effective only when they have voting power on the board of directors and when the disabled representatives who vote have sufficient information and skills to understand, evaluate, and attack the issues at hand. Otherwise, powerless advisory boards and uninformed, unskilled representatives can be easily manipulated, coopted, and used as "rubber stamps" for professionals' decisions (Thursz, 1969).

Of course, the only "consumer participation" model that would give the disabled control over their fates would include their option to organize the rehabilitation facilities they need and to choose rehabilitation practitioners who are sensitive and attuned to disabled persons' needs, preferences, and potentials. The opportunity to organize and manage rehabilitation facilities with a great number of practitioners and consultants would not only create new, responsible, and prestigious careers for qualified disabled persons, but would also eventually greatly improve the degree of communication and understanding between practitioners and disabled (Thursz, 1969). Furthermore, the fact that the disabled would be holding the purse strings might greatly increase the practitioners' sensitivity to the needs of the disabled and thus improve the quality of rehabilitation care.

A final very important note concerns the role of social scientists, and especially sociologists, vis-à-vis the fermenting social movement of the disabled. The old question has been, "Should they?" but, as Julius Roth has pointed out, the relevant question is, "Can they?"[11]

Looking at the role sociologists played and continue to play in the Women's Movement demonstrates that the contributions of some (mostly women) sociologists have been considerable. While it is true that these sociologists did not start the movement, their professional expertise has been quite crucial in providing valid, pertinent facts and insights into the nature of discriminatory behavior at the macro- and micro-sociological levels. Similarly, it can be expected that some sociologists (probably those with some kind of disability) will be able to use their professional expertise to facilitate the social movement of the disabled by making sophisticated macro-sociological analyses of the social systems affecting rehabilitation and of the power structure involved. Thus, sociologists can help pinpoint the loci for change, analyze and evaluate the social action strategies of other movements, and help formulate social policy backed by scientific expertise as well as by ideology. Sociologists can have significant impact through their professional role—and not only as political activists—if they choose to use their expertise within the ideology of a social movement.

NOTES

1. From Julius Roth's initial comments on this essay.
2. One is struck with the similarity of attitudes toward the disabled and women. Witness the many conferences, discussions, speeches, and books on the "role," and in earlier years on the place, of women in society. Like the disabled, women have had to accept and adjust to a stereotyped role if they were to receive the approval of men and the rewards men were controlling. This "feminine" role, like the "disabled" role, was restrictive in that it allowed women very few options, namely only the less desirable, less prestigious, more tedious and time-consuming ones (Safilios-Rothschild, 1974).

3. The noncongenitally disabled share with the old this particular characteristic.

4. In the case of the poor, both models are possible, although socialization into the minority status from birth is the most usual process.

5. See also the articles by Wilfred B. Race, who is Director of Programme Services of the Canadian Rehabilitation Council for the Disabled.

6. In Detroit, for example, disabled college students and other high-status citizens asked for a Common Council hearing at which they presented systematic evidence of discrimination against them. (See Don Lenhausen, "Handicapped Cite Bias," *Detroit Free Press*, September 9, 1973.) In New York City, different groups of well-educated and militant disabled persons are becoming organized for political action. (See P. L. Montgomery, "Five Groups of the Disabled Plan City-wide Alliance," *The New York Times*, June 19, 1972.)

7. For an account of the very recent French protest movement of the disabled, see Bernard Guetta, "Le marché noir des handicapés," *Le Nouvel Observateur*, no. 448 (June 9–17, 1973).

8. Bernard Kutner has discussed an ongoing experimental program in which the disabled are bused into a rehabilitation center for necessary treatment but live at home. Some programs include specific "role therapy" for the practitioners to help them emerge from their encrusted professional roles. Through this therapy, clients are also encouraged to assume active roles in the rehabilitation process. These various treatment arrangements could help change the nature of the interaction between practitioners and disabled.

9. It is interesting to note that the "direct expertise" power of professionals has seldom been challenged even by sociologists. See, for example, Haug and Sussman, 1969.

10. From Julius Roth's initial comments on this essay.

11. Ibid.

BIBLIOGRAPHY

Guetta, B.
     1973.   Le marché noir des handicapés. *Le Nouvel Observateur*, no. 448, June
              9–17.
Haug, M., and Sussman, M. B.
     1969.   Professional autonomy and the revolt of the client. *Social Problems*,
              17:153–161.
Jones, J. S.
     1972.   Accept my disability? Never. Letter published in *American Journal
              of Nursing*, 72:1412–1415.
Kerr, N.
     1970.   Self expectations for disabled persons: Helpful or harmful? *Rehabili-
              tation Counseling Bulletin*, 14:85–94.

Krause, E. A.
  1972. The future of rehabilitation research. *American Archives of Rehabilitation Therapy,* 20:19–32.
Kriegel, L.
  1969. Uncle Tom and Tiny Tim: Some reflections on the cripple as Negro. *The American Scholar,* 38:412–430.
Lenhausen, D.
  1973. Handicapped cite bias. *Detroit Free Press,* September 9.
Leviton, G.
  1972. *Professional and Client Viewpoints on Rehabilitation Issues.* Final Report to the Social and Rehabilitation Service of Project 15-P-55183/5, October.
Ludwig, E. G., and Adams, S. D.
  1968. Patient cooperation in a rehabilitation center: Assumption of the client role. *Journal of Health and Social Behavior,* 9:328–336.
Martin, J.
  1972. Why not straighten out an up-and-down world? *Washington Post,* December.
Martin, J., and Psomopoulos, P.
  1972. Human disability and human settlements. Paper presented at the Twelfth World Congress of Rehabilitation International, Sydney, Australia, August 27–September 1.
Montgomery, P. L.
  1972. Five groups of the disabled plan city-wide alliance. *The New York Times,* June 19.
Orzack, L. H.
  1969. Social changes, minorities, and the mentally retarded. *Mental Retardation,* 5:2–6.
Race, W. B.
  1972a. Social action. Proceedings preview—Twelfth World Congress of Rehabilitation International, Sydney, Australia, August 27–September 1:221–223.
  1972b. The roles of the disabled. Paper presented at the International Seminar on Social Planning for the Disabled, Brisbane, Australia, August 20–24.
Roth, J. and Eddy, E. M.
  1967. *Rehabilitation for the Unwanted.* New York: Atherton Press.
Safilios-Rothschild, C.
  1970. *The Sociology and Social Psychology of Disability and Rehabilitation.* New York: Random House.
  1974. *Women and Social Policy.* Englewood Cliffs, N.J.: Prentice-Hall.
Safilios-Rothschild, C., and Yehia, M. A.
  1972. The social implications of new bioengineering technology for the

handicapped. Proceedings preview—Twelfth World Congress of Rehabilitation International, Sydney, Australia, August 27–September 1:215–220.

Scott, R.
  1970. *The Making of Blind Men.* New York: Russell Sage Foundation.
Thursz, D.
  1969. *Consumer Involvement in Rehabilitation.* National Citizens Conference on Rehabilitation of the Disabled and Disadvantaged, Washington, D.C.: U.S. Department of Health, Education and Welfare, Social and Rehabilitation Service.
Truzzi, M.
  1968. Lilliputians' land: The social role of the dwarf. In *Sociology of Everyday Life*, edited by M. Truzzi, pp. 197–211. Englewood Cliffs, N.J.: Prentice-Hall.
Williams, J. I.
  1971. Disease as illness. *Social Science and Medicine*, 5:219–226.
Wolff, I. S.
  1972. Acceptance. *American Journal of Nursing*, 72:1412–1415.

CHAPTER 3

Societal Reaction Theory and Disability

Walter R. Gove

Deviance and Societal Reaction Theory

While societal reaction (or labeling) theory is one of the most popular theories of deviance, its application to the area of disability and rehabilitation has not been sufficiently explored. One of the most fundamental distinctions made by the societal reaction theorists is between primary deviance, which is behavior that may cause someone to be labeled as deviant, and secondary deviance, which is the behavior produced by the individual's being placed in a deviant role. According to Lemert (1967:17), primary deviation "at best has only marginal implications for the psychic structure of the individual; it does not lead to symbolic reorganization of self-regarding attitudes and social roles. Secondary deviation is deviant behavior, or social roles based upon it which become a means of defense, attack or adaptation to the overt and covert problems created by the societal reaction to primary deviation."

The societal reaction theorists attach little significance to primary deviance except insofar as others react to it. As Erikson (1964:11) states, "Deviance is not a property *inherent in* certain forms of behavior, it is the property *conferred upon* these forms by the audiences which directly or indirectly witness them. The critical variable in the study of deviance then is the social audience which eventually determines whether or not any episode of behavior or any class of episodes is labeled deviant." Similarly Becker (1963:9) states, "*Social groups create deviance by making rules where infractions constitute deviant behavior,* and by applying those

57

rules to particular people and labeling them as outsiders. From
this point of view, deviance is not a quality of the act a person
commits, but rather a consequence of the application by others of
rules and sanctions to an 'offender.' "

According to the societal reaction theorists, usually the most
crucial step in the development of a stable pattern of deviant
behavior is the experience of being caught and publicly labeled as
deviant. Whether this happens "depends not so much on what he
does as on what others do" (Becker, 1963:31). Erikson (1964:16),
writing about the labeling process, states, "The community's decision to bring deviant sanctions against the individual . . . is a
sharp rite of transition at once moving him out of his normal
position in society and transferring him into a distinctive deviant
role. The ceremonies which accomplish this change of status,
ordinarily, have three related phases. They provide a formal
confrontation between the deviant suspect and representatives of
his community; they announce some judgment about the nature
of his deviancy; and they perform an act of social placement,
assigning him a special role which redefines his position in society."

Erikson (1964:16) goes on to state, "An important feature of
these ceremonies is that they are almost irreversible." Why might
this be the case? According to societal reaction theorists, the status
of deviant is a master status which overrides other statuses in
determining how others will act towards an individual (Becker,
1963:33).[1] Once a person is stigmatized by being labeled deviant,
a self-fulfilling prophecy is initiated, with others perceiving and
responding to the person as a deviant (Becker, 1963, Erikson,
1964). Furthermore, once persons are publicly processed as deviants, they are typically forced into a deviant group, often by
being placed in an institution. As Becker notes (1963), such
groups have one thing in common, their deviance. They have a
common fate, they face the same problems, and, because of this,
they develop a deviant subculture. It is argued that the development of a deviant identity and deviant subculture will be greatly
accelerated if, as often happens, the individuals are placed in an

institution where the setting and procedures tend to strip them of their identities and define them as incapable and/or irresponsible (for example, see Goffman, 1961). According to Becker (1963:38), "membership in such a group solidifies a deviant identity" and leads to a rationalization of one's deviant behaviors.

In the view of the societal reaction theorists, once this has occurred it is extremely difficult for the individual to break out of his deviant status. As Lemert (1967:55) states, "Once deviance becomes a way of life, the personal issue often becomes the cost of making a change rather than the higher status to be gained through rehabilitation or reform. Such costs are calculated in terms of the time, energy, and distress seen as necessary for change." The deviant has learned to carry on his deviant activities with a minimum of trouble (Becker, 1963). He has already failed in the normal world and now faces that world as a stigmatized person. Furthermore, if he is returned to the community, he will face an audience that anticipates the worst, and he is likely to be placed on a form of probation where the slightest failure will be grounds for reinstitutionalization.

In summary, the argument of the societal reaction theorists is that persons who have passed through a degradation ceremony and who have been forced to become members of a deviant group have experienced a profound and frequently irreversible socialization process. They have acquired an inferior status and have developed a deviant self-image which is rooted in the image of themselves reflected by the actions of others.

The Societal Reaction Model Versus the Rehabilitation Model

The societal reaction approach appears to have considerable appeal in the area of disability and rehabilitation. For example, the widely cited paper by Friedson (1965), "Disability as Social Deviance," essentially applies the societal reaction perspective to disability. Similarly, Scott's (1969) work with the blind clearly fits within this perspective, as does some of the work by Safilios-Rothschild (1970:109–125). Furthermore, when we look at the role of the disabled in our society, it is readily apparent that there are characteristics which fit into the societal reaction perspective. The disabled are typically stigmatized, and their stigma often appears to act as a master status which determines the nature of their interaction with others (for example, Goffman, 1963; Davis, 1961).

Furthermore, the concept of disability has been institutionalized into our social structure, and persons are processed by various government and private agencies and found to be either disabled or not disabled. Those who are found to be disabled are then often channeled into an institutional setting, which may have many of the characteristics of a total institution. Typically, a major focus of the institutionalization processes is getting the person to accept that he is disabled and to incorporate his disability into his life style. Furthermore, one of the consequences of acknowledged disability, particularly in an institutionalized setting, is the development of a subculture in which the disabled person often becomes immersed.

However, as the task of rehabilitation is to "help the handicapped achieve the greatest physical, social and economic usefulness of which they are capable," most persons who work with the disabled probably do not see the tasks they perform as establishing and institutionalizing deviant behavior. Quite the contrary, in their view most of the individuals they work with have serious impairments which make it difficult, if not impossible, for them to function effectively in the open community—at least in the absence of special training. Persons who work with the disabled would argue that they are maximizing the extent to which the impaired individual can function in a normal fashion; that individuals are placed in an institution only when it is necessary for them to receive treatment or training; that getting the individual to acknowledge his impairment and its inherent limitations is essential if the individual is to adapt to his condition and develop effective compensatory modes of behavior; that the proclivity of the disabled to cluster together in social groups is natural in light of the fact that they experience common problems and have similar capabilities; and that, in fact, this grouping tends to maximize rather than minimize the disabled persons' involvement in healthy social relationships.

In short, both the societal reaction theorists and the rehabilitation theorists see disability behavior as largely a product of role relationships. However, the societal reaction theorists, who typically see the social system as oppressing the underdog, view the societal procedures for processing and assisting the disabled as creating and stabilizing deviant behavior. In contrast, rehabilitation theorists interpret the same procedures and processes as helping the disabled individual develop the ability to lead a normal life.

To some extent the differences between the societal reaction theorists and the rehabilitation theorists may be semantic. That is, the societal reaction theorists may simply be choosing to label as deviant the protected and circumscribed role characteristics of many of the disabled, whereas the rehabilitation theorists may be choosing to label the same role behavior as appropriate and effective. By and large, however, the differences are quite real. The question of whether these processes are primarily beneficial or detrimental is, in principle, an empirical question.

Aspects of Rehabilitation: Interpersonal and Formal

Various paths or careers may be followed by someone who has a physical or mental impairment. The processes involved are complex, and both the societal reaction and rehabilitation perspectives have limitations in the area of disability.

A distinction needs to be made between interpersonal reactions and formal societal reactions. The term "formal societal reaction" is used here to refer to those reactions which either are official acts by persons who in some sense represent the established social structure or are actions that occur in an institutional setting such as a hospital or government agency. "Interpersonal reactions" is used to refer to those reactions to an individual which are not tied to the formal social structure but which instead occur in ordinary settings while the person goes about his daily activities. Societal reaction theorists have, of course, dealt with both formal societal reactions and interpersonal reactions. However, in their analysis of the development of stabilized deviant behavior, they have treated formal societal reactions as pivotal. It has been their argument that interpersonal reactions which treat a person as deviant are primarily a consequence of prior formal societal reactions which have labeled a person as deviant.

Persons who interact with an individual who has a physical or mental impairment may adopt one of three strategies. They may make an effort to interact in a normal fashion, they may withdraw from the impaired individual, or they may confront the individual with the fact that he is impaired. It is, of course, likely that persons dealing with the impaired will utilize a combination of these three strategies.

If others interact with the impaired person as if he were normal, this should lead to his integration into the social structure and promote a feeling of normality (for example, Davis, 1961). In those instances in which the individual's impairment does not affect his ability to perform, as is the case with certain physical disfigurements, this probably should be viewed as a positive reaction. However, if the effort at normalization means that certain corrective actions are not taken, these efforts in the long run may be detrimental. For example, the data presented by Lowe and Hodges (1972) suggest that although blacks are as likely as whites to be alcoholics, alcoholism is more likely to be normalized in the black subculture than in the white. One consequence of this is that blacks are less likely to be labeled as alcoholics; however, this also means that black alcoholics are much less likely to be linked into the health care system. As the authors point out, societal reaction theory would view this as a form of "benign neglect"; however, this neglect would appear to be far from benign, for blacks are much more likely than whites to die from their alcohol abuse (Lowe and Hodges, 1972).

The point, of course, is that many impairments are serious and that individuals often benefit from corrective action even if such action involves their being officially labeled as deviant and/or impaired. This is particularly obvious with certain physical impairments; the acceptance of special training by the blind, for example, may enable them to live a relatively normal life.

Attempts at normalization are probably fairly common when persons have close interpersonal ties to the impaired individual. However, if the impairment creates serious and continuing problems, eventually those close to the impaired individual will respond to the impairment. This response may channel the impaired individual along one of two paths. The first path is toward isolation. Here others simply disengage, leaving the impaired individual with few, if any, close social ties. The second path involves directing the individual toward institutions within the social system that specialize in dealing with the impaired. This path may also potentially lead to disengagement, and the desire for disengagement may be one of the reasons it is initiated. This path, however, is probably more typically chosen in an effort to obtain assistance for the impaired individual. Depending on the characteristics of the agencies involved, this second path may lead to the impaired individual's reengagement with those close to him, to involvement in a new group, or to isolation.

From the medical and rehabilitation perspectives, the greater the social, economic, and educational resources of the individual, the greater the likelihood that he will be directed toward the appropriate medical and rehabilitative facilities. In contrast, the societal reaction perspective clearly suggests that the greater the resources of the individual, the greater the likelihood he can avoid being channeled into a deviant role, in this case the role of the impaired and disabled (see, for example, Gove and Howell, 1974). If the resources of the individual are positively related to the rapidity and persistence with which efforts are made to initiate and maintain involvement with facilities dealing with the disabled, the participants see this path as beneficial. In contrast, if the resources of the impaired individual are negatively related to the rapidity and persistence of such contact, the participants probably have a negative view of such facilities, essentially seeing them as a way of removing the impaired from the community.

A formal societal reaction has definite consequences. The impaired individual may come in contact with agents of the community because he initiates contact, because those close to him initiate contact, or because community agents take action. If contact is through the action of officials, it may be the result of surveillance, of a screening device, or of a response to a complaint by lay members of the community. In at least some instances, the response of the officials will be to indicate that the individual who comes in contact with them is not sufficiently impaired to warrant their attention. Such a response would appear to affirm the normality of the individual. However, in most instances we know very little about the condition of the individuals who are rejected by agencies as being not sufficiently impaired, nor do we know much about the consequences of such rejection.

If the individual, after being processed, is accepted as a client by the agency, the individual's impairment has been officially acknowledged, and he has been labeled as disabled. As the societal reaction theorists have pointed out, the screening procedures may take on the characteristics of a degradation ceremony, and the institutional role in which the individual is placed may act to strip him of his former identity and to produce a sense of stigmatization and incompetence.

In contrast, from the rehabilitation professionals' perspective, the procedures of the agency are likely to be viewed as part of the endeavor to overcome those physical impairments, psychological maladjustments, and vocational inadequacies which make it impossible for the impaired individual to lead a normal life. From the point of view of the professionals, if the impaired individual is to be rehabilitated, he must make a realistic appraisal of his impairment. Furthermore, he frequently must renounce what may have become a comfortable state of dependency and go through the painful process of relearning the skills necessary to perform the elementary activities of daily life.

The range of rehabilitation services varies widely. In some cases the disability may be largely eliminated, as for example when plastic surgery eliminates a physical disfigurement or when treatment makes a case of tuberculosis inactive. With many impairments the goals of rehabilitation will be more modest, generally because a cure is impossible. In such cases the ideal goal may be to provide the individual with the tools and skills that will maximize the degree to which he is able to function. For the blind this might involve such things as learning to read Braille, learning to eat in a relatively normal fashion, and learning to walk with a cane. For the paraplegic it might mean learning to use a wheelchair or braces or perhaps learning a vocational skill.

Although rehabilitation may be aimed at returning the impaired individual to a relatively normal role in the community, there is often the belief, which may in fact be quite accurate, that even with new skills the impaired individual will have to live in a fairly circumscribed world. In such cases it may be felt that teaching the impaired individual to live a sheltered existence in a setting where he associates with others like himself may be the most realistic and desirable goal. In some cases, of course, agencies may make no effort at rehabilitation and simply provide the impaired individual with means for subsistence.

A formal societal reaction that defines an individual as impaired and in need of special assistance has implications for the type of interpersonal reaction the person experiences in the community. As the labeling theorists are fond of pointing out, a formal societal reaction acts as a signification process which marks the person as a deviant. This process, in the view of the labeling theorists, structures the way others regard the individual and causes them to treat him as a deviant. However, when a physical impairment is readily visible, it is doubtful that an official societal reaction has much effect on the degree to which persons in the community see the impaired individual as deviant.

In areas where the impairment is less obvious, it is possible to argue that the certification of disability serves to normalize exceptional behavior and to avoid a definition of deviance (for example, Haber and Smith, 1971). Sampson, Messinger, and Townes (1961, 1964) found important restitutive processes associated with mental hospitalization. In short, they found that mental hospitalization interrupted a situation which was experienced as untenable and, in doing so, blocked actions which threatened irreparable damage to interpersonal relationships. It did this primarily by redefining the problem. Initially the disturbed person was perceived as a responsible being who was behaving in an intolerable fashion. Mental hospitalization, however, labeled the person as ill and not responsible for his disruptive acts. In addition, it caused others to act toward the disturbed individual in the solicitous and helpful manner that is appropriate when dealing with someone who is ill. Similarly, research has found that mental hospitalization is often associated with improved social relations (Gove and Fain, 1973).

With certain impairments, then, a formal societal reaction which labels someone as impaired and disabled may initiate a relabeling process by modifying a definition of deviance that had been established at the interpersonal level.

Stigmatization

There is a stigma associated with many mental and physical impairments. From the societal reaction perspective, the impaired are highly stigmatized, and this stigma permeates, in a very detrimental fashion, the way others interact with the individual. Friedson (1965:81), for example, states that the amputee "is pressed to be a 'good Indian' rather than a bad, but good or bad, an Indian he remains and as everyone knows the only really good Indian is a dead one." Similarly, Scott (1972:16), when discussing pity, states, "The pity we often feel toward those who are blind, or crippled or mad, is in reality anger and hatred that has been disguised in a form that is more acceptable to us." A much more benign view is that, when persons deal with those they know are impaired, they wish to be solicitous and helpful, but at the same time the person's impairment makes him different, and they do not know what to expect or how to act.

This latter view is consistent with what we know about many

forms of stigma (Gove and Fain, 1973; Kleck, Ono, and Hastorf, 1966; Davis, 1961). If this view is correct, then a formal societal reaction which labels the person as ill or disabled may establish some of the general parameters for appropriate behavior. Regarding this possibility, it is interesting to note that societies, such as the United States, which have developed formal processes for dealing with the disabled tend to be more tolerant of disability than those that have no such processes (Jordan and Friesen, 1968; Hanks and Hanks, 1948).

One of the recurrent themes in the literature is that stigmatized persons have to take the initiative in defining the situation for others if they are to engage with them in normal interaction (see, for example, Davis, 1961). Rehabilitation therapists could assist the disabled by teaching them how to go about defining the situation for others. Further, they could teach those close to the disabled to construct situations so as to promote normal interaction. However, although officials concerned with rehabilitation rarely deal with these issues in a systematic way, it is very likely that the disabled learn a great deal about interaction strategies from their peers. Thus, a formal societal reaction which brings the disabled together may indirectly play an important role in teaching the disabled how to structure their interaction with the nondisabled.

Conclusion

The evaluation of the consequences of a formal societal reaction to an impaired individual is a complex process. It involves specifying what the individual's life would be like in the absence of a formal societal reaction and comparing it with what his life would be like with such a reaction. One of the keys to this evaluation would be the determination of what the nature of the interpersonal reaction would be in both instances. Such an evaluation would include all major segments of the person's life: his network of social relations, his mental status and self-esteem, his health, and his material well-being. Particular attention should be paid to the degree to which the person's impairment interferes with his social relations, his daily activities, and his performance of instrumental tasks. Detailed evaluations of this nature have not been made, in part because they would require a true control group, which would mean denying seriously impaired individuals the assistance that is regarded as essential. However, even with the limited knowledge available, some reasonably accurate conclusions can be drawn regarding the societal reaction and rehabilitation perspectives.

Societal reaction theory appears to have three readily apparent inadequacies. First, it is the societal reaction position that primary deviance is unimportant except insofar as it causes one to be labeled as deviant. However, it is obvious that this is not a valid assessment of the impairments that cause most people to be classified as disabled. In most instances, an impairment imposes severe limitations on the impaired individual's ability to function in a normal manner. Thus, in the area of disability, primary deviance is typically very important.

Second, societal reaction theory appears to view the acts of agents of the social system as the prime factors in establishing the deviance or disability of the impaired individual. However, it is quite clear that the individual's impairment often leads to an interpersonal reaction before any formal societal reaction has occurred and that this interpersonal reaction frequently leads both to isolation and to the development of a sense of inferiority and stigmatization. Thus it appears that the critical step in the signification process often occurs prior to any official societal reaction.

Third, societal reaction theory has focused almost totally on negative consequences of labeling. However, with disability it is obvious that a formal societal reaction often has many positive effects. These positive effects include such things as economic support, special training, and the acquisition of new implements such as braces and hearing aids, as well as the often effective treatment of such disorders as tuberculosis and mental illness. Furthermore, a formal societal reaction may initiate an important relabeling process. Societal reaction theory would greatly benefit from a serious consideration of these issues, and such a consideration would lead to major modifications of the theory.

Rehabilitation practitioners, on the other hand, are often not sufficiently cognizant of the debilitative processes described by the societal reaction theorists. Rehabilitation facilities often seem to have many of the characteristics of total institutions which are discussed by the societal reaction theorists, and, further, these characteristics frequently are unnecessary. Such facilities all too often have procedures that unnecessarily strip the impaired individual of his former identity, for they too often segregate the impaired individual from the community; and their procedures are often unnecessarily rigid, authoritarian, and ill-adapted to the particular needs and concerns of their clients. Furthermore, rehabilitation agencies frequently do not effectively confront the issue of stigma.

In summary, in a choice between the rehabilitation model, which suggests society should intervene, and the societal reaction model, which suggests society should not intervene, it is clear that the rehabilitation model is preferable. However, making that choice does not mean that societal reaction theory should be disregarded. The processes this perspective points to are real, and they are often debilitating. Disregard of these processes all too frequently keeps rehabilitation efforts from reaching their potential.

NOTE

1. This chapter draws on Becker's (1963) original statements regarding the societal reaction or labeling perspective. It should be noted that recently Becker has developed some second thoughts regarding the generality of his statements (Becker, 1971).

BIBLIOGRAPHY

Becker, H.
  1963. *Outsiders: Studies in the Sociology of Deviance.* New York: Free Press.
  1971. Labeling theory reconsidered. Paper presented at the British Sociological Association meetings, London, England.
Davis, F.
  1961. Deviance disavowal: The management of strained interaction by the visibly handicapped. *Social Problems,* 9:120–132.
Erikson, K.
  1964. Notes on the sociology of deviance. In *The Other Side,* edited by Howard Becker, pp. 9–21. New York: Free Press.
Friedson, E.
  1965. Disability as social deviance. In *Sociology and Rehabilitation,* edited by Marvin Sussman, pp. 71–99. Washington, D.C.: American Sociological Association.
Goffman, E.
  1961. *Asylums: Essays on the Social Situation of Mental Patients and Other Inmates.* Garden City, N.Y.: Anchor Books.
  1963. *Stigma: Notes on the Management of Spoiled Identity.* Englewood Cliffs, N.J.: Prentice-Hall.
Gove, W., and Fain, T.
  1973. The stigma of mental hospitalization: An attempt to evaluate its consequences. *Archives of General Psychiatry,* 28:494–500.
Gove, W., and Howell, P.
  1974. Individual resources and mental hospitalization: A comparison and evaluation of the societal reaction and psychiatric perspectives. *American Sociological Review,* 39:86–100.
Haber, L., and Smith, R.
  1971. Disability and deviance: Normative adaptations in role behavior. *American Sociological Review,* 36:87–97.
Hanks, J., and Hanks, L. M.
  1948. The physically handicapped in certain non-occidental societies. *Journal of Social Issues,* 4:11–20.
Jordan, J., and Friesen, E. W.
  1968. Attitudes of rehabilitation personnel toward physically disabled persons in Colombia, Peru, and the United States. *Journal of Social Psychology,* 74:151–161.
Kleck, R.; Ono, H.; and Hastorf, A.
  1966. The effects of physical deviance upon face-to-face interaction. *Human Relations,* 19:425–436.

Lemert, E.
    1967.   *Human Deviance, Social Problems, and Social Control.* Englewood Cliffs,
        N.J.: Prentice-Hall.
Lowe, G., and Hodges, H. E.
    1972.   Race and the treatment of alcoholism in a southern state. *Social
        Problems,* 20:240–252.
Safilios-Rothschild, C.
    1970.   *The Sociology and Social Psychology of Disability and Rehabilitation.* New
        York: Random House.
Sampson, H.; Messinger, S.; and Townes, R.
    1961.   The mental hospital and marital family ties. *Social Problems,*
        9:141–155.
    1964.   *Schizophrenic Women: Studies in Marital Crises.* New York: Atherton
        Press.
Scott, R.
    1969.   *The Making of Blind Men.* New York: Russell Sage Foundation.
    1972.   A proposed framework for analyzing deviance as a property of social
        order. In *Theoretical Perspectives on Deviance,* edited by Robert Scott
        and Jack Douglas, pp. 9–35. New York: Basic Books.

CHAPTER 4

A Behavioral Perspective on Rehabilitation

Wilbert E. Fordyce

The process of rehabilitation is a long and arduous one for both the disabled individual and the professional staff members who treat him. Patients must face the problems of life with disability, and rehabilitation professionals must deal with the problems faced by the patients. By definition, the best rehabilitation program is the one which most effectively helps its patients cope with the problems of losing and regaining physical and social functions. While virtually all rehabilitation systems have articulated these central goals, many have been sidetracked into dealing with what they have perceived as underlying issues in the rehabilitation process. Hence, a great deal of emphasis is often placed on such matters as patient cooperation and motivation. The traditional perspective on cooperation and motivation has failed to yield effective methods for helping many kinds of patients cope with their problems of life with disability. At times, traditional conceptualizations of motivation may, in fact, become an obstacle to patient performance. Perhaps a new analysis of the goals and methods of rehabilitation is in order.

In recent years, behavioral analysis of human activities has gained much attention as an approach to psychological problems. The behavioral modification approach has piled up strong evi-

This chapter incorporates valuable comments offered by Rodney Coe, Albert Wessen, Elliot Krause, Bernard Kutner, Harold P. Lyons, and Byron Hamilton. This project was supported in part by Social and Rehabilitation Service Grant 16-P-56818/0-10.

dence of its effectiveness in predicting and altering human behavior. In light of the obstacles encountered by physical rehabilitation programs in their efforts to optimize patient performance, perhaps it is time to give the behavioral perspective on rehabilitation careful examination.

The physical, psychological, and social problems involved in the rehabilitation of the physically disabled are complex and interrelated, and a full understanding of their various aspects and stages of development is certainly essential before any treatment model is applied to their solution.

Assimilation of Disability

Perhaps a diagram like the one shown in figure 1 can best describe the rehabilitation process in behavioral terms. The ordinate of the diagram represents what is called output, that is, a person's responses or actions. The abcissa is a time line. As de-

FIGURE 1. Psychological Factors in Disability:
Assimilation of Disability—a Behavioral Analysis

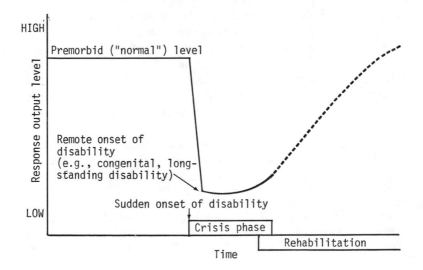

picted, a person's output of behavior is at some level of activity until he sustains a disability. At that point he enters what might be called a crisis phase, and then embarks on the rehabilitation process. Despite its name, the crisis phase is by no means the only period during which there are problems with which the individual must contend.

The disabled person faces four major problems. One concerns the forced entry into the rehabilitation process. A second problem consists of relinquishing behaviors which were appropriate before the onset of disability but which no longer fit; in other words, the extinction of disability-inappropriate behaviors. A third kind of problem is the acquisition of disability-appropriate behaviors, the learning of ways to be effectively disabled. Finally, there are the problems of maintenance of performance. It is not sufficient for disabled persons to learn ways of managing with a disability. They must be able to maintain their level of performance. These four aspects of the disability-rehabilitation process are of special interest from the point of view of behavioral science.

The entry into disability and rehabilitation is almost without exception a forced or involuntary one. The recently disabled person is "asked" to do something he does not want to do; he is forced by circumstances to "play" a disability and rehabilitation game.

Prior to his beginning rehabilitation, the disabled person's behaviors were maintained by payoffs that were part of his way of life. When he begins rehabilitation, some of these payoffs persist. However, the disability cuts off many of these payoffs or reinforcers. In addition, the person must acquire a repertoire of low frequency, low strength, low value, (that is, low payoff) behaviors when he becomes disabled. He must learn to perform actions he rarely did before, actions which previously resulted in little or no reinforcement, actions which he did not value at all. In the light of the individual's previous reward structure and behavior patterns, it is no wonder that such learning can be a difficult task and that motivational or low performance problems are so commonplace.

The Motivational Model

The recently disabled person must deal with a rehabilitation system based on a disease or motivational model, which may entail a number of disadvantages. Figure 2 illustrates this model.

FIGURE 2. Disease-Medical Model View of Symptom Control[1]

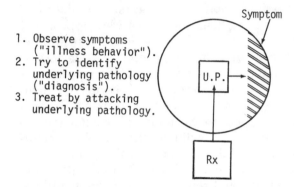

1. Observe symptoms ("illness behavior").
2. Try to identify underlying pathology ("diagnosis").
3. Treat by attacking underlying pathology.

The disease or motivational model makes the assumption that behaviors are under the control of or guided by some kind of underlying mechanism which usually is called "the personality" or "the motivational structure." If his behaviors are not those which are perceived as appropriate and necessary in a given situation, the patient is often deemed unmotivated, motivated by the wrong desires, or even as having some kind of pathological motivation (for example, self-destructive impulses). In order to effect change under this disease model, rehabilitation must presumably change the patient's personality or his motivations. In essence, motivation is viewed as the patient's problem. If he doesn't do the right kind of things, there is something wrong with his motivation.

This conceptualization, as often employed by the health care system and other related systems, tends to cast a patient in the role of child in a parent-child relationship. Of course, the parent role is filled by the professional who tells the child what to do and instructs him in how to proceed with his life. But professionals, like parents, expect the child (that is, the patient) to generate and provide his own motivation (Leviton, 1971).

Finally, the rehabilitation system using the disease or motivational model assumes that when the patient leaves the rehabilitation setting, the maintenance of performance and continuance of necessary activities are once again his own affair. Sustaining motivation is the problem of the patient rather than of the rehabilitation system.

The Learning Model

The assumptions of the motivational model and their ramifications differ from those provided by a behavioral or contingency management perspective, as shown in figure 3. The patient be-

FIGURE 3. Behavioral Model View of Symptom Control[1]

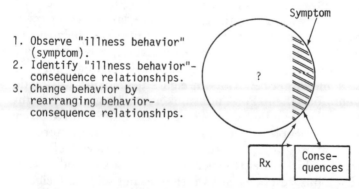

1. Observe "illness behavior" (symptom).
2. Identify "illness behavior"- consequence relationships.
3. Change behavior by rearranging behavior- consequence relationships.

haviors expected by this type of rehabilitation system are essentially operants. By definition, operants are subject to influence by consequences. The logical application of the operant approach to helping a person change his behavior entails rearranging the consequences of his behavior instead of attempting to change his personality or his motivation. Thus, this approach does not attempt to change personality or motivation. Quite the contrary, the strategy of intervention is to change the consequences of behaviors by changing the environment.

A person is helped to increase a desired behavior by employing a strategy that allows the behavior to be followed by a favorable consequence, a reinforcer or a payoff. To help a person decrease the rate of a behavior, two possible strategies may be applied. One is the withdrawal of reinforcers for that behavior; the other is the reinforcement of some behavior that is incompatible with the undesirable behavior. For example, a patient spending too much time in bed might be helped to rest in bed less by the withdrawal of reinforcers for bed rest. An alternative strategy would attach reinforcers to walking, because it is impossible to walk and lie down at the same time.

A reinforcer is something that effectively influences the rate of the behavior it follows. While there is an extensive technology about the definition and identification of reinforcers, the key element is called the "Premack principle" (Premack, 1959). This is the principle, simply stated, that high-strength behavior can be used to reinforce low-strength behavior. A behavior that a person engages in frequently, if made contingent upon the behavior to be increased, likely will serve to increase that target behavior. For a heavy smoker, cigarettes are a reinforcer which might serve to increase some target behaviors, if cigarette smoking was made contingent upon them. For a nonsmoker, smoking is not a high-strength behavior and would not be expected to reinforce other behaviors. For people who like to rest a lot, often encountered in rehabilitation programs, time spent in bed can be a very effective reinforcer by which to help the person to increase some other kind of activity. Thus, rest behavior, which does not seem to facilitate independent activities, may be effectively used as a reinforcer for more activity.

The application of behavioral reinforcers for physically disabled individuals should be used with caution because the interlocking patterns of human behavior are extremely complex. When reinforcement is applied, entire behavioral systems may be affected. Therefore, the employment of behavioral techniques, like any other intervention system, should be preceded by careful study, planning, and preparation. The objectives of rehabilitation are to help patients decrease certain behaviors and to increase certain other behaviors. To accomplish these objectives, a thoroughgoing programing of contingencies or consequences, that is, a contingency management paradigm, should be helpful.

Disability as Punishment

As stated, the entry into disability and rehabilitation is involuntary and aversive, thus corresponding in essence to the concept of punishment. Punishment has two definitions from a behavioral perspective: the deprivation or loss of positive reinforcers and the onset of aversive stimuli. Both are exactly what occur when a person suffers a disability.

First, the disabled individual immediately loses access to many of the payoffs available to him prior to his disablement. He is removed from work, separated from leisure activities, blocked from achieving goals in life, and secluded from people who are important to him. In short, he immediately enters into a state of deprivation of reinforcers.

Simultaneously, he enters into a state carrying with it many aversive stimuli. There are the cosmetic effects of disability, the pain, and the forced practice of various laborious self-care and physical restoration procedures, many of which are initially repugnant to him. He faces the prejudices of both self and others toward disability. Some individuals encounter the additional burden of excessive sympathy and overprotection by those around them. Indeed, the person with a disability really is functioning in a punishment paradigm.

Essentially two kinds of behavior have been shown to follow punishment. One is escape or avoidance; the other is counteraggression or attack. In the presence of punishment, a person tries to engage in behaviors which will extricate him from the situation. The recently disabled patient may use all kinds of avoidance and escape behaviors, including withdrawal into fantasy and denial of actual disability. He may also resort to attack and counteraggression. A patient may "pick a fight" with any of a variety of elements of the rehabilitation system. By doing so, he extricates himself from a punishing situation. For example, if he fights often enough with his physical therapist, he "buys time out" from physical therapy. At the same time, he engages in behavior characteristic of almost all primates. When trapped in an aversive situation where no obvious escape is possible, he hits back (Azrin, Hake, and Hutchinson, 1965; Jolly, 1972:169–194; Bandura, 1973).

Traditional reactions to these rebellious or recalcitrant behaviors, which really are escape and avoidance behaviors sanctioned by the rehabilitation system, have often been in error. One of the errors professionals and, to an even larger extent, nonprofessionals such as family members tend to make is the "attribution of bravery." That is, the disabled person is seen in terms of how the viewers would feel if the disability occurred to them. Visitors enter the paraplegic's room thinking, "If that had happened to me, I would be decimated and I would be crying. But this paraplegic is not crying. He must be very brave." Instead, the patient may be trying to avoid his aversive dilemma by withdrawing into reverie, daydreams, and denial fantasies. The visitors' praise provides social reinforcement, not for realistic bravery, but for fantasy and withdrawal.

Professionals also often err in reaction to a patient's counteraggressive attacks. When a patient trapped in the punishment paradigm "strikes out" at them, they "hit" back. For example, professionals may get angry at the "uncooperative patient" and punish him even more. They may employ a variety of negative sanctions which they justify in terms of "setting limits" to "help" the patient. They may deliberately punish the patient by withdrawing privileges if he swears or yells or throws something at them. By doing so they may further isolate him, inducing even greater deprivation, confusion, and disorganization.

The behavioral reinforcement approach to rehabilitation strives to strengthen active participation in the rehabilitation process by positive reinforcement and to minimize avoidance and withdrawal. In this process, emphasis is placed on ignoring unwanted behaviors and on removing their positive reinforcers rather than on punishing the patient for his undesirable behaviors. The behavioral perspective perceives crisis phase behaviors as expected parts of the relearning process, and seeks to create a favorable learning environment.

This approach implies an initial tolerance of hostility. It demands a particular effort by all the professionals involved to establish rapport and communication with the disabled individual, particularly in the early stages of the process. At these stages, rehabilitation professionals are often the only source or reinforcement the patient can depend upon. Rather than misuse this pivotal position, professionals must emphasize their support, encouragement, and communication to promote maximally reinforceable, goal-directed behaviors. Each element of progress toward rehabilitation should receive much reinforcement.

Extinction of Disability-Inappropriate Behavior

Along with the strengthening of participatory behavior, the extinction of premorbid disability-inappropriate behavior must occur. This extinction corresponds approximately to the concept of "adjustment to disability." From a behavioral perspective, the extinguishing of disability-appropriate behaviors is accomplished by the withdrawal of reinforcers to those behaviors. Paradoxically, the initial effect of the withdrawal of reinforcers to a target behavior is a temporary increase in the rate of the behavior. This is not so strange as it seems. For example, experienced dieters know that their first response to the curtailment of the reinforcer, food, is an increase of appetite. For the smoker who suddenly quits, the itch for a cigarette gets stronger. But such reactions are only temporary. The extinction of behavior proceeds if the system effectively keeps the reinforcers withdrawn.

With reference to the extinction process, it is important to make the distinction between what might be called "verbal" and "performance" behaviors. That is to say, there is a difference between what a person says and what he does. Although in our society these two behaviors tend to have a positive correlation, it appears to be a relatively low-power relationship. Hence, verbal and performance behavior are by no means the same. In the case of the disabled patient, performance behavior often changes at a somewhat more rapid rate than verbal behavior. The patient usually will do disability-appropriate things sooner than he will say disability-appropriate things. Conversely, he will continue to talk as if the disability had not happened to him long after he is beginning to behave in a way that is appropriate to the disability (Fordyce, 1971).

A major error committed by rehabilitation professionals and others is related to their misunderstanding of this lag between attitudinal and behavioral change. If a patient says, "It really didn't happen to me. I am going to walk out the front door," professionals sometimes assume with great concern, "He is not adjusted to his disability." They may furthermore take special steps to help him adjust, unnecessarily involving him in psychotherapy, group therapy, and other verbal behavior remedies while failing to see that the patient's performance behavior is already quite appropriate to the disability.

In contrast, a behavioral perspective suggests that what a person does leads rather than follows what he says, and, hence, the best action to take is to help him emphasize changing what, in fact, he does. What he says eventually will tend to take care of itself. Such an approach to rehabilitation not only proves effective, but saves considerable staff time and resources.

While many professionals have been oversensitive to their patients' failure to verbalize adjustment to disability, they sometimes have been only vaguely aware of the process by which patients move into their disability-related role (perhaps to an extreme). Sociologists describe this process as assuming the "sick role," which was first described some years ago by Talcott Parsons (1951).

As has been stated, the rehabilitation process includes forced entry into disability, extinction of repertoires of predisability behavior, and acquisition of disability-appropriate behavior. These stages are strikingly similar to the stages of the sick role model outlined by Parsons. There are the fundamental injunctions of the sick role upon the person to behave as if he were sick, to enact sets of behaviors other than those relevant to ordinary life, and to appear as if he were dependent (Kassebaum and Baumann, 1965).

A peculiar aspect of the process is that many of the behaviors chosen for coping with sickness or disability may not always be punishing. In fact, the phrase "secondary gain," referring to the advantages of the sick role, indicates that entry into illness may, depending upon the consequences of being sick, evoke ambivalence in many persons. While certainly many of the sick role's aspects exemplify punishment, other elements of disability may provide relief, if not outright pleasure. That is, a patient allowed to play the sick role and indulged with continued dependence on others may begin to find the pain and deprivation of illness or disability balanced or even outweighed by the compensations. For instance, Cole and Lejeune (1972) demonstrated that women on welfare used "illness" and playing the sick role to justify their failures in the performance of other roles. Similarly, even involuntary entry into disability can bring certain rewards, even though those rewards may not be initially apparent to the patient.

The discussion of extinction of predisability repertoires of behavior under the behavioral model has an analog in Parsons' conceptualization. According to Parsons the sick role, if adopted, exempts qualified individuals from performing their preillness roles. However, identification with the sick role also implies that individuals must perform new roles and meet new expectations. The learning of these new roles and rules is equivalent, of course, to the acquisition of disability-appropriate behaviors. In terms of the sick role, this learning is manifested in the development of a new set of relationships with therapists, physicians, staff, and family.[2]

The family has a central role in the behavioral process because

it can be a powerful reinforcer of rehabilitation-appropriate behaviors. If the family is not actively included in the rehabilitation
program, it may well continue to reinforce old behaviors that are
counterproductive to rehabilitation success. Active family involvement in the behavioral program can be a source of strong
positive reinforcement for the individual patient. However, it is
important to guide the family so that it reinforces behaviors
consistent with rehabilitation goals.

Motivation: A Reexamination

Because the behavioral perspective focuses on specific behaviors, critics often confront the behavioristic approach with
questions about motivation, which presuppose a different model.
A motivational or disease model assumes that underlying motivations have great influence over a person's behavior. This motivational model is represented by figure 4. Some variance in be-

FIGURE 4. Behavior Influence Factors: Motivational Model[3]

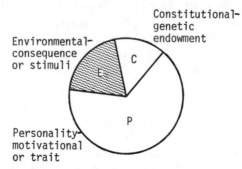

havior is attributed to genetic factors and some to environmental
factors. Traditionally, motivation theorists argue that a person's
behavior is principally influenced by his personality structure or
underlying motivations.

A behavioral perspective conceptualizes and distributes the
variance in individual behavior in a somewhat different manner.

It "slices the pie" of behavior influence factors in a way graphically represented in figure 5. This model recognizes genetic and personality factors but gives them reduced importance. According to the behavioral perspective, the behaviors a person engages in are governed to a considerable extent by the immediate environmental consequences of those behaviors. To change the rate of a given behavior, its environmental consequences must be altered. In the light of this, a motivation problem in the rehabilitation process becomes conceptually, if not tactically, a simple issue.

Tactically, treatment of the motivational problem in the rehabilitation process is essentially an exercise in programing the consequences of behaviors that need to be changed. Applying the behavioral perspective, rehabilitation professionals pinpoint which behaviors need to be increased, which behaviors need to be decreased, and which behaviors that are not in the repertoire need to be taught or shaped into it. Then they examine the consequences of those behaviors and determine which consequences might be utilized to change the rate of the behaviors.

Case Illustrations

The application of some of these principles is best illustrated by a few examples. The first concerns the case of a teen-age girl whose jaw was shattered in an automobile accident when she was a

FIGURE 5. Behavior Influence Factors: Behavioral Model[3]

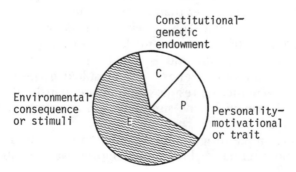

child. Over a seven-year period, her jaw essentially froze shut. She could not undergo dental repair, and she had limited ability to eat and speak. Surgery was performed to restore jaw function, but exercise to stretch the jaw muscles was also essential. The exercise was extremely painful for the girl. A therapeutic program was selected to improve her jaw function enough to allow her to open her mouth forty-eight millimeters with the help of a special device or forty-three millimeters without it. Her treatment emphasized opening the device until pain was intolerable, that is, working to tolerance. She was gradually induced to open her mouth about twenty-eight millimeters; however, as time progressed her performance fell to the point where she was opening her jaw a mere fourteen millimeters. When she inserted the device designed to open her mouth, she would scream with pain. The device was then removed. Her rate of opening began consistently to fall.

At that point, a behavioral management team began a contingency management program. It was obvious that "time out" from opening her mouth was something she very much wanted and, therefore, was a high-strength behavior. Opening her mouth was a low-strength behavior because of the pain involved. Therefore, "time out" from opening her mouth was programed to become contingent upon mouth-opening behavior. The end of a practice session was determined by accumulation of a predetermined amount of time at a selected oral aperture, instead of by her reported pain tolerance. Thus, rest or "time out" was contingent upon performance, rather than contingent upon pain. The girl had four trials a day, five days a week. Figure 6 shows the average aperture for all trials in each week of treatment. The slight decrease depicted at the end is actually an artifact, since she missed part of one day's exercise, which resulted in a lower week's average. In general, the results demonstrate that she did reach her target behavior, by the simple tactical adjustment of programing rest.

Similarly, simple programing was used in the case of a teenage boy who, after having brain cysts removed, was described by a

FIGURE 6. Mean Weekly Jaw Aperture[4]

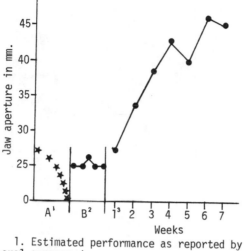

1. Estimated performance as reported by oral surgeon.
2. Base line; five trials.
3. Discrepancy between base line and first week's average reflects treatment progress.

referring physician as a "virtual vegetable." While this was an exaggerated statement, it reflected the marked lethargy and extremely limited efforts he displayed, even under conditions of intense exhortation. Asked to exercise, he seemingly could not perform at all. Again, the behavior management team arranged a contract with the boy whereby he could earn "time out" to rest by exercising on a bicycle. The reinforcement was time off the ward and out of the hospital. The results indicated by figure 7 were once again positive, showing a dramatic improvement from a level of nearly total nonperformance.

Critics of the approach utilized in these examples often cite as its limitation that it focuses on single or discrete kinds of behaviors which exist in an environment that can be artificially

FIGURE 7. Bicycle-riding[5]

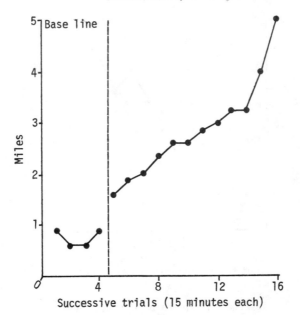

Successive trials (15 minutes each)

simplified and controlled to a large degree. If it could be shown
that behavioral methods always focus only on single or discrete
behaviors *and* that to do so results in only limited, if any, help in
solving the patient's problem, this would be valid criticism. The
major difficulty with such a criticism is that it is so sweepingly
general as virtually to defy response. The evidence is that focusing on discrete behaviors does work (for example, see Ullmann
and Krasner, 1965).

What is the evidence relating discrete behaviors to more complex clusters of behaviors and indicating whether changing one
does or does not change the other? What is the evidence that
alternative methods of assistance, presumably focusing on more
complex clusters of behavior, indeed provide greater assistance?
The behaviorist would contend that his critics have yet to come
forth with data which convincingly support the criticisms implied

by these questions. A second issue relates to the extent to which demonstrations of the utility of behavioral methods stem virtually exclusively from their application in controlled or semicontrolled environments. This criticism is burdened by the critics' lack of familiarity with the extensive behaviorally-based work which has been and is being done outside of institutional settings or with minimal institutional controls. The example of the girl with jaw pain is a case in point. There are innumerable other examples (see, for example, Bushell and Jacobson, 1968; Franks and Wilson, 1974; Stuart, 1967; Wahler, 1969).

Discussion

The behavioral approach is sometimes accused of dictating in an autocratic or even Machiavellian manner the directions and forms the changes in behavior are to take. Serious questions are raised: "Which behaviors are chosen for either extinction or reinforcement?" "Who does the choosing?" It has been pointed out that these questions would become particularly salient were the rehabilitation system to emphasize acquisition of a limited set of behaviors or behaviors that were inconsistent with those reinforced by the larger society. Such a criticism, of course, rests on the assumption that the patient and his family do not participate in defining treatment objectives or target behaviors. All treatment interventions should be examined to see how arbitrary, narrow, or unresponsive to the patient's natural environment the goals might be.

The behavioral approach can be viewed as no more manipulative in orientation than the traditional models used by the rehabilitation system and people in general. For example, what right does a parent have to say "thank you," in the hope of increasing the probability that his youngster will repeat a thoughtful behavior? Certainly that parent is manipulating that child. Likewise, in most teaching, the "teacher" manipulates the behaviors of the students. The surgeon manipulates his patient. Perhaps any form of professional intervention must be acknowledged as manipulation. In this context, the critical question is not whether the rehabilitation system uses manipulative techniques, but to what extent it can use them in a manner that allows all involved parties to participate as effectively as possible in the manipulation.

Professionals using behavioral techniques attempt, as much as possible, to identify the objectives of the rehabilitation program, to clarify what the program staff thinks the patient's objectives ought to be, and to establish what the program can do to help the patient determine what his objectives are. Certainly this is not manipulation in the Machiavellian sense. It is, instead, specification of arrangement of optimal relationships between behavioral objectives and environment. The patient must then decide whether to participate.

After achieving patient participation in rehabilitation, professionals face the problem of helping the clients maintain performance after they leave the system. Rehabilitation programs tend to fail to discriminate between the capability for a behavior and the probability that the behavior will occur (Fordyce, 1971). Programs often teach a person certain activities and discharge him with the hope that he will continue to perform. In fact, he often does not. In that case, he is deemed unmotivated.

The motivational model previously described is often invoked to suggest that there are aspects of rehabilitation maintenance which behavioral manipulation of stimuli and consequences cannot effectively handle. Motivation theorists insist that human beings do not always respond to immediate stimuli (a point with which behaviorists entirely agree). They respond to plans, future aspirations, expectations, and goals. They have to be motivated, and the sick role analysis suggests that this aspect of the process involves the motivation to get well, to want to get "back to normal." The behavioral perspective regards differences with alternative conceptions as they relate to the influence of remote consequences as largely a matter of semantics. Because man has the capacity to symbolize, that is, to anticipate remote consequences as well as immediate ones, remote consequences are indeed capable of influencing behavior. The question, then, becomes one not of instilling motivation, but of discovering the extent to which a person can program his life so that those remote consequences will be effective reinforcers.

The behavioral perspective, on the basis of the foregoing assumptions, argues that the maintenance of performance is just as much a responsibility of the rehabilitation process as is the initial teaching of that performance. A patient's seeming "lack of motivation" cannot be regarded as an insurmountable obstacle for any rehabilitation program. The maintenance of performance essentially requires examination of the environmental consequences of disability-appropriate behavior outside of the rehabilitation center. Those environmental consequences may not function in a way that will maintain disability-appropriate behavior and, in fact, may promote or reinforce disability-inappropriate behavior. In that case, the rehabilitation system ought to do what it can to reprogram that environment so that it will most effectively reinforce desirable responses and cease to reinforce undesirable ones.

Thus, rehabilitation professionals must give special emphasis to the environment outside of institutional walls (Baer and Wolf, 1967). The patient needs to be able to do things *out there*. He does not need to be able to transfer from bed to wheelchair in a physical therapy gymnasium or on a nursing unit. He needs to be able to transfer in his home. He needs to regain his payoffs from interacting with others, from leisure-time activities, and from having a job. Mobility is one of many requisite skills to accomplish in order to achieve those ends.

Practitioners concerned with extending the rewards of the therapeutic setting into the community and outside environment have attempted to teach and train people with whom the individual will have to relate after leaving the hospital, especially families (Bushell and Jacobson, 1968; Fordyce et al., 1968). This has been a difficult goal to accomplish, and sometimes there is only partial success. For example, a behavioral management team selected chronic pain patients for an operant-conditioning program on the condition that the patients' spouses agreed to participate in the training process. The spouses were taught to be as socially nonresponsive to pain behaviors and as socially responsive to well behaviors as possible. Results showed that in cases of female patients and male spouses the approach was quite successful. The continuation or generalization of effective well behavior, increased activity levels, and lower medication intake evidenced in these cases were proof of accomplishment, even after two years. But for cases of male patients and female spouses success rates were significantly lower. Perhaps this difference is explained by the observation that, in present American society, the husband has a more important part in social reinforcement for his wife than she has for him. As a consequence, husbands can successfully reprogram their spouses' behavior, but wives' actions do not seem to have as much effect. There are a number of other possible explanations.

Since special difficulties may be encountered in family reinforcement programs, professionals often attempt to emphasize other interpersonal reward relationships as well.

Without doubt programs reinforcing skills which will be of value to the patient outside of the rehabilitation system are beneficial, if still sometimes neglected or underemphasized, enterprises. Vocational rehabilitation is one area in which this attempt to help a person gain access to reinforcers in the natural environment has been stressed. An individual is not aided to enter an employment setting because work is moral and virtuous, but because a work situation involves special kinds of reinforcers which will maintain a host of behaviors and skills in addition to the work skill itself. For example, a job will help a paraplegic maintain behaviors such as fluid intake, skin care, effective transfer, mobility, and bladder care simply because without such maintenance he will not gain access to the payoffs of the job.

Even more crucial but much more neglected is the area of

leisure and socializing. A program offering leisure activities which are available and rewarded in the outside environment will help the patient maintain a variety of self-care behaviors. From a wider perspective, social skills of patients being rehabilitated must be reinforced so that other people will want to include the patients in a variety of interpersonal and social situations. The skill of communicating with others in a socially attractive fashion is a learnable skill. Furthermore, it is a portable skill which when learned helps in the reprograming of a person so that he, in turn, can influence his environment.[6]

The behavioral approach has been criticized as being mechanistic, oversimplified, Machiavellian, and limited in scope, while the motivational approach has been traditionally viewed as dynamic, conceptually rich and complex, respectful of patients' individuality and future-oriented. On the contrary, the analysis undertaken here suggests that motivational techniques may be too vague and nonspecific to be of much help except to a small subset of verbally and ideationally oriented patients and that such techniques may result in the professionals' denying responsibility for failures (that is, the "unmotivated" patients). The utilization of behavioristic techniques seeks to change discrete behaviors, to involve patients in their own rehabilitation, and, if the techniques are employed with foresight, to prepare them for life outside of the rehabilitation facility.

The problems of patients within institutional rehabilitation programs, defined as entry into the process, extinction of rehabilitation-inappropriate behaviors, and learning of rehabilitation-appropriate behaviors, have already received much attention. The problems of extrainstitutional maintenance of performance, including the development of family participation, work and play adjustment, and social skills, require more study and experimentation. Thus, at this time, behavioral analysis has taken a first step in the area of rehabilitation. It has begun to ask precision questions.

NOTES

1. Slightly modified from W. E. Fordyce, "Psychological Assessment and Management," in *Handbook of Physical Medicine and Rehabilitation,* ed. F. H. Krusen, F. Kottke, and P. Ellwood, 2nd ed. (Philadelphia: W. B. Saunders, 1971). Used by permission.

2. In the actual treatment of physically disabled individuals there remains the problem of helping patients to move ahead. The behavioral approach provides concrete methods to help patients change individual behaviors.

3. Slightly modified from W. E. Fordyce, *Behavioral Methods for Chronic Pain and Illness* (St. Louis: C. V. Mosby, 1976). Used by permission.

4. Slightly modified from R. Barach, B. Buech, and W. E. Fordyce, "Rest and 'Time Out' from Treatment as Reinforcers to Decrease Jaw Muscle Pain," *Rehabilitation Psychology* (in press).

5. Slightly modified from R. Berni and W. E. Fordyce, *Behavior Modification and the Nursing Process* (St. Louis, C. V. Mosby, 1973). Used by permission.

6. It is particularly difficult to modify the disabled individual's environment outside of an institutional setting. There is no reward system to encourage researchers and practitioners to bridge the gap between hospital and community. For example, it is extremely difficult, if not impossible, to obtain funding from Medicare or Medicaid to pay for home treatment. This situation underlines the obvious gap between research findings and treatment practices.

BIBLIOGRAPHY

Azrin N.; Hake, D.; and Hutchinson, R.
    1965.   Elicitation of aggression by a physical blow. *Journal of the Experimental Analysis of Behavior,* 8:55–57.
Baer, D., and Wolf, M.
    1967.   The entry into natural communities of reinforcement. In *Achieving Generality of Behavioral Change,* symposium presented at the American Psychological Association meetings, Washington, D.C., September.
Bandura, A.
    1973.   *Aggressions: A Social Learning Analysis.* Englewood Cliffs, N.J.: Prentice-Hall.
Bushell, D., and Jacobson, J.
    1968.   The simultaneous rehabilitation of mothers and their children. In *A Working Model for Psychologists in Rehabilitation,* symposium presented at the American Psychological Association meetings, San Francisco, Calif., August.

Cole, S., and Lejeune, R.
  1972. Illness and the legitimization of failure. *American Sociological Review*, 37:347–356.
Fordyce, W.
  1971. Behavioral methods in rehabilitation. In *Rehabilitation Psychology*, edited by W. S. Neff, pp. 74–108. New York: American Psychological Association.
Fordyce, W.; Fowler, R.; Lehmann, J.; and DeLateur, B.
  1968. Some implications of learning in problems of chronic pain. *Journal of Chronic Diseases*, 21:170–190.
Franks, C., and Wilson, G., eds.
  1974. *Annual Review of Behavior Therapy*, pp. 1–40. Vol. 2. New York: Brunner/Mazel.
Jolly, A.
  1972. *The Evolution of Primate Behavior*. New York: Macmillan.
Kassebaum, G., and Baumann, B.
  1965. Dimensions of the sick role in chronic illness. *Journal of Health and Human Behavior*, 6:16–27.
Leviton, G. L.
  1971. Professional-client relations in a rehabilitation hospital setting. In *Rehabilitation Psychology*, edited by W. S. Neff, pp. 215–247. New York: American Psychological Association.
Michael, J.
  1970. Rehabilitation. In *Behavior Modification in Clinical Psychology*, edited by C. Neuringer and J. Michael, pp. 52–85. New York: Appleton-Century-Crofts.
Parsons, T.
  1951. *The Social System*. New York: Free Press.
Premack, D.
  1959. Toward empirical behavior laws: I. Positive reinforcement. *Psychological Review*, 66:219–233.
Reese, E.
  1966. *The Analysis of Human Operant Behavior*. Dubuque, Iowa: Brown.
Stuart, R.
  1967. Behavioral control of overeating. *Behavior Research Therapy*, 5:357–365.
Ullmann, L., and Krasner, L., eds.
  1965. *Case Studies in Behavior Modification*. New York: Holt, Rinehart and Winston.
Wahler, R.
  1969. Oppositional children. A quest for parental reinforcement control. *Journal of Applied Behavior Analysis*, 2:159–170.

CHAPTER 5

Coping and Adaptive Behaviors of the Disabled

Israel Goldiamond

In these days, when only women are supposed to write about women's problems, and blacks about blacks', I come with an unfair advantage over others who write about disability—I am writing from a wheelchair. In these days when authority is legitimized only through personal experience, I present impeccable credentials: for nine consecutive months I was hospitalized for a spinal injury. During that time I shared observations, roles, and treatments with other patients. More importantly, we were to share similar futures upon discharge, possibly to be disabled for the remainder of our lives. It was this which fundamentally distinguished us from the newspaper reporter who attempted to understand us by spending almost a week with us, much of it in a wheelchair; most of the patients ignored him as a phony.

What I am writing now I might have written if I had simply spent the same amount of time as an observer. But I doubt very much if I would have written it at all, or at least not this intensively. The injury forced it upon me. I experienced the pain and discomfort. The pain is mostly gone, but I still frequently experience the discomfort; it is present right now. This private experience could not have come from observation, and I can think of nothing in my past life that would have prepared me for it and that might have formed a basis for empathy, as defined experien-

The research on self-control was performed under a grant from the State of Illinois, Department of Mental Health, entitled "Self-control Procedures: Variables in Recording and Intervention."

tially. However, arrangements can be made so that the continual discomfort not only does not get in my way, but is not even experienced. These arrangements derive from knowledge which I had prior to my current state and for which empathy is not always necessary. Arrangements could also be made so that I would experience the discomfort and it would be incapacitating.

I shall present some observations of my behavior and that of other patients while I was a patient and after discharge; I also observed patients who had not been in the hospital with me. Observations and relations are derived from context, and no observer starts out with a *tabula rasa* whether his role is as therapist or as patient. A blind roommate of mine systematized his observations and their relations through a purposive God. He drew to his bedside many nursing students whom he impressed by the sustaining power of his faith. A professional systematized his observations psychoanalytically and found depression to be a necessary developmental stage in rehabilitation; he subsequently presented a paper before a psychiatric audience. My approach stems from the experimental analysis of behavior, or what might be called functional behaviorism (or radical behaviorism, to distinguish it from classical behaviorism [Skinner, 1974]).

This approach deals with the meaning or motivation of behavior by considering a pattern of behavior in terms of its maintaining consequences. The pattern may be required for these consequences to occur, under certain conditions. The rhythmic foot-tap of the saxophonist when he is playing may be motivated by the necessity to keep time. The identical beat of a child's foot under the dinner table when the family is eating may be motivated by the parental annoyance it produces, or the same beat by a stroke patient in his room may be motivated by the muscle recovery it may produce. Although the beats are identical, they are somehow in different classes. They do not have the same meaning for the persons involved, are motivated differently, are intended differently, or serve different functions. We can also say that, despite similar topographies, the beats are different operants; that is, they are maintained by different consequences

(Skinner, 1953). The five languages of meaning, motivation, intent, function, and behavior-consequence contingency cover similar ground. The behavior-consequence language, however, deals directly with observables and potentially manipulatable events.

Once we have assessed the meaning of a current behavior, we may utilize this information to develop programs which change it or produce other desirable ends. Out of the systematic development of such procedures, a technology of behavior is emerging with a common conceptual system. Derived in the laboratory, this technology is known as the experimental analysis of behavior (cf. Skinner, 1938). Applied to clinical problems (Neuringer and Michael, 1970) and classroom problems (Sulzer and Mayer, 1972), it is known as behavior modification (Goodall, 1972). Applied to curricular problems, it is known as programed learning or instruction (Hendershot, 1967). Applied to pharmacological problems, it is known as behavior pharmacology (Thompson and Schuster, 1968). Applied to muscular and other physiological problems, it is known as biofeedback (Barber et al., 1971).

The field of rehabilitation and disability appears to be an ideal area of application for a technology of behavior. For the past few years, in our laboratory and clinic at the University of Chicago, we have been applying this approach to emotional and other living problems of outpatients, as part of the outpatient service of the Department of Psychiatry. In essence, a contract is signed by two consenting adults which specifies the agreed-upon outcome to be obtained, ascertains the current repertoire which is relevant to it, and tries to develop a program which converts the current repertoire to the desired repertoire in a step-by-step manner. The program requires self-control and self-analysis, which involve training patients to change the contingencies governing their own behavior and, having identified these contingencies, to analyze their own behavior and understand it (Goldiamond, 1965a). The contingencies governing behavior are defined as the *relationships* between the *behavior* patterns at issue which are required to produce certain *consequences* and the class of *conditions* under which this relationship is likely to hold. In the process of developing programs which produce change and insight, we believe that we, too, have gained some new insights into and understanding of behavior, the contingencies of which it is a part, and their relation to experiential states.

One afternoon when I found myself on my back with one leg bent back under my arm and devoid of feeling, I realized that I might have suffered a spinal injury. When I had been transferred to a stretcher and was told by the neurosurgeon who had rushed to the scene of the accident that I could be treated in that town or be flown to my own hospital—to arrive in about three hours—I realized that delay would directly affect recovery, and I agreed to be treated there. When I awoke in the intensive-care unit after surgery, I knew that if I were to get back to the work I enjoy and feel is important, I would have to exert for myself the type of self-control and self-analysis we had been applying with other consenting adults.

Starting in early October 1970, I spent a little less than a month in a hospital in a small town near the site of my accident. I was later transferred to another hospital where I remained until the end of June 1971. The first hospital was an excellent general hospital serving the community from which its staff and patients were drawn. Prior to or following their hospitalization, patients might meet staff members in the local supermarket. The atmosphere in the hospital was one of kindness, consideration, and efficiency. However, because it was not primarily a rehabilitation hospital, the neurologist and my wife joined in a search for possible places to which to transfer me once acute treatment was over. Neither was previously aware of the existence of the facility which was to be my home for eight months. If they had not found this facility and if I had not been transferred there, the remainder of my story might have been utterly different.

Recently we learned of a patient with a lesser injury who had been returned home from an acute-care hospital without rehabilitation training. She is bedridden at home and requires increasing care. Apparently neither her physician nor her family was aware of facilities which could train her to transfer to a wheelchair and to increase her mobility. In the absence of such training, deterioration, physiological as well as behavioral, is occurring.

The ignorance of acute-care hospital personnel sometimes does not concern only special facilities (such as rehabilitation) available for disabled persons. Sometimes it extends to special medical requirements for those persons. At the acute-care hospital I was in, because I could not initially turn myself in bed I was log-rolled every two hours to avoid the skin breakdowns called decubitus ulcers. At the rehabilitation unit I later entered a large number of patients came in with such ulcers because they had not been log-rolled while they were in acute-care hospitals.

The rehabilitation hospital to which I was transferred was in the large city in which I live, with staff and patients drawn from different parts of the metropolitan area. The likelihood that anybody there would meet or would have met any other patient or staff member on the outside was remote, with the obvious consequences for relations within the institution. While there was a community on the outside, there was also a community evident on the inside. It would be nice to say that the divisions between the communities were overridden by the common treatment mission of the staff, but this would confuse social mission with the different contingencies for the individuals involved.

The patients enrolled in our self-control clinic have been required to keep daily logs of their behaviors and other events, and I assigned myself this task as well. I kept graphs. I recorded my muscle movements. Thus, I noted that shortly after arrival I was told to lie motionless and not to move my torso: "Don't move; we'll move you." Within these limitations I noted some exercises I imposed for myself; "9:15–9:21 A.M., shrugged shoulders 10 times." But after a while it was a struggle even to lift a two-pound weight. I was thus immobilized for more than three months. Toward the end of that period I could move, provided I wore a painful body brace. Much later, I noted that when one crawls forward movement of arms and legs is in contralateral pairs, but when one crawls backward it is in ipsilateral pairs. This information was useful in learning to walk both forward and backward with the aid of a reciprocal walker.

I recorded social interactions in the hospital. Thus I noted the dismissal of a male attendant when he was caught with the hand of a female paraplegic patient on his knee. The attendant and the patient had been carrying on a love affair, both in the hospital and when she was home on leave. I recorded medications, surgery, and the fact that X rays indicated dislocation of spinal segment T12 ⅜'' from L1. I also recorded the occurrence of feelings of elation, annoyance, and so forth; the contingencies responsible were quite clear. In one instance they were not, and the records I kept were valuable in clarifying them.

Staff members log-rolled me every two hours during my sleep. This wakened me, of course, but I promptly fell asleep again. On a Wednesday in February, I was unable to fall asleep after the final log-roll and was sleepless for two hours. On Thursday, I was sleepless for four hours. On Friday, it was six hours, and Saturday night was totally sleepless. Nor could I sleep during the Sunday following. I mentioned this to the nurse, who immediately attributed my mounting sleeplessness to mounting anxiety. What was I worried about? What was I thinking about that kept me awake? Of course I was worried; if one cannot sleep, one is liable to worry about it. True, many of the thoughts were not pleasant. There is no reason why thoughts in a hospital when one is sleepless should be pleasant. But, as I had successfully taught outpatients in our self-control program, emotions do not cause behavior; rather, emotions *and* behavior are governed by contingencies. The solution might be that something was increasingly keeping me awake at night.

The nurse could find nothing in her record, and I looked in mine. For the past four months I had been receiving 40 mg. of Valium a day, which my physician said I could kick at will, just as I previously had kicked other medications. On Monday that week, the dosage was 40 mg. On Tuesday, I reduced it by taking three pills of 10 mg. each. On Wednesday, I took no pills. That night had contained the first sleepless period. The ensuing pattern checked with one of the many withdrawal symptoms listed in the Physician's Desk Reference. I promptly reinstated myself on 5 mg. a day and slept soundly all night thereafter. I faded that out completely within a month. Without the records and without a contingency view of emotions as meters of observable contingency relations rather than as causes of behavior, I might have delved into past anxieties and discomforting events and had something to stay awake about. Withdrawal might then have run its course, and the changes might have been attributed to my quest into the past.

Consequences and Behavioral Requirements

While I was in the rehabilitation hospital, I kept up my professional activities. On December 14, although I was immobilized, a site visit for a grant was made in my hospital room. Within a month, I had dictated a progress report and a forty-page grant proposal. By the start of the spring quarter, I was allowed to make weekend home visits and so could resume my graduate seminar at home. When a small skin ulcer appeard on my buttock, my wife drove me home anyhow, with me lying on my side on the back seat of the station wagon. I conducted the class while lying on a living-room couch. During one weekend, I addressed the annual banquet of the Association for Precision Teaching. One year and one day after the accident I spoke at a convention in Los Angeles. I ran the laboratory and clinic from my hospital room, with research assistants, staff, students, and colleagues constantly there during visiting hours. I also took on a client in a self-control weight program.

That spring a new roommate entered the scene. He was John McWethy, midwest editor of the *Wall Street Journal* and a severely impaired quadriplegic. John rapidly caught my bad habit and began to run his office from the same room. The room was now also crowded with newspaper reporters, public relations officials, and others from both our staffs. There was no trouble telling the two staffs apart. The members of one set were Ivy League—well dressed, clean shaven and clean-cut—and the members of the other were a motley bunch who wore jeans and had straggly beards and long hair. John has since returned home, and he puts in a full week as editor of his paper. He represents one of the very few cases of such functioning by a quadriplegic.

Resumption of our professional lives was critical to both of us; in order to achieve that goal we had to participate wholeheartedly in the rehabilitation program of the hospital. The existence of such a contingency relation or its absence was what, from my observation, distinguished those patients whom the staff described as "motivated" from those whom they described as "unmotivated" or "impossible to reach" or, in less charitable moments, "goof-offs." When a critical consequence was contingent upon participation, there was participation. When such a critical consequence did not exist, or was not strong enough to maintain the effort required to produce it, participation was absent or lackadaisical.

The small college in which a quadriplegic honor student was enrolled as a freshman prior to his injury constructed special ramps for his return, and he learned to operate a typewriter with splints and took college courses at the hospital. On the other hand, a peer with nothing in particular to return to simply watched others and created a social life of his own in the hospital. Two other patients were involved in lawsuits, in which size of settlement was related to extent of injury. These two patients engaged in few recovery programs. These cases puzzled the staff tremendously. People should *want* to get better and should *want* to stay alive longer; the staff knew how to help produce such outcomes; and the patients should *want* to cooperate. The causes of negative attitudes were believed to be hostility, depression, or other attitudinal or underlying psychodynamic formulations. Recalcitrant patients were given pep talks or scare talks that warned of the dire consequences of degeneration, shown movies, and reasoned with, all to no avail. None of these analyses, of course, overcame or was relevant to the absence of consequences important enough to sustain the high response cost required to produce the outcomes desired by staff members.

Nor were the patients unaware of this. They talked pessimistically or optimistically to staff, depending on which was required, and then, to other patients, of how they had "psyched out" the professionals. It would be naive to assume that they revealed their "true" selves either to other patients or to professional staff members. Both sets of behaviors were under "audience control" (Skinner, 1957), that is, tended to accord with audience contingencies or what has been described elsewhere as the "demand characteristics" (Orne, 1959). Some psychologists and social workers tried to assess and change attitudes or gave projective tests such as the House-Tree-Person. Other social workers tried to make job or educational arrangements, which included finding opportunities for work and trying to reduce the behavioral requirements of these jobs. The patients appreciated the efforts of the latter group, but not of the former.

For some patients for whom critical consequences outside the institution could not be found, maintenance of institutionalization became the incentive that governed behavior. One staff conference was concerned with a patient who, it was felt, had been there too long; the hospital was too much of a good thing for him. The solution reached was the mistake often made under such circumstances: to make it less of a good thing, remove the privileges, and start to ignore him. This is a mistake, because as I have noted elsewhere (Goldiamond, 1969), if a critical consequence is withdrawn and the patient is desperate, he will display other behaviors which force the institution to provide the consequence. In this case, the patient was log-rolled at night, but during the day he persistently lay on the same side. He shortly developed decubitus ulcers, which required frequent attention, and thereby frustrated plans to discharge him.

An even more dramatic case was that of a female paraplegic who had married a man so objectionable to her parents that they had disowned her. The previous year she had pointed a pistol to her chest, and the bullet had entered her spine rather than her heart. She was determined to return to her parents and not to her husband, and was making little progress because she had little to do with the therapies available. The staff was wondering into whose hands she could be discharged. The patient took matters into her own hands. She denounced the hairdressers who came in once a week as part of a Mafia conspiracy and spread this information. No one acted on this. The following week she attached a sign to the back of her wheelchair. It read: "Don't blow for the—commies. Hitler and Eichmann were right, but didn't finish the job." This was written notification; it was written into the nursing chart. Some of the psychologists said all this was just talk and she could be given scissors for the grooming she liked.

The institution not having "listened" early in the escalation process, the patient now forced its hand. That Thursday, when the ward door was wide open and "luckily" when three male attendants were passing by, she was observed bending over the bed of an aphasic patient, a pair of sharp scissors in her upraised hand, stabbing at the patient. She was, of course, instantly seized and transferred to the nearest mental hospital. This is not the end of the story. Her parents took her back.

It should not be supposed that the behaviors produced were necessarily planned. There is ample evidence in the operant laboratory literature that consequences appropriately defined and programed will influence behavior whether or not the subject is aware of their relation to behavior (Hefferline, Keenan, and Harford, 1959; Goldiamond, 1965b[1]). Accordingly, the conscious-unconscious continuum is not relevant to this model. Knowledge of contingencies relevant to behavior can, of course, be used to plan and establish those contingencies and thereby to control behavior, either one's own or that of others. But once the contingencies are there, the behavior comes under their control, whether or not one is aware of them. Very often, environmental agents unwittingly set up a program which can produce behaviors that are contrary to the aims of these agents. Very often, the progressive interactions between agents and person produce a patterned escalation of undesirable behavior very much like the step-by-step programing which characterizes programed instruction.

One of my roommates was a boy, aged thirteen. He tied up elevators. He jammed a seventy-year-old wheelchair patient into a bathroom in such a manner that attendants had to spend close to an hour to extricate him. The boy offered a loosely rolled newspaper to a brain-damaged patient who asked for a cigarette and roared with laughter as the high flame produced when the newspaper was lighted almost singed the patient's hair. The boy could generally be described as malicious. Staff members' lectures, reprimands, and hostile comments which were intended to decrease the behavior only increased it. The boy was getting the adult attention so critical to children of his age.

Usually he got along well with his roommates: we told him, in essence, not to foul his home nest behaviorally and tried to reinforce positive behaviors. My wife paid him a dollar for a crayon still life he made of the city landscape outside our window (it still hangs in our house), and for a week thereafter he spent most of his free time drawing landscapes. One of the aides set up a wall graph to record positive behaviors, but to be effective a token economy requires concerted staff action, which was not available.

Another of my roommates, a factory superintendent in his fifties, was transferred to the hospital after surgery for a brain tumor. He was regarded as disoriented: he urinated against the wall of our room, wondered what he hell he was doing in Panama, and wandered about. What was not noted was that this disorientation was absent in the cafeteria, where he lined up at the counter with his tray and ate appropriately at his table.

In the laboratory, disruption of behavior occurs during "stimulus change" (Azrin, 1958), that is, when certain hitherto pervasive and ambient stimuli are changed. This can be the introduction of noise, the flickering of a light, or often a minor physiological change. When stimuli are changed in this manner, the initial reaction may be disruption of the behavior pattern. Which pattern is disrupted is probably a function not only of such changes but of variables related to the histories of the different patterns. In Azrin's experiment, with human subjects, introduction of noise disrupted a temporal pattern of button-pressing established during the experiment but did not disrupt the button-pressing itself. If the consequences and the behavioral requirements for those consequences are not changed, the pattern appropriate to them may return, that is, may be reestablished under the new conditions. As Azrin notes, we then say that the disrupting effects of the novel stimulus have worn off and the subject has adapted or habituated; the temporal pattern established in the absence of noise has now also been established in its presence. If, however, the consequences are changed by the experimenter or as a result of the behavior of the audience, new patterns of behavior may be established.

Cafeteria requirements are the same under a variety of conditions, and the behavior of my roommate there was not "disoriented." However, hospitalization and hospital rooms were new to a hitherto vigorous man whose brain damage was also new. There was sense to his "disoriented" behaviors there. Our hospital window overlooked factory and warehousing areas adjacent to a lake; a naval pier was nearby. "What the hell am I doing in Panama?" is a question that seems to be responsive to these stimuli.

The lower walls of our room were tiled, the curtains between the beds hung probably on shower rings, and, come to think of it, sarcastic visitors did compare our room to a latrine. To keep the patient from urinating against the wall, the staff confined him to his bed, and he promptly soiled his pants. Several attendants had to hold him down to change him at least four times daily. He was allowed up, and then he wet both wall and pants. He did not use the urinal supplied. One of the attendants, who was taking psychology courses and had discussed them with me, said that surely we could do better. As the patient was constantly begging for cigarettes, it was recommended that his being given a cigarette be made contingent upon delivery to the attendant of a urinal, with the required content gradually to be increased. The effects were remarkable. On occasion, the patient, who was supposed to have loss of recent memory, searched over a good part of the floor for the attendant, with urinal in hand substituting for Diogenes' lamp, in order to collect his cigarette. Another episode showed that the patient had recent memory, provided it was consequential. He was enraged by the thirteen-year-old's prank with the flaming newspaper. About three days later, the boy was alone in a room with the patient, who pushed the youngster on the bed and started to beat him up.

The patient, or rather, the nonunderstanding environment, began to present other problems, however. Society's typical response when it does not control an individual's behavior by its own behavior was employed: control by physical means. The patient wandered all over the floor and was caught going down the back staircase. He was then strapped into a wheelchair. The final solution for the urination problem was of a similar kind. Rather than programing use of the urinal for a variety of attendants under a variety of conditions for consequences other than cigarettes, the staff had him catheterized. His rage increased, and it seemed that he was in the initial stages of developing an organic psychosis.

The staff members were not unfeeling or badly intentioned. Most were highly dedicated, and they put up with a great deal. Behavior analysis cannot be applied too successfully by one individual when the remainder of the staff is operating under different premises. To turn the whole system around to provide support for behavior analysis is a formidable undertaking, especially when the system is already straining its resources under current standard operating procedures. However, it should be noted that a unit in which the behavior analysis approach is used can be set up as readily as the type of unit in which such analysis is an intrusion. Demonstrably different outcomes have been obtained when behavior analysis has been routinely employed (Ayllon and Azrin, 1968).

Turning from this social microcosm to the social macrocosm, one wonders about the inevitability of many problems of the disabled. To what extent are organic psychoses, deterioration, and debility programed? To what extent can we reverse trends toward such problems by appropriate behavior analysis and control? And how do the costs compare? Certainly, the suffering was far greater in the case of the man who had had surgery for a brain tumor when behavior analysis was not employed. Everyone was unhappy about the patient's behavior, and the solution chosen by the staff produced misery and guilt all around.

Laboratory experiments have demonstrated that there is a distinction between impairment of memory and impairment of learning in brain-damaged animals. Animals trained in a task may not perform it after brain surgery, but they can often be retrained in that task. Schools are available for brain-damaged children. I am aware of none to which one can refer a fifty-year-old adult for retraining.

Programing

The terms "program" and "programing" are applied in a variety of ways. I shall restrict my definition to their use in operant laboratory research and its extensions to programed instruction, behavior modification, and biofeedback.

A program, as defined in these areas, includes specification in observables of the outcome to be obtained, or *target*; explicit specification of the repertoire currently available to the organism which can be used as a starting point, or *current relevant repertoire;* and explicit specification of the *steps* which will mediate between current and target repertoires. The steps include a presented stimulus and a defined behavioral requirement. Each step itself is a subprogram containing these three elements: the target toward whose production the step is aimed, the starting point, and the procedures producing the change. The outcome of any step is the starting point of the next one, just as the starting point of that step was the outcome of the preceding one.

Merely having an admirable sequence of steps does not guarantee that the subject will go through them. Accordingly, the program also requires the development of a system of *response-contingent-consequences* attached to the behavioral requirements of each step and of the program itself. These positive reinforcers can be material, such as financial rewards, food, trinkets, or candy; surrogates such as tokens or points; social, in the form of approval or opportunity to be with certain groups; behavioral, such as the opportunity to do certain things; program-specific, for example, the outcome of the program itself, with presentation of the next step being the reinforcer for meeting the requirements of the preceding steps; or combinations of these.

In the operant laboratory, such programs are used to establish behavioral patterns which can then be used for investigative purposes. For example, to investigate the effects of a drug on retention, we might use delayed "match-to-sample." A monkey is confronted by a small wall panel on which an illuminated circle is projected. When he presses the panel, the illumination goes out. Five seconds later, two panels light up. One contains a circle and the other an ellipse. The subject is rewarded for matching what appeared on the sample five seconds earlier, that is, food is given to him only if he presses the circle panel. If he does so reliably, we can say the drug dosage has not affected his retention for this task under these conditions, and we can investigate when and how it does. How to get the subject to engage in the necessary "match-to-sample" behavior is not immediately evident, however. The procedures which do so are not hit-or-miss, nor are they established through trial and error. Rather, the experimenter uses a program of the kind specified, which he can follow from a colleague's scientific report.

Initially, the targets of such laboratory programs were relatively simple. Outcomes of laboratory investigations starting with such targets made it possible to progressively extend these targets for further investigation. Some of the investigators realized that programing procedures could be applied to establish target patterns for human beings. Then the usefulness of the target was not as a starting point for experimental investigations; the goal was the *attainment of the target itself:* for example, getting a mute patient to speak, establishing proficiency in an academic subject, getting a hitherto resistant community to request well-baby care, or decreasing heart rate. Hence, the various subfields of applied behavior analysis and their relation to the experimental analysis of behavior were established. This relationship is continuing. In order to investigate certain linguistic issues, Premack (1970) has been programing language for a chimpanzee. Others suggest that his procedures can be used to teach language to mentally retarded children.

One of the discoveries of the examination of programing itself has been that it is often critical whether the training agency establishes the target through allowing subjects to make errors and correct themselves, that is, trial and error, or establishes the target through an errorless program, or trial and success (Terrace, 1963). In the trial-and-success case, the behavior is being continually reinforced. Through the use of this procedure, target behaviors have been established which were impossible to establish using trial and error. Such behaviors had hitherto been considered outside the subject's capacity (Sidman and Stoddard, 1966).

In other cases, the same targets have been established, and target outcomes established through trial and error cannot be distinguished from target outcomes established through trial and success. However, when one tries to alter the task or the conditions, for example, no longer reinforcing the discrimination learned, there are critical differences related to the programing history (Terrace, 1969). The program itself is a variable.

Because I was acquainted with the literature in this area and aware of the numerous contributions of Fordyce (1968, 1971), Myerson, Kerr, and Michael (1967), and Michael (1970) to rehabilitation, it was disappointing not to see behavior procedures explicitly applied at the hospital, especially in view of the fact that the area lends itself, as few areas do, to a programing approach. However, such an approach was implicit in many of the rehabilitation areas. In physical therapy, for example, we were told that we could start the walking program only when we could press at least fifty pounds with each arm. The barbells were nicely graduated for a series of steps. Walking followed an implicit program. It started with standing at the parallel bars and then went on to making a few steps, and finally to using crutches or a walker outside. The success of this program attracted invalids from miles around, many of whom saved money for years in order to come to learn; some townships ran special programs to raise funds for disabled citizens.

On days when patients progressed in physical therapy, their morale was high; on days when they did not make progress or they failed, their morale was often low. Progress was to a large extent related to the procedures used. One could see progress in arm muscles by the evident size of dumbbells used. But when the physical therapist asked the patient to push a leg against the therapist's pressing arm, there was absolutely no feedback as to whether the patient was advancing. There was no explicit way to handle trace movements. The possibilities seemed to cry for research in explicit programing with biofeedback, for assay of instruments to provide the evidence of progress that can maintain behavior which will help achieve goals desired by both patients and staff.[2]

There were step-by-step sequences in sitting and standing, in transfers from bed to wheelchair to car, in use of eating utensils (with special assistive devices provided for quadriplegics). There were carefully planned medical sequences in decatherization and bowel control, among other areas. In the area of social behavior, there were sequences directed toward home return, starting with a visit of a few hours and continuing to a longer stay, to overnight, to weekends, and finally to discharge. There was an active recreation department; participation in activities might be contingent on acquisition of behavior patterns in other areas. For example, a patient had to be able to transfer to and from a car in order to go to the movies. Where the sequences were successful they were designated by their targets, for example, eating, driving, home return. They started with assessment of the current relevant repertoire.

Some of the assumptions underlying these successful programs are made explicit by research in operant programing. The attitudes implied by this approach are often 180 degrees from those explicitly required and explicitly indoctrinated by other approaches. Differing attitudes have profound implications for the patient's recovery, as well as for societal reactions to disability.

In our self-control clinic, we are trying to apply programing procedures and rationale to the problems of patients whose presenting complaints range from anxiety states to xenophobia. Our approach may best be illustrated by reference to a hypothetical patient who applies for alleviation of her anxiety. Further investigation reveals that her husband will shortly be assigned to Moscow, and she is terrified because she speaks no Russian at all. This deficit is good reason to be anxious. We now try to ascertain the competence required to define her target outcome, speaking Russian, and ascertain her current relevant repertoire. If she speaks Bulgarian fluently, we can attain the target within a week. If she speaks German and French instead, we shall start from there, and our task may take longer. If she speaks only English, it will take even longer. We classify the patient *by what is to be acquired and by the nature of the program and not by the deficit.* We do not say she suffers from Hyposlavophonia. That is quite evident to her and to us.

Similarly, rather than attempting to eliminate stuttering, which many people can do, including the stutterer himself, we establish a pattern of fluency that the speaker has not used before and which we are pretty good at doing.[3] Rather than eliminating obesity or establishing dieting (which is just a change in words), we establish new eating patterns which are not intuitively evident. Almost anyone for whom the contingencies are sufficiently critical can eliminate patterns. But not everyone can program new patterns effectively, let alone know which patterns are to be programed. If establishing fluency substitutes for eliminating stuttering and establishing new eating patterns substitutes for dieting, what substitutes for relief from anxiety? This is a more complex question, but can be similarly analyzed.

The programs to be used and the successful application of programing require attention to the current relevant repertoires. Stated otherwise, we look for strengths. As one patient said after the initial interview, "Do all your patients leave feeling this euphoric?"

The 180-degree turn in attitudes called for is not simply in terms of intervention, for example, that one can intervene more effectively by concentrating on what is to be established and by looking at strengths, rather than concentrating on what is to be eliminated and then looking at weaknesses. The former approach I have designated as constructional, in contrast with the pathological approach of the latter (Goldiamond, 1974). A constructional approach compels reinterpreting the nature of the symptom and its relevance to the contingencies of the patient's behavior. Rather than considering the presenting problem as indicative of pathology, we may think of such patterns as eminently sensible and possibly the most sensible possible for existing contingencies. The behavior patterns which disturb us may be the equivalent of the key peck or lever press maintained by positive reinforcement. If a pigeon pecks at a disk only when the previous peck produced shock it is not because it is masochistic. It does so because the environmental program is such that he will occasionally get food that way but not after a peck that does not produce a shock (Holz and Azrin, 1961).

An example mentioned earlier was the patient whose parents had disowned her. In one system of discourse, she would be described as paranoid, and the emphasis might have been on understanding her history. However, if her behavior is analyzed in terms of contingencies, her behavior becomes not only sensible but remarkably so: she apparently pressed exactly the right levers to get back home. The young man for whom continued institutionalization was a critical consequence developed decubitus ulcers when the staff tried to deprive him of that consequence. Again, we could describe the behavior as suicidal and classify him in terms such as passive-aggressive, but if we analyze his behavior in terms of its contingencies, it becomes eminently sensible: he apparently pressed exactly the right levers to stay in the hospital. The two patients' efforts were heroic, and the cost was tremendous, but the efforts were apparently called for.

Several questions are raised by such an approach to behavior. An immediate one is, why should we require such heroic efforts? When we try to deprive individuals of certain critical consequences, many can apparently find other means to attain them, sometimes at tremendous cost to themselves and tremendous cost to society.

A few weeks ago, I was asked by the medical service at our hospital to consult on a case in which the patient was driving the staff crazy by her constant calls; her light lit up more than twenty times a day. Their analysis, which agreed with mine, was that she was doing this for attention, and her psychiatric history clearly indicated why this would be a critical reinforcer. The staff members' reaction was the perfectly natural one of refusing to be manipulated this way, and the intervention they proposed was to withdraw attention. This approach is often found in the behavior modification literature, where it is called extinction. In the animal laboratory, if we stop reinforcing the pigeon for pecking at the disk, it will eventually stop, but it has no alternative; it is literally in a box. This patient, I suggested, *did* have an alternative. If the staff stopped paying attention when she put on her light, she could make them come by ripping her bed, vomiting, and so forth. As a matter of fact, she later turned over the television set and broke it. By denying the critical consequence, the staff would force her to escalate behaviors which would produce it, along with outcomes which would be increasingly costly to her and to the social agency they represented. Coming when the light goes on is comparatively cheap.

I recommended a program which would start with this repertoire. They were to set up a written chart scheduling twenty-five daily visits at times *they* set. When the schedule called for their arrival at times when her light was not on, they were to tell her how they appreciated not having been called because such visits often had to be limited since they had been called from something else, but now they had some time for a chat. The program *started* this way but was to pursue a different course designed ultimately to free the staff. This was to include constructional psychotherapy (Goldiamond, 1974) which would be continued on an outpatient basis after she was discharged from the hospital.

Another consultation for which the solution was not easily available was a kidney patient on regular dialysis. Upon coming home, he drank a six-pack of a cola drink and had to be rushed back. He later drank witch hazel. He was diagnosed as suicidal, and the inevitable psychiatric consultation was called for. It turned out that his system had rejected a kidney transplant, and, as far as his family was concerned, he was the equivalent of a terminal cancer patient. They felt he would die but not before he had gone through their savings, home equity, and other resources. When he came home, all members of his lower-middle-class family except his mother greeted him with the guilt-ridden hope that he would die soon—an uncomfortable situation, to say the least. He engaged in exactly the right behavior to get him out of there and into the hospital, where people wanted him to live. By regarding his behavior in terms of the sense it makes, in terms of the requirement for reinforcement it represents, we classify him not as suicidal but as highly desirous of life.

When I was writing to a friend in England about the program we were developing, I realized that this case would not have occurred there. Because of the British health plan, a patient in England would not have been bankrupting his family. Its members might therefore have welcomed him when he came home, and society would have been saved the costs and efforts of medical treatment, hospitalization, consultation, and other procedures.[4] The costs of the present ways of dealing with disability, in terms of the heroic and expensive behaviors they require, are somehow seldom computed.

Similarly, if some way had been figured out of assuring the young man who kept the hospital from discharging him that he would be taken care of or that a future outside the hospital was brighter than one within, society would have been saved the costs and efforts that his ulcers required. What effective approach could have been applied for the woman whose parents had disowned her I do not know. But the question of what is an effective approach can be raised when we view behaviors in terms of the sense they make, rather than in terms of disabilities, pathologies, or maladjustments.

Independence and Affect

An issue that is continually raised with regard to people classified as disabled or aged is independence. Independence is often considered to be a desirable outcome of intervention. When this is stated, it is often part of a mixed message: both "striving for" independence and accepting the fact that one will now be dependent are regarded as signs of adjustment.

The difficulty with setting independence or its quest as a goal is not that it is unrealistic or that it involves false expectations; it is simply that it is a false issue or pseudo issue. Neither the disabled nor the able-bodied, neither the young nor the old are independent of their environment. If I am dependent on an elevator to get me to my office, so, too, are others. If they are independent of the elevator, they are dependent on an unblocked staircase. Stating aims in terms of independence, relative independence, or as much independence as possible poses alternatives in nonexistent terms. It also obscures attention to classification in terms that are congruent with events, point out real problems, and may even suggest solutions which are available or which should be programed.

My laboratory office is on the second floor of a museum. I can take myself to the museum and down the loading ramp. In order to get into the basement, I (or anyone else) must telephone in advance to ask that the basement door be unlocked. I also make sure that the freight elevator will be available. If calling every day became bothersome, I would arrange to arrive at definite hours so that my arrival could be anticipated, as is the arrival of visitors to the regular museum every morning, when the main gates are unlocked. They, too, are dependent on the guard's completion of his duly appointed rounds.

The appropriate form of the dependency question is: With regard to what behavioral patterns, and under what conditions, are disabled people dependent on the environment in ways different from before? If they or society value certain behavior patterns, what should be done to make the behavior possible? My friend, John, whose newspaper experience is treasured, is driven to work every morning and driven home every evening. His morale is high. Neither his morale nor mine would be high if we concentrated on the obstacles in our way.

I was recently asked by a nurse to discuss such difficulties, because some patients were "not being realistic about them." I declined indignantly for four reasons. First, I believe it is far more sensible, useful, and fulfilling to define problems in terms of goals and ways to program the achievement of goals rather than in terms of overcoming obstacles. New conditions, physiological or other, merely mean that more time and different efforts may be required for us to attain our goals. The appropriate approach is one which stresses problem solving in the form of questions such as: What do I have to do to get where I want to go? What is available, or what has to be provided? The solutions for a disabled person are often unique because they have not been handed down to us by the more general environment, which is pro gramed for others. The approach optimizes ingenuity. This is something society sorely needs, and it may profit from carefully observing the unique solutions which people in unique positions are required to find in order to attain their goals.

Second, when the professional refers to patients as "being unaware of," "being unrealistic about," or "repressing" their problems, it is the *professional* who is often being unrealistic. If I am not discussing pains, problems, and infections to which I am susceptible, it is not because I am unaware, unrealistic, or repressing. At times, I am painfully aware of them, and I mean that literally; I am sure other persons also do not discuss problems when they could. If they do not, in discussions with professionals, "face up" to these issues, it is because of the same good sense: They are facing, or trying to face, in a different direction, namely one that can help them program attainment of their goals.

I believe strongly that it should be the task of professionals to help the disabled develop such programs. I discussed physical therapy earlier. Physical therapy was popular with most patients precisely because the concerted effort of the staff was in this direction. I believe that, if staff members learned operant programing, they could do even better. Nevertheless, their efforts were not devoted to discussing shortcomings but to building behavioral repertoires on what was available. Pain could result from the stretching of contracted muscles, and sometimes patients screamed, but they came back and were proud of their therapists and themselves. The place was always a bustle of activity.

If 80 percent of patients who are fitted with leg braces do not wear them, it is not because they are unaware of the importance of standing upright for the function of internal organs, retardation of osteoporosis, and general health (Olson, 1967). It is because most leg braces are made by individuals who are competent in the structural properties of metal and design braces accordingly, but who generally totally lack an understanding of the behavioral requirements of the patient. And why should the makers of braces develop competence in this area? They are amply rewarded by payment on delivery for their present level of incompetence. A rental or use-contingent payment system might serve otherwise. Patients are aware of future complications if they do not stand. But, like the cigarette smoker, they take the cash and let the credit go. The public health task is to devise braces that people will readily wear.

The same point is tellingly made by Sharples (1971) with regard to artificial limbs. He asked patients and providers to rank order five criteria for the development of artificial limbs. What the patients ranked first, the providers ranked last; what the patients ranked last, the providers ranked second. With the exception of one pairing (physical function) the rankings were exactly reversed. Sharples commented that "the nonalignment of priorities between these two groups accounts for much nonutilization of prostheses and the concomitant wasting of time, talent, and more tangible resources" (1971:60).

Third, while a description of situations in terms of what cannot be done or what deficits exist may serve to indicate limitations, it may also be demoralizing and depressing. I have often puzzled over the reinforcers our society must be providing to keep such negating discourse going. I recall once being driven through a downpour in Miami. The cab radio said "Probability of sunshine, 5 percent." It makes sense to talk this way when your economy depends on tourism. But what is the critical variable when my radio reports, "Probability of precipitation, 5 percent," rather than "Probability of sunshine, 95 percent"?

An insight occurred to me once in dealing with a patient, classified as obsessive, who talked rapidly and almost without cessation. If one must talk and one is not particularly gifted or educated, much of the talk will not make sense, but will be verbal garbage, anything to meet the requirement of high output. Breaking into her harangue, I pointed to the desk calender and said, "Today is Wednesday, January 7, 1970." "I don't want to talk about that," she said. "Of course you don't," I answered. "When you talk about what today's date is, that's about all you can say about it. But think of all the ways you can talk about what it's not. You can say it's not Tuesday, January 6, or it's not 1588, or not March 15, 44 B.C. You can be fanciful and imaginative; it's not February 73, 2066. Let's not talk about what is not in your life and what is not making you happy. Let's talk about what is, and what you want, and what we can try to do." She then said much less, but made sense each time.

Fourth, then, we can write endlessly about deficits and obstacles and develop numberless theories about them. We may gain professional audiences and attention. We provide opportunities for rebuttal and counter-rebuttal. In the absence of progress toward solution, the locus of difficulty may be assigned to the problem or the patient, but it may be in the approach.

Absence of progress can, of course, depress patients. They can also be depressed by treatment by the staff, by invasion of privacy, and by any of a variety of other degradations visited upon inmates of institutions. I recall, when I was once "grounded" and was moved by cart, that a student nurse suddenly grabbed a professional journal I was reading out of my hands. She bubbled, "What are you reading?" I presume this was her way of establishing rapport with children, and I recalled the effects of powerlessness then.

By considering apathy, depression, or aggression as developmental stages in injury (or for that matter in aging or other causes for institutionalization), staff members are relieved of the necessity for asking how their actions might have helped cause these reactions. Ameliorative change is thereby precluded. The theories are pervasive. My wife, for example, was told to expect me to be profoundly depressed. When she protested that I was not depressed, she was greeted with the same skepticism that would greet someone disputing cephalocaudal sequences of infantile development.[5]

It is, in part, reaction to one's own injury that is supposed to contribute to depression. But I submit that depression may result because the injury may reduce the availability of consequences that had hitherto been the critical maintainers of behavior. The injury may impose a high response effort to obtain what had hitherto been less difficult to obtain. The depression may produce concern and attention. Actively programing alternative consequences or behavior patterns is a different reaction to injury—with different emotional effects.

Aphasia produces, we are told, profound personality changes and emotional lability. An effect of aphasia is diminution or loss of accustomed ways to control the social environment through speech. In the laboratory similar losses of control are often accompanied by reinstatement of behavior patterns which had in the past been successful in attaining control. Thus, a powerful businessman who had brought straying followers into line by threats and displays of temper often threatened hospital staff members with dire consequences and was irascible. A factory worker who had learned the safe army way out when things had not worked out—"No excuse, sir"—shrugged his shoulders philosophically when the wrong sounds occurred. One woman wept and whined continually. These behavioral patterns and their accompanying emotional lability were present a high proportion of the time; so were the reinforcement losses.

The wife of an aphasic physician commented that her husband's personality had changed markedly since he became ill. He had been a very sweet person and was not continually irritating and insulting. "You're telling me about yourself, and not him," I said. "You're saying that you had always set things up for him so that he got what he was after. How did he behave in the past on the rare occasions when he didn't get it? Those are commonplace now." She thought for a moment and then said, "You're right. He hasn't changed."

The handling of pain and discomfort, and its relation to consequences, is another area that bears inspection. Seated in the wheelchair, I very often feel a discomfort in my seat. It might be called pain. This occurs especially when I am not working. One way to talk about it would be to say that the pain keeps me from working. Thereby, I could get sympathy and support from a variety of people who are proponents of classical theories of emotion. A second way to talk about it would be to say that, because I am not working, my attention is turned to my seat and I feel discomfort. Thereby, I could get sympathy and support from proponents of the James-Lange theory of emotions. I submit that neither approach is particularly helpful.

A third way to talk about it is to say that I am not working because the contingencies which maintain productive work have not been instituted or are somehow crumbling. My discomfort is a signal to me that something is lacking contingency-wise. My seat is apparently more sensitive to the crumbling trend of these contingencies than is my intellect. When I start feeling the discomfort, I should immediately attend to the contingencies before they break down completely. I should set up working conditions so that my writing progresses.

When I use a contingency theory of emotions in this manner, I do not get sympathy, but my behavior receives the same support from my colleagues that maintained it at a high rate before. I valued the support then and value it now.

Transitive and Intransitive Approaches

The title of this chapter is "Coping and Adaptive Behaviors of the Disabled." It raises the questions of coping with what and adapting to what. To understand adaptation we must understand the environment which sets up behavioral requirements and consequences contingent upon them. There is a limited number of ways to change behavior by changing contingencies. When we use environment-free statements in discussing people, we can generate an infinite number of statements, as many as the not-today dates of the obsessive patient mentioned earlier. The environment-free statements generally employ intransitive verbs and give credit (or blame) to the subject of an intransitive sentence: the *child* learns (or does not); *corn* grows (or does not); the *child* develops; *people* age; *older* people deteriorate; in nursing homes, *they* become depressed. We can include the environment by transforming the statements into transitive ones: the *teacher* instructs (or does not) the child; the *farmer* grows (or does not) corn; *something* ages people and develops children; *nursing homes* deteriorate older people and depress them. When we make this transformation, we seem to get a handle on the problem, but the statements are rough on teachers, professionals, and nursing homes and unduly blame them, because following this syntax, it is they who are accountable for undesirable outcomes. They may be victims of the same passive theories and may be equally unhappy about the outcomes.

Accordingly, a second transformation is in order: the teacher's *procedures* instruct the child (or do not), the farmer's *procedures* grow corn (or do not), nursing home *arrangements* deteriorate older people and depress them. The stress has now changed. If the child is not learning and the teacher is not teaching, we should look to the *procedures* used in the transaction and change them to produce the effects desired. This is something we may be able to teach the teacher or the professionals in a hospital.

However, the second transformation also has inadequacies. It lacks parallelism between subject and predicate. With regard to the subject, it is not the total teacher that the transformation involves but those procedures she uses which are relevant to her role in fulfilling the requirements of her contract with the school board. Similarly, the total child is not the object of these procedures. There are other behaviors, for example, those related to religion, that the school is explicitly enjoined from affecting. The behaviors of concern are those relevant to the social contract implied in the establishment of a school system. Accordingly, by the same token that the teacher is not the manipulating subject, the child is also not the manipulated object. This provides our third transformation, which is the programing statement. The *procedures* of the teacher program the *target behaviors* of the child or do not; they may program others in addition or instead. The arrangements of the hospital program target behaviors of the patient or do not; they may program other behaviors which are not in the implicit contract or are contrary to it. The target can be agreed upon by mutually consenting adults or can be determined in other ways. Competence is required in programing, in setting targets, in assessing current repertoires, in using or establishing necessary facilities, and so on. In successful self-control, the procedures of the programer establish such programing and analytic competence in clients regarding their target behaviors. The client's involvement with the professional and reliance on interventive institutions is phased out as the client becomes increasingly competent.

We are all familiar with the nursery rhyme, "Oats, peas, beans, and barley grow, / Oats, peas, beans, and barley grow, / Neither you nor I, nor anyone know / How oats, peas, beans and barley grow." When the process is expressed intransitively, it is mysterious and unknowable. Not so the procedures, however. Went (1957) reports results obtained with plant growth in a Climatron, an environmental chamber in which there is considerable control over variables normally uncontrolled in a greenhouse or outside it. He was able to produce pea plants almost to specifications. Presumably, by changing the settings of his variables to those values which hold outside, he could have grown all the different pea patterns whose diversity has led to the nursery rhyme I quoted.

Where the conventional settings of typical variables produce conventional behavior patterns and progressions, it may not matter much for practical purposes if we view behavioral changes as possessing regularities of their own; that is, they need be only grossly related to the environment. Because the environment seems to be a constant, for practical purposes it can be ignored. Instransitive forms can be used for purposes of understanding. However, when the behavior patterns produced are not conventional, practical procedures deriving from an intransitive statement which ignores the environment break down. In the search for transitive forms, for the functional relation of behavior to its environmental contingencies, we may uncover the transitive relations which also govern the conventional cases whose controlling environment we have been taking for granted and have been ignoring. We thereby extend knowledge and understanding even when intervention is unnecessary.

Accordingly, whether one's interests are knowledge or intervention, theory or practice, I would like to solicit members for the Society for Abolition of Intransitive Verbs for describing people. The name is in the negative form which I have opposed up to now, but I have chosen it because its initials, applied to persons, form the acronym SAIV. The message is clear.

Adaptive Behaviors and Social Institutions

It appears to be far more costly and time-consuming to develop successful social programing for the disabled than it is to explore failures ascribed to autonomous psychological processes. If we deal with social programing requirements, we may be able to attain goals not hitherto attained. But at what social cost would the benefit be attained, and how would this compare with the outcome of a cost-benefit analysis of the present system? What other demands are being placed on our limited social resources? Certain outcomes, like degradation or suffering, are difficult to cost account, and I shall therefore confine my comments to those which are capable of more ready analysis. I do not know whether the consequences of transitive programing views are less costly than those of intransitive disability views. We have no such information at present. To get it requires us to think through goals, priorities, available procedures, and procedures that might become available. What I do suggest is that even the *appearance* of the costliness (as compared to the status quo) of this effort may be illusory.

It is expensive to train professionals and provide professional intervention. To the extent that the disabled person does not rely on such social institutions, he is not draining their resources and not requiring a society harassed by other obligations to provide yet more. One may be independent of a professional intervention system, but one is not independent of the social environment. The question that must be raised is the comparative cost of alternative systems.

Rather than discussing such alternatives to hospitalization as home visitors, personal care organizations, and the like, which others can do far more capably, I shall confine my discussion to the alternatives to current nonprograming interventions that are provided by programing procedures and analysis.

A standard item of equipment in physical therapy is a chair in which, through a complex pulley system, weights are attached to the patient's legs to assist or resist movement. It is the leg equivalent of the barbells. In one device, the weights are behind the patient's back and so must be controlled by a physical therapist. This system is far more costly than a system which would substitute, whenever possible, patient control for professional control.

At home, the high cost of the device, plus the fact that another person had to help me use it, seemed to preclude such exercise on my own. However, I purchased a portable clothes-rack which has no bottom bar, so that I can wheel into it. With pulleys and weights, the total cost of the device was less than thirty dollars. It may not do all that the expensive chair can do, but I can exercise my leg and can program an increasing weight requirement by myself. It would seem that redesign of such equipment would save costs for physical therapists, who might then turn their attention to other areas and more adequately use their unique skills.[6] Such redesign might also influence patient recovery.

The costs for hospitalization for the consequences of immobility can be staggering. A patient's physiological processes can be affected by his mobility and by his regularly putting weight on the bones through assuming an upright position. The lack of competence of brace makers has been noted. But the price of such incompetence is a bill which is staggering, not only in terms of hospitalization and loss in employment but also in terms of misery and suffering. Surely, it would be less costly to support a *sustained* research effort concentrated on producing braces which people will wear.

Consider the case of the brain-damaged patient who urinated against the walls of his room and in bed. To follow through on the token system which worked would have been too costly because of the institutional structure available. The patient was catheterized, at considerable saving. However, catheterization involves insertion of a foreign substance into the bladder and makes bacterial invasion possible, indeed highly probable. The resultant infection will require intervention which will become extremely expensive if renal involvement occurs. One hospitalization for a short time will be far more costly than a token economy run over six months would have been, and the token economy might deal with other targets as well.

One insurance company, with considerable experience in rehabilitation costs, reports spending close to $5 million on rehabilitation for fewer than two hundred insured wheelchair cases, or more than $25 thousand per average case. The company's estimate, based on other cases, is that, if the patients had not had rehabilitation training, costs to the company would have *exceeded* the cost of rehabilitation by almost $50 thousand per case, on the average. The 1965 estimate based on about one hundred thousand civilian paraplegics suggests that the savings are not insignificant (Barrie, 1970). A pilot study in Israel on costs of nonrehabilitation of persons with other types of disability makes a similar point and attempts an explicit cost-benefit analysis (Silberstein, et al., 1964). The need for raising the question of the cost of nonrehabilitation in the United States is suggested by Morris' (1973) estimate that there are "six million Americans with handicaps so severe and incurable that they cannot carry on all or part of their normal activities."

Rehabilitation facilities are distinguished from acute-care hospitals to a large extent by the emphasis the former place on attempting to replace institutional intervention with other types of intervention. The considerable success they have achieved, as judged solely by the insurance figures cited, suggests that the success can be extended by more explicit attention to a programing analysis and to research in programing.

Social contingencies can also deteriorate the behaviors of the disabled. A professional who enjoyed her work but whose multiple sclerosis made her unable "to cope with public transportation to and from work" asked for a small subsidy to augment what she could afford for substitute transportation. "I was candidly told by the Welfare Department," Saxon (1973:112–113) writes, "that they would be happy to wholly subsidize me when I gave up work, but could not arrange to help me with $20 per week to prevent my becoming a public charge. . . . [I] do not want to be forced to stop contributing through circumstances beyond my control." Another example, a report for the Special Committee on Aging of the United States Senate, by the Levinson Gerontological Policy Institute (1971:5), notes that average payments under Old Age Assistance for the severely handicapped living at home are $77.60 a month, but that "our programs . . . will readily pay an average of perhaps $400–$500 a month to keep the same person in an institution." As the requirement to get the help unobtainable at $77.60 is behavioral deterioration, deterioration is being programed. In addition to these individual effects, "the entire burden is placed upon family and neighbors who usually help for a time, until they are virtually bankrupted in money and energy. . . . Instead of reinforcing and conserving these natural family and friendship supports, they are permitted to exhaust themselves until only much more costly alternatives remain available" (1971:5)—including drinking a pack of soft drinks to return to the hospital for dialysis or drinking witch hazel to stay there, as I mentioned earlier.

Setting up Personal Care Organizations (Caro and Morris, 1971) which provide support at home not only may be more economical but may produce marked behavioral and physiological differences. Caro and Morris suggest a voucher procedure whereby the disabled may choose among a variety of delivery systems and suggest other well-considered alternatives. To the extent that such investigations increase the programing repertoire of the environment, they are to be welcomed. However, I should like to point out that the system may simply produce alternatives between types of custodial care unless the paraprofessionals involved utilize programing procedures. The extensive use of paraprofessionals (often operating at distances considerably removed from the professionals) to program behavior is reported by Tharp and Wetzel (1969).

Institutions are currently under attack. It should be pointed out, however, that the establishment of behaviors which are the opposite of those targeted by the social contract is not confined to institutions such as asylums, hospitals, and schools. Nor is it confined to currently established professional groups. It can occur equally well at home, in the community, and elsewhere under the well-meaning aegis of parents, neighborhood groups, and new orders of paraprofessionals. What is at issue is not the type of institution or professional but the type of programing.

We can, like the obsessional mentioned, talk endlessly of programs which do not produce the outcomes targeted, or we can program competing outcomes and denounce the programs which exist. We might more profitably direct our attention to the procedures used in programs that produce outcomes in accord with the targets and to those which produce outcomes which compete with the targets. We might utilize effective procedures in different programs, and we might ascertain the conditions under which institutionalization is the intervention of choice. What this boils down to is that I suggest we start treating institutions which present disturbing patterns with the same programing courtesy with which we treat individuals who present disturbing patterns. What is needed is a marriage of social analysis and behavior analysis.

If deteriorated behavior of individuals can be shaped by reinforcement of invalidism, institutional behavior can be similarly shaped by short-sighted policy. Presumably a patient flat on his back needs more care than one on his feet. To get institutions to accept and care for the bedridden, Illinois Welfare paid nursing homes an allotment scaled according to degree of disability; they were paid more for supine patients than for ambulatory ones. The contingencies for keeping patients bedridden were thereby neatly set up. A contingency analysis suggests that the allotment might be scaled according to degree of progress toward ambulation, with so fat a bonus paid when the patient *walks* out that the institution will set up a research laboratory to develop new devices. An interesting analysis of the relation between institutional care and social and other payoffs for the institution is provided by Ullmann (1967).

More is required than the building of "a barrier free community environment" (Molinaro, 1973). While such human engineering to eliminate "physical barriers . . . in the design and construction of our buildings and communities" is of great importance, such change is insufficient by itself. Architects and engineers should concern themselves with contingencies. For example, when the Sermon on the Mount is printed in unreadable type, it cannot be read. Printing it handsomely in legible type does not, however, guarantee that it will be read. To assure that it will be read requires motivation-incentive-meaningfulness, or attention to the contingencies, social contexts, and systems which provide consequences and set behavioral requirements for them. Unless these are set up, no one may read the Sermon on the Mount. It might then be falsely concluded that one should not attempt to set legible type because it makes no difference anyway, except for occasional heroes, such as Lincoln, who read by candlelight. One *should* set legible type, and one *should also* set contingencies appropriate to the task.

A programing approach does not mean the establishment of uniform programs which ignore differences between individuals.[7] Where there is such deindividualization, I suggest we look to the present approaches, which posit uniform reactive states, life problems, and deficits as the result of disability. Such approaches may set up uniform social contingencies which provide self-fulfillment for the hypotheses. A programing approach requires meticulous attention to the different repertoires people bring to their disability, to differences in targets they require or desire, to differences in the procedures which will be necessary for change, and to the different consequences which maintain behavior. A programing approach suggests procedures whereby individuals themselves can learn how to analyze and control the contingencies governing their own behavior.

None of the foregoing, I trust, will be interpreted as advocacy of some simple-minded procedures for reinforcing here and extinguishing there. The branch of applied behavior analysis which offers closest parallels is programed instruction, which not only requires application of contingencies of reinforcement but also defines the contingencies in terms of a program, or complex curriculum, whose establishment requires expertise in the curricular area.

In self-control, it is assumed that the people closest to the curricular area, ones who have the greatest expertise, are the people involved. The task for the professional programer is to teach them how to develop programs for themselves by keeping records so that they can relate changes in their own patterns to changes in procedures. In short, the purpose is to help them form their own analyses. In this process, setbacks are not occasions for despair but occasions for unscheduled learning, just as equipment breakdowns in operant laboratories have at times produced significant breakthroughs.

Much of rehabilitation is already disposed toward such analysis; the contrast with acute-care hospitals is often striking. Research which develops programing for the disabled may increase happiness as defined in classic Greece: "Happiness is striving one's utmost under favorable conditions." This definition calls upon us to ascertain and possibly program the favorable conditions which will maintain behavior in the strength desired. In the process of producing such happiness, we may learn to understand it better.

The coping and adaptive behaviors of the disabled are, in the terms of the third transformation from the passive to the programing active, the target outcomes, unwitting or witting, of the programing procedures of the social system. That is, the specific programing procedures program and produce the adaptive behaviors of the disabled. When the significant attention is to deterioration, the system programs the adaptive behavior of deterioration. Patients may then express pessimism and depression. Using other programs, the system may program ingenuity. Patients may then express optimism. Investigators will then find statistically significant and intriguing correlations between coping behaviors and those verbal behaviors we call attitudes. By examining social systems in terms of the programing procedures they institute, we may become able to program both behavior *and* attitudes. We may become better able to analyze and systematize our knowledge. The behaviors of the disabled are adaptive now, as they will be when we have more knowledge.

Perhaps what we should be talking about are the adapting and coping repertoires of the environment. We might then talk of environments with limited talents and resources, of environments which are not living up to their potentials, and of environments which are ingenious. We might then attempt to set up environments which program target behaviors in accord with social contracts mutually agreed upon by consenting adults.[8] Programs of a sort exist now, but they are often unsystematic and inexplicit and can produce outcomes which are the exact opposite of the targets stated in the social contract. When we shift our approach toward the direction suggested in this discussion, we shall still have a long way to go. We shall be changing the explicitness whereby we describe the functional elements of a program, the degree to which we can learn how to find those elements, and, we hope, the extent to which we can manipulate them. Closing on the same personal note with which I began and speaking only for myself, I conclude: Hasten the day!

NOTES

1. See especially pp. 111–112.

2. Since the writing of this paper, an exploratory report has been published describing use of biofeedback to increase mobility in a paraplegic and a paraparetic (Schneider et al., 1975). One of the patients reports continued progress (Herbert, 1975).

3. Results of the present program, in which fluency has been established with lifelong stutterers in a median of 29 sessions, will be reported in a monograph in preparation. For an earlier report, based mainly on the prior experimental analysis, see Goldiamond (1965*b*).

4. Since this chapter was written, the federal government has undertaken much of the financial underwriting of kidney dialysis. Had this been in effect at the time, the behaviors mentioned might not have occurred or the cost been incurred. However, the general point still holds for similar situations.

5. *Newsweek* (March 5, 1973) notes the case of a Marine corporal who, upon being told after surgery for removal of a bullet that he would be paralyzed for life, was not depressed, but happy to be alive at all. "I adjusted to the fact so quickly," he reports, "that they sent me to a psychiatrist to find out if I was okay" (p. 23).

6. The author is indebted to Robert T. Babbs, Jr., Director of Rehabilitation at the University of Chicago, and Mrs. Adrienne Peterson and Donald Olson, registered physical therapists, for suggestions.

Currently, much of therapy time for patients consists of waiting, since the therapists usually have more than one patient at a time and divide their time between patients. This is built into a system where the patient cannot adjust equipment for himself. An alternate system, based on a model designed for academic material (Cohen and Filipczak, 1971), suggests itself. In that model, the teacher became a program checker, adviser, and editor. She could visually monitor as many as thirty carrels at the same time. The carrels were used for programed material. When the student arrived, he checked in at the teacher's desk and was given the appropriate unit. When he left, he brought the records to the teacher, who checked them with him and then noted which unit he should have next (either the same unit or an earlier one).

In physical therapy, this would involve equipment which the patient could adjust himself or which the therapist might adjust at program points dictated by the preceding record. This might be a cumulative record of behaviors, or other print-out. If the recording system could not provide immediate feedback to the patient concerning progress toward his goal, at least it might produce records which could be compared with records previously obtained. In the educational system, the program checkers were able to note not only the progress of the students but possible program improvements. They used their knowledge of subject matter and teaching skills for continual program revision and improvement. The carrels were supplemented by classrooms and other facilities when explicit programs were not yet available. The use of such a systems approach in physical therapy naturally imposes behavioral requirements on therapists to be more explicit, something which patients also desire. The presence of explicit evidence of progress, no matter how minute, can sustain behaviors which often crumble otherwise because the patient feels too discouraged to continue.

7. The reader may substitute "institution" throughout this paragraph wherever "individual" appears or is implied for a ready verbal extension of behavior analysis of individual organisms to behavior analysis of institutions. Developing the appropriate procedures is a more difficult matter and is, of course, a direction required by behavior analysis.

8. This is the thrust of B. F. Skinner's *Beyond Freedom and Dignity* (1971).

BIBLIOGRAPHY

Ayllon, T., and Azrin, N.
   1968.   *The Token Economy*. New York: Appleton-Century-Crofts.
Azrin, N.
   1958.   Some effects of noise on human behavior. *Journal of the Experimental Analysis of Behavior,* 1:183–200.
Barber, T.; DiCara, I.; Kamiya, J.; Miller, N. E.; Shapiro, D.; and Stoya, J., eds.
   1971.   *Biofeedback and Self-control, 1970*. Chicago: Aldine.

Barrie, D.
   1970.   The economics and management of spinal cord injury. Paper pre-
           sented at Input Conference, Spinal Injury Service, Phoenix, Ariz.,
           June 25–26.
Caro, F. G., and Morris, R.
   1971.   *Personal Care for the Severely Disabled: Organizing and Financing Care.*
           Waltham, Mass.: Levinson Gerontological Policy Institute, Brandeis
           University.
Cohen, H. L., and Filipczak, J.
   1971.   *A New Learning Environment.* San Francisco: Jossey-Bass.
Fordyce, W. E.
   1968.   Psychology and rehabilitation. In *Rehabilitation and Medicine,* edited
           by E. Licht, pp. 129–151. New Haven: Elizabeth Licht.
   1971.   Psychological assessment and management. In *Handbook of Physical
           Medicine and Rehabilitation,* edited by F. H. Krusen, F. J. Kottke, and P.
           Ellwood. Philadelphia: W.B. Saunders.
   1973.   Intervention in the disability process. Paper delivered at conference
           on Socialization in the Disability Process. Department of Sociology,
           Northwestern University, Chicago, Ill., March 5–6.
Goldiamond, I.
   1965a. Self-control procedures in personal behavior problems. *Psychological
           Reports,* 17 (Monogr. Suppl. 3):851–868.
   1965b. Stuttering and fluency as manipulatable operant response classes. In
           Research in Behavior Modification, edited by L. Krasner and L. P.
           Ullmann, pp. 106–156. New York: Holt, Rinehart and Winston.
   1969.   Applications of operant conditioning. In *Current Trends in Army Medi-
           cal Psychology,* edited by C. A. Thomas, pp. 198–231. Denver: Fitz-
           simmons General Hospital.
   1974.   Toward a constructional approach to social problems. *Behaviorism,* 2,
           no. 1:1–84.
Goodall, K.
   1972.   Shapers at work. *Psychology Today,* 6, no. 6:53–63, 132–138.
Hefferline, R. F.; Keenan, B.; and Harford, R.
   1959.   Escape and avoidance conditioning in human subjects without their
           observation of the response. *Science,* 130:1338–1339.
Hendershot, C. H.
   1967.   *Programmed Learning: A Bibliography of Programs and Presentation
           Devices.* Bay City, Mich.: Carl H. Hendershot.
Herbert, L.
   1975.   Biofeedback: Post script. *Squeaky Wheel,* 4, no.4:10, 12.
Holz, W. C., and Azrin, N. H.
   1961.   Discriminative properties or punishment. *Journal of the Experimental
           Analysis of Behavior,* 4:225–232.

Levinson Gerontological Policy Institute
　1971.　*Alternatives to Nursing Home Care: A Proposal.* United States Senate, Special Committee on Aging, G.P.O., Stock No. 5270–1248.
Michael, J. L.
　1970.　Rehabilitation. In *Behavior Modification in Clinical Psychology*, edited by C. Neuringer and J. L. Michael, pp. 52–85. New York: Appleton-Century-Crofts.
Molinaro, L.
　1973.　Building a barrier-free community environment. Announcement for workshop sponsored by The American City Corporation, Columbia, Md., March 21–23.
Morris. R.
　1973.　What do you do after the doctor leaves? *Harper's Magazine*, 246, no. 1472:88–89.
Myerson, L.; Kerr, N.; and Michael, J. L.
　1967.　Behavior modification in rehabilitation. In *Child Development*, edited by S. W. Bijou and D. M. Baer, pp. 214–239. New York: Appleton-Century-Crofts.
Neuringer, C., and Michael, J. L., eds.
　1970.　*Behavior Modification in Clinical Psychology.* New York: Appleton-Century-Crofts.
Olson, E. V.
　1967.　The hazards of immobility. *American Journal of Nursing*, 67:779–797.
Orne, M. T.
　1959.　The nature of hypnosis: Artifact and essence. *Journal of Abnormal and Social Psychology*, 58:277–299.
Premack, D.
　1970.　A functional analysis of language. *Journal of the Experimental Analysis of Behavior*, 14:107–125.
Saxon, B.
　1973.　A public charge charges the public. *Harper's Magazine*, 247, no. 1482:112–115.
Schneider, C.; Scaer, R.; Groenewald, P. T.; and Atkinson, H.
　1975.　EMG techniques in neuromuscular rehabilitation with cord injured, patients. *Squeaky Wheel*, 4 no. 4:4–10.
Sharples, N.
　1971.　Prosthetic technology and patient use. *Inquiry*, 8:60–70.
Sidman, J., and Stoddard, L. T.
　1966.　Programming preception and learning for retarded children. *International Review of Research in Mental Retardation*, 2:151–208.
Silberstein, J.; Margulec, I.; Eliahu, Y.; Gaspar, E.; Hovneh, A.; Huppert, E.; Pinkerfield, E.; Gottlieb, E.; and Kossowsky, R.
　1964.　Costs of non-rehabilitation in Israel. *Journal of Chronic Disability*, 17:991–1018.

Skinner, B. F.
    1938. *The Behavior of Organisms*. New York: Appleton-Century-Crofts.
    1953. *Science and Human Behavior*. New York: Macmillan.
    1957. *Verbal Behavior*. New York: Appleton-Century-Crofts.
    1968. *The Technology of Teaching*. New York: Appleton-Century-Crofts.
    1971. *Beyond Freedom and Dignity*. New York: Alfred A. Knopf.
    1974. *About Behaviorism*. New York: Alfred A. Knopf.
Sulzer, B., and Mayer, R. G.
    1972. *Behavior Modification Procedures for School Personnel*. Hinsdale, Ill.: Dryden.
Terrace, H. S.
    1963. Discrimination learning with and without "errors." *Journal of the Experimental Analysis of Behavior*, 6:1–27.
    1969. Extinction of a discriminative operant following discrimination learning with and without errors. *Journal of the Experimental Analysis of Behavior*, 12:571–582.
Tharp, R. G., and Wetzel, R. J.
    1969. *Behavior Modification in the Natural Environment*. New York: Academic Press.
Thompson, T., and Schuster, C. R.
    1968. *Behavioral Pharmacology*. Englewood Cliffs, N.J.: Prentice-Hall.
Ullmann, L.P.
    1967. *Institution and Outcome*. Oxford: Pergamon Press.
Went, F.
    1957. *The Experimental Control of Plant Growth*. Waltham, Mass.: Chronica Botanica.

CHAPTER 6

Conceptual Model of Family as a Group: Family Response to Disability

Betty E. Cogswell

This chapter has two objectives. The first is theoretical: to develop a conceptual approach for viewing the family as a group, as a small system in process of change. The second is substantive: to describe families' responses to the disability of one of their members. These two objectives are closely interrelated, for the theoretical perspective has been developed inductively from an intensive study of twelve families. This study fits the grounded theory orientation (Glaser and Strauss, 1967) whereby there is a constant search for concepts which seem sufficiently accurate and useful to systematically describe what occurs in families with a disabled member.

As other researchers have found, it is extremely difficult to assay the reactions of families to disability within some kind of comprehensive framework if the intent is to describe the many vicissitudes families undergo as they proceed from the onset of disability through convalescence and rehabilitation. In an attempt to organize these data, I have drawn concepts, directions, and insights from four sources: general sociology, family theory and studies, general systems theory, and the arts—a play and a film.

This chapter includes revisions of earlier presentations, incorporating selected portions of a paper presented at the annual meeting of the American Psychological Association in Montreal, August 30, 1973. This work was supported by Health Resources Administration, U.S. Department of Health, Education and Welfare, Grant No. H-00559.

Design of Study

An exploratory study was made of twelve households, each of which had a disabled family member. While there were elaborate criteria for selecting the families, those most pertinent to this chapter were a disability that included visible, restricted body movement and was unlikely to result in death within five years. Two other criteria included the patient's return to the family after initial hospitalization and family residence within a fifty-mile radius of the university where the study was based. Data were collected from fifty-eight individual family members and from approximately twenty rehabilitation workers, either hospital-based professionals or home visitors, who worked with the families. Families were followed for two-to-three-year periods. Three of the families, studied previously in the late fifties, were selected for this study because of their value in providing information on the long-term effects of disability on the family. Table 1 contains a social profile of the twelve families.

The use of households as a unit of data collection does not imply that the definition of family for this study was restricted to only those individuals in residence. The importance of other family members was recognized by the investigators, and as much information as possible was obtained about kin who came forward at the time of disability. Both time and financial limitations precluded interviewing kin who neither lived nor visited frequently in the households under study.

A variety of data collection techniques were used: open-ended individual and group interviews, fixed-form questions, observations in the home, and standardized family measurement scales. Individual data collection techniques permitted the recording of perspectives of each family member toward the family group. Only group observations and group interviews captured actual group behavior.

An advantage of using a variety of data collection techniques is that each method is useful in interpreting data collected by other techniques. For example, data obtained on the family measure-

TABLE 1. Description of Family

Family	Unit	Member's Roles	Age: Disability	Age 1972	Type of Disability	Duration	Occupation Predisability	Occupation 1972
Smith	A.	Husband/Father	36	43	Arthritis	7 years	Mechanic	Self-employed
		*Wife/Mother	34	41			Salesclerk	Bookkeeper (pt. time)
		Son/Brother	10	17			Student	Student/Mechanic (pt. time)
		Daughter/Sister	7	14			Student	Student
James	A.	*Husband/Father/Uncle	31	34	Paraplegia	3 years	Architectural Draftsman	Architectural Draftsman
		Wife/Mother/Aunt	27	30			Housewife	Switchboard Operator
		Niece/Cousin	16	19			Student	Student
		Son/Brother/Cousin	7	10			Student	Student
		Son/Brother/Cousin	4	7				
Dobson	A.	Husband/Father	54	57			Retired/Disabled	Retired/Disabled
		Wife/Mother	46	49			Clerk	Unemployed
		*Son/Brother	20	23	Paraplegia	3 years	Enlisted Military	Unemployed
		Son/Brother	19	22			Construction (pt. time)	Construction (full time)
		Son/Brother	10	13			Student	Student

*Disabled person.

Unk. = Unknown.

N.A. In "Age: Disability" column "N.A." signifies the person was not part of the family at the time of the disability. Under "Age 1972" it means that the person had left the home by 1972.

TABLE 1—*Continued*

Family	Unit	Member's Roles	Age:Disability	Age 1972	Type of Disability	Duration	Occupation Predisability	Occupation 1972
Kaiser	A.	*Husband/Father	39	41	Hemiplegia	3 years	Clerk	Unemployed
		Wife/Mother	Unk.	Unk.			Sales (pt. time)	Sales (pt. time)
		Daughter/Sister	15	17				
		Son/Brother	13	15				
		Son/Brother	12	14				
		Son/Brother	9	11				
		Daughter/Sister	Unk.	Unk.				
		Daughter/Sister	2	4				
Borden	A.	Husband/Father	65	68			Retired/Disabled	Retired/Disabled
		*Wife/Mother	63	65	Hemiplegia	2 years	Domestic	Domestic
		Daughter	40	42			Secretary } (2 jobs)	Secretary } (2 jobs)
							Domestic	Domestic
Jordan	A.	Husband/Father	44	46	Multiple	2 years	Handyman	Unemployed
		*Wife/Mother	30	32	Sclerosis		Housewife	Housewife
		Daughter/Sister	6	8			Student	Student
		Daughter/Sister	4	6			Student	Student
		Son/Brother	3	5				
Gaston	A.	*Husband/Father	26	27	Paraplegia	1 year	Spinner	Draftsman
		Wife/Mother	28	29			Unknown	Unknown
		Son/Brother	4	5				
		Son/Brother	4	5				

Warren	A.	*Husband/Father	20	21	Paraplegia	1 year	Skilled/Foreman	Contractor
		Wife/Mother	19	20			Housewife	Housewife
		Son/Brother	1	2				
		Son/Brother	N.A.	1				
Gordon	A.	Husband/Father	51	65			Supervisor	Retired
		Wife/Mother	45	Dec'd			Clerk/Mgr.	
		*Son/Brother	16	30	Paraplegia	14 years	Student	Bookkeeper/Mgr.
		Daughter/Sister	16	Mar.				
	B.	Father						
		*Son						
Merton	A.	Mother	Unk.	N.A.				
		Daughter/Sister/Wife	21	N.A.				
		Husband/Brother-in-Law/Son-in-Law	23	N.A.			Sales	
		Daughter/Sister/Sister-in-Law	17	N.A.				
		*Son/Brother/Brother-in-Law	19	36	Paraplegia	17 years		
	B.	*Husband	19	36	Paraplegia	17 years	Clerk	Draftsman / Sales (self-emp.) (2 jobs)
		Wife	N.A.	34				Beautician
Howard	A.	Mother	Unk.	Unk.				
		*Son	33	36	Diabetic/Amputee	3 years	Auto Mechanic	Unemployed

TABLE 1—*Continued*

Family Unit	Member's Roles	Age: Disability	Age 1972	Type of Disability	Duration	Occupation Predisability	Occupation 1972
B	Husband/Cousin	Unk.	Unk.				
	Wife/Cousin	Unk.	Unk.				
	*Cousin	33	36				
	Daughter	Unk.	Unk.				
	Daughter	Unk.	Unk.				
	Daughter	Unk.	Unk.				
	Son	2	5				
Erwin A.	Husband/Father	Unk.	N.A.			Insurance Broker	
	Wife/Mother	Unk.	N.A.			Sales (pt.time)	
	Daughter/Sister	Unk.	N.A.			Student	
	*Son/Brother	17	34	Paraplegia	17 years	Student	Accountant
B.	*Husband/Father	17	34				
	Wife/Mother	N.A.	Unk.				
	Daughter	N.A.	3				Housewife
C.	*Ex-husband/Father (divorced)	17	34				

ment scales called our attention to the need for some more subtle interpretations of the open-ended data. The open-ended data helped to ground more concretely some of the items on the scales. Separate interviews with individual family members shed light on observations of the group as well as on group interviews including two or more family members. A further advantage of using multiple-data techniques is that consistency of findings from several techniques strengthens conclusions on validity of data.

The general guidelines used in this research design can be illustrated best by a contrast of our approach with others in the field of family research. Such a comparison will also point out the uniqueness of our design. In brief summary, the highest proportion of family studies are based on data taken from one respondent. Most others, concentrating on dyadic relationships, are based on data from two respondents; and a few, notably those of Strodtbeck (1954) and Straus (1968), deal with three family members. Our unit of research was the family group, and our method was to collect data from all family members. Further, our study, unlike those of Strodtbeck and Straus, concentrated on natural rather than experimental behavior.

In studies of family group therapy (for example, Satir, 1964, and Jackson, 1956), where the family is the unit of research, data collection usually occurs in an institutional setting,[1] and there is a heavy emphasis on family psychopathology. We studied families in their natural habitat—the home—without particular emphasis on psychopathology. Hess and Handel (1959) did study whole families in their investigations of family worlds, using case-study data collection and analysis. Our study differs from theirs because, while we used case-study data collection, we attempted analysis across families, concentrating on family properties, patterns, and processes.

In instances where the family rather than the individual is the unit for research, data analysis presents some unexplored problems. Existing data collection techniques as well as statistical techniques are more easily applicable to analysis of characteristics and attributes of individuals than to analysis of small groups. One can, as we did, use family measurement scales to obtain each member's perspective on self, other family members, and family issues. Then one can ascertain degrees of consensus or concordance. Further exploration and work, however, is needed to construct instruments which weight the varying degrees of influence of each family member's perspectives on group interaction and dynamics.

Perhaps the most difficult problem of analysis was the objective of the study itself—to develop inductively a conceptual framework for studying families as groups in process, as small social systems. This required a constant interplay between conceptualization and data ordering and reordering as new insights occurred. Sensitive to the problems of measurement and conceptualization, I developed a working analytic framework which advances the study of whole families beyond mere case description. Further refinements of this and other family group models, however, could easily require a career of investigation.

In conceptualizing family as a group, modern systems theory serves well as an understructure which forces one's thinking toward holistic, dynamic, and process perspectives. Systems theory, however, is general and nonsubstantive; therefore, I have drawn concepts from both general and family sociology. The current level of theoretical development in family sociology and general systems theory[2] is such that systems theory is most useful as a tool in inductive, analytic description of vast arrays of data. As yet, it is not a particularly useful approach for deductive studies because of the difficulties in operationalizing concepts. Systems theory, however, has been a useful approach for ordering data about these twelve families, for their responses and behavior seemed to approximate an open, purposive, goal-seeking, self-adaptive system.

Reuben Hill (1974) has explored the use of modern systems theory as an approach for increasing our understanding of family phenomena. He indicated that a basic shortcoming of all existing conceptual frameworks[3] about the family, with the exception of the family development approach, is their failure to cope systematically with the social time dimension. The thrust of Hill's paper is to juxtapose a description and delineation of the framework of family development and general systems theory. In this exercise, Hill found that even the family development framework has several limitations:

1. It is too simple in organization and rigid in interrelationships to allow for the complexity and fluidity of families.

2. It views family as a closed rather than open system and takes the position that events occurring within the family are likely to be explained better by internal antecedent family events than by external events.

3. It views family as a system with a relatively static equilibrium and thus with little capacity to make structural changes when, in actuality, a family's capacities for growth, development, adaptation, and structural change may be the very attributes by which it remains a viable system.

To these limitations of the family development framework, I would add a fourth particularly pertinent to this study. Most previous research using this framework has concentrated on macroanalysis of broad institutional patterns connected with lengthy stages in the family life cycle (for example, Duvall, 1962; Glick, 1957; Lansing and Kish, 1957) rather than on microanalysis of day-to-day changes in the dynamics of family interaction and structure.

Art and Science in Investigation

As diverse as art and science are in approaches to phenomena, they are similar in that each turns to advantage selective views of reality. Scientific theories reflect only the essentials of phenomena, by necessity focusing attention on some aspects of reality to the neglect of others; likewise art, in helping to clarify the myriad details of everyday occurrences, often strips life to its barest essentials, or it may exaggerate some aspect of life in order to convey a message. In this context, the main difference between the two approaches is the extent to which individual interpreters may manipulate and modify the elements used to interpret or represent phenomena. Scientists are not allowed either to distort data to fit a particular theory or to omit data which do not support a theory, while artists are granted poetic license to highlight messages and intents. By virtue of this poetic license, art sometimes is able to point more clearly than science toward new views of reality.

In this study insights gained through viewing and studying a play and a film were extremely useful in helping me to clarify some of the properties of family group phenomena (see table 2 on page 154) and from this clarification to develop a conceptual scheme (see table 3 on page 157) to order the masses of data collected on the twelve families with disabled members. This was a two-step process: use of art to grasp more clearly the phenomena of groups followed by use of these insights to construct a scheme to analyze family response to disability.

I was led to this somewhat unorthodox course through a series of events. Early in my career as a student, Laura Thompson discussed with me many times a useful working hypothesis: art often precedes science in depicting new views of reality. Having initiated this study with full awareness that behavioral science had little to offer in the way of conceptual schemes for viewing family as a group and being dissatisifed with the schemes I had been able to abstract from my data, I was searching for new leads. Fortuitously, I came upon a play and a film that epitomized family as a group rather than as a collection of individuals. This suggested a tentative organizational scheme for this study.

Laura Thompson had also given me a second useful hypothesis: that basic fundamentals of a holistic problem-solving approach are best observed by studying groups on the razor's edge of survival, groups where life or death is problematic. When group survival becomes problematic among people with a strong group identification, it is my impression that group structures, dynamics, and processes are reduced to essential necessities. Problem-solving is a day-to-day occurrence, with individual and group competence and potential likely to be used to the maximum. Social elaborations based on previous roles, norms, status, and prestige are less salient than in groups where survival is not threatened. These types of groups bear some similiarities to families with a newly disabled member.

For the purposes of this study I have chosen to contrast two works of art, a play and a film, in order to obtain a firmer grasp on family group phenomena. In 1966, when Edward Albee's play *A Delicate Balance* was first produced, I was strongly convinced that it was the best portrayal, not excluding sociological and anthropological studies, of the anatomy of a family as a group. Albee, through artistic structuring, had succeeded where behavioral scientists had failed. The existence of each of the four family members in the play depends on an intertwining of the emotions and behaviors of the others. Consequently, the gestalt of the group rather than the discreteness of the individuals is the essence of the play.

Recently I saw the film *Sounder* (Metro-Goldwyn-Mayer, 1972), which is also a classic in describing family as a group; however, if one compares the two families on a variety of properties, one finds that in almost every instance they fall toward opposite ends of each property continuum. *Sounder* is similar to the play in that the life of each family member is closely interrelated with the lives of the other members; but in contrast to the play, this film has the analytic advantage of dealing with a family on the razor's edge of survival.

A Delicate Balance is difficult to summarize in substantive terms, because it is basically a continuing series of bantering conversations. The play portrays an upper-middle-class family composed of four neurotic individuals—Tobias, a husband/father who has retired from work; Agnes, a domineering wife/mother; Julia, an ever-divorcing daughter; and Claire, the wife/mother's alcoholic sister. These four individuals are locked into a pathological family system. Three themes are apparent: the individuals are neurotic; despite the deficits of the individuals, the family group offers satisfaction, comfort, and security to its members; and the family considers change undesirable and all members attempt to maintain the status quo.

CLAIRE: We can't have changes—throws the balance off. . . . Just think, Tobias, what would happen if the patterns changed: you wouldn't know where you stood, and the world would be full of strangers; that would never do. (Albee, 1966:144–45)

The play conveys the notion that belonging to any group is preferable to social isolation; in this instance, if the group dissolved, so would each of its members. What was not apparent until *Sounder* was contrasted with *A Delicate Balance* was that the family in *A Delicate Balance,* although tightly constructed to control internal dynamics, would be maladaptive in handling any impingements from the outside environment. Within this context some of the system properties became more apparent.

In *A Delicate Balance* the family operates with a static equilibrium within a tightly bounded system where roles are rigid. Although events and situations vary, family responses tend to be recurring and predictable. Psychiatry, in speaking of individuals, defines neuroticism as the inability of the individual to vary responses and behaviors in the face of different situations, events, and people. This definition seems equally appropriate for this particular family group. Interrelationships among members are based on rights, not love, and one obtains these rights merely through longevity. As Agnes states, "The years we have put up with each others' wiles and crotchets have earned us each others' company" (Albee, 1966:11).

The system provides the members with a known framework of behavior and interrelationships which support each individual's delusions about self and others. For this family, delusions become reality. In essence the family group provides an arena for expressing socially unacceptable emotions such as mutual hate, disdain, intolerance, and uninhibited catharsis. These expressions, however, negate neither any individual's acceptance by the group nor his or her right to be a part of the system. Although the group is patterned to handle ever recurring internal crises (self-invoked), one suspects that this family's survival potential would be minimal in crises impinging from the outside environment. Through the centuries, flexibility and adaptation have been the key to survival in changing environments. This family's ability to make modifications contingent on outside influences—the ability to cope—appears nonexistent. In all probability the group would not have the capacity to adapt to outside changes.

Sounder[4] is a beautiful and poetic portrayal of a very simple but heroic black sharecropper family (father, mother, two sons, and a daughter) who respond to and overcome a series of crises originating in the outside environment. The secret of this family's survival in the face of adverse social and physical circumstances is family properties which lie at polar extremes to those of *A Delicate Balance*. The *Sounder* family, united both by geographic isolation and by mutual love and respect, may be characterized as having a dynamic equilibrium, high role flexibility, and a self-adapting stance toward unexpected events impinging from the outside world. The internal family system changes in order to cope with adversity and to take advantage of the few opportunities offered by the social system. Behavior is modified and regulated by attempts to cope with crises as well as opportunities. As events occur, roles spill over traditional age and sex boundaries, and an individual or the group rises to meet the deficit of one member's inability to perform his or her normal role. In contrast to *A Delicate Balance* where problems are created through internal family dynamics and through the neurotic personalities of the members, *Sounder* shows no evidence of family problems initiated internally.

The *Sounder* family shows incredible resilience in response to a series of crises. As the film begins, the family is close to starvation, and the father is arrested for stealing a ham from a local white landowner. The father is first placed in the local jail and later sent away to a prison workcamp. Disregarding usual age and sex norms, the mother and children "do what they have to do" for group survival.

On several occasions we see the spillover of roles. When the mother leaves the cabin to go to town to visit the father in jail, she leaves the older boy, who appears to be around ten or twelve, in charge of the other two children. The oldest girl, who would normally assume this responsibility, is too young. When the mother finds that women are not permitted to visit the jail, she sends the older boy, who is very young for this task. Later when the father is moved to a prison camp, the older son walks approximately fifty miles, unsuccessfully searching for him. The planting season comes, and the father is still absent. Mother and children, even the smallest (five to seven years old), take on the chores of heavy labor so that the farm can produce. No help in the way of food or labor comes from friends and neighbors, who are perhaps too close to the razor's edge of survival themselves to offer assistance.

Responses to the outside white social system evidence more coping behavior than might have been expected among black families living in the South in the early 1930s. The older boy makes maximum use of his link with a white woman who sends her washing to his mother. In order to help the boy the woman secretly goes through the sheriff's files and finds the approximate location of the father's prison camp. She also gives the boy books. In the face of odds imposed by the white world that prevent successful action or reaction, the family quietly resigns itself to the situation. This stance is poignantly illustrated by the quiet inner strength, pathos, mutual love, and support expressed by the mother and children as they witness the sheriff chaining the father and taking him away and a deputy shooting the family dog which tries to follow.

The family not only accommodates hardship but also musters its strengths to take advantage of the few available opportunities in the outside world. Prior to his father's imprisonment, the older boy had attended the local white school, sitting on the back row reserved for black children. Despite rebuffs from the other children, he persevered and became the only one in the family who could read. During the course of searching for his father's prison camp, he is befriended by a black teacher who has her own school for black children. She invites him to come back and live with her so that he may attend her school, which is obviously superior to the local school. The boy wants to take advantage of this opportunity but feels that he is needed at home and cannot leave.

Before the new term begins, the father returns home, having been released from prison early since he had been severely crippled by a dynamite blast. It is toward the end of the harvest season; as he attempts to help, it becomes apparent that he can contribute very little to the necessary heavy labor. Despite the father's deficits, he decides that the boy should go away to school and that somehow the family will make it, as they always had in the past when a contributing family member was missing. The beauty of this decision is the willingness of each family member to struggle in order to help the boy grow and develop beyond the limited circumstances of the parents and other children.

Family System Properties

A perspective on family as a group has been established more easily by contrasting this play and this film than by studying the masses of our own data. Illustrations are more pristine and more poignant. Insights are gained and conceptualization facilitated. These insights in turn have directed our attention to particular events occurring in the lives of the families studied and have been useful in describing how families manage disability as well as how some families grow and mature in this process. These properties abstracted from the play and film are summarized in table 2.

In the table the term "morphostasis" refers to those processes which tend to preserve a system's given form, organization, or state (Buckley, 1967:58) despite impinging events initiated either within or outside the family. "Morphogenesis" refers to processes by which a system tends to elaborate, modify, or change its current form, structure, or state (Buckley, 1967:58) in response to new events. The other terms flow from these two general definitions. Detailed definitions can be found in Buckley.

Table 2 serves as a heuristic model to lead us closer to one of

TABLE 2. Family System Properties

Properties	A Delicate Balance	Sounder
General system characteristics	Morphostasis	Morphogenesis
Structural organizations	Static	Self-regulatory, adaptive
Goals	Maintain status quo	Survival and benefits for the group
Roles	Rigid	Flexible
Events leading to action and reaction (crisis or opportunity)	Internal family dynamics	Environmental (outside) events
Etiologies of action	Antecedent events within family system	Antecedent, current, and future internal and external events
Boundaries	Closed (impermeable)	Open (permeable)

our original objectives—to describe families as a group or a small social system. Several characteristics of this model should be stated. (1) The model provides a basis for description of families in global summarizing terms but is not adequate to capture detail. (2) It forces one's thinking toward family rather than individual properties and toward interrelationships of these properties. (3) It requires specification and modification to deal with our second objective of describing the processes of family change over time. (4) Because of the very nature of these two families, *A Delicate Balance* tends to represent family pathology and *Sounder,* family health.

Relationship to Study Families

Neither the *Delicate Balance* family nor the *Sounder* family represents any of our twelve families; however, with one possible exception, which is discussed later, the families studied approach the *Sounder* end of the continuum. In response to the event of disability of one member, the families tended to be adaptive, to take on group goals, to move toward more flexible role structures, to use antecedent and current experiences and future expectations as a basis for action, and to manifest changes over time in the permeability of their boundaries. The families in the study can be more aptly characterized as morphogenic than morphostatic.

Families in Process of Change: Accommodation to Disability

Using the framework abstracted from *A Delicate Balance* and *Sounder,* I shall now turn to the data on the twelve study families to develop a conceptual scheme which captures in some substantive detail the processes of family change which proceed from onset of disability through convalescence and rehabilitation. In this scheme all designated family properties are interrelated; thus a cause-effect linear model must be replaced by a transactional or synergistic one. Each property is illustrated in terms of five broad stages in the process of adaptation: I. precrisis, II. crisis, III. transition, IV. temporary stabilization, and V. readaptation. Absolute time for these stages is meaningless. There are neither set time limits for families to remain in each of these stages nor exact amounts of time for families to move from Stage I through Stage V. Wide time variations occur among families. This fact presents difficulties if one chooses to investigate family change through panel surveys.

When changes that occur in these stages are assessed, each family serves as its own control, and changes described are relative to previous stages. Obviously there were variations among these families before disability which continued after disability. Families can be placed on continua that range from relatively morphostatic to morphogenic systems, from impermeable to permeable boundaries, from network to group organization, and from role rigidity to role flexibility. There are also variations in composition and stages in family life cycle. Even so, analyzing each family in terms of changes in that particular family system, one can identify patterns that transcend families. Disability of one member is the common event which requires adaptation and necessitates change within the group.

Our intent is that work on conceptual frameworks will continue beyond the scope of this paper. Ultimately, our objectives, which in themselves have recently been redefined as a consequence of analyses presented here, are to describe family systems in terms of salient properties and to indicate the interrelationships of these properties at different stages in the process of adjustment. To achieve these goals fully requires more analysis and thought than space permits. While we are confident at this point that a systems approach is fruitful, our analysis is not sufficiently advanced and our data may not be sufficiently focused to reveal all property interrelationships occurring in each stage. In fact, the stages themselves may require some revision as analysis proceeds. As Hill and Rodgers appropriately caution:

Stages are a convenience to permit stopping the process of development and concentrating on the properties of the family at this and that point in its development. In actuality, the stages merge into one another imperceptibly, so one gets the impression rather of continuity than of stages with sharp breaks, yet there are analytical advantages in such breaks. (1964:189)

Presentation of this conceptual scheme within the space limitations of this chapter perhaps can best be achieved by the use of a word chart (table 3) which indicates general changes in family properties by stages of adjustment. This will be followed by a narrative giving only a brief description of events occurring during each stage. A full reanalysis of our data in terms of this scheme has not yet been completed. The next step will be to return to the data and recode all findings by means of the word chart. The expectations, on the basis of this reanalysis, are that other family properties will be added and that both properties and stages may be amplified. *(Continued on page 161)*

TABLE 3. Stages of Adjustment

Systematic (Group) Properties	I Precrisis	II Crisis	III Transition	IV Temporary Stabilization	V Readaptation
A. Family priorities					
1. Concern	Usual	Possible death of member	Disability of member	Disabled member	Approximates precrisis
2. Definitional response	Usual	Vacillation	Diffuse	Specified	Approximates precrisis
B. Family composition	Household-immediate	Immediate minus disabled	Immediate plus aides	Immediate	Immediate
C. Family Dynamics					
1. Group organization	Network	Group formation/affect	Group development/tasks	Group development/division of labor	Network/group
2. Role behavior	Regular	Truncated	Unspecified	Respecified/caretaker	Regular
D. Family Goals	Varied/individualistic	Diffuse/group	Specific/group	Specific/group	Varied/individualistic
E. Family entry boundaries	Low permeability	High permeability	High permeability	Impermeability	Low permeability
F. Family exit boundaries	High permeability	Impermeability	Less impermeability	Low permeability	Permeability

Explanations of Properties in Table 3

A. Family Priorities

I.   Usually there is no single family priority. Individual members' priorities are honored by the group to the extent that they do not interfere with or jeopardize the priorities of other family members.

II.   The patient is hospitalized for a period of time, during which diagnosis, acute care, and some physical rehabilitation take place. Although death is seldom imminent in the diagnoses of the patients in this study, the families' first major concern is the possibility of death. Perhaps because most of the families associate hospitalization with acute illness, they tend to respond in keeping with an underlying assumption of the sick role (Parsons, 1951:433–437) that the two potential outcomes of illness are death or complete recovery. The tendency is to vacillate between these two possible outcomes, with little consideration of the possibility of permanent disability. Acceptance of the family member as disabled develops gradually over the next two or three stages.

III.   The disabled member returns home for further convalescence. The immediate concern of the family is personal care of the disabled person; almost all family members over the age of six to ten contribute to the care of the disabled member. Definitions of how to manage this care and how to respond to the disabled member are diffuse.

IV.   The performance of the necessary tasks involved in the care of the disabled person becomes better defined and routinized. Family concern begins to focus on handling financial problems, social and psychological consequences of disability, and usual problems of other family members. Families begin to accept the definition of permanent disability and concommitant definitions of rehabilitation.

V.   Priorities become more individual, less centralized. The situation approximates the precrisis state.

B. Family Composition

I.   Most families are composed of a household kin unit, with, occasionally, a nonresident member in frequent contact.

II.   The family as a functioning unit no longer includes the hospitalized disabled member, who becomes the object of family anxiety rather than a family participant.

III.   Either kin take up temporary residence in the household or someone is hired to assist in the care of the disabled member and to assume some household tasks. In one of the families studied, because neither alternative was possible, the disabled person (wife/mother) moved to her mother's home and the father and small children moved to his mother's home for the duration of Stage III, the transition period.

IV.   Aides and kin leave.

V.   The precrisis household kin unit is resumed.

C. Family Dyamics

I. 1. The structure of the family approximates a social network. There is little evidence of group characteristics or central purpose or direction, and group activities are minimal.

2. Role behavior varies from family to family but is the result of family interaction over time.

II. 1. As a result of the hospitalization of the disabled person, the central purpose of mutual support and a common emotional response consolidate the family into a group. The disabled person becomes the affective focus of the family group.

2. The disabled member's roles are held in abeyance, and other family members carry on some of their regular outside roles as well as family roles, but all nonessential tasks and activities are dropped.

III. 1. The group becomes centralized with regard to tasks as it seeks to maintain household functions, to care for the disabled member, and to assume some of the disabled person's previous role responsibilities. The disabled person becomes the hub of family activity. The family, at first through trial and error, begins to move toward a planning and problem-solving orientation.

2. The roles tend to be unstable, shared, and nonspecific to a single person. All members over six to ten years old help to care for the disabled person. Tasks during this period, with few exceptions, are interchangeable among family members.

IV. 1. Grouping is maintained by the establishment of a division of labor.

2. In contrast to Stage III, the diffuse family responsibilities are transferred to a single person, a caretaker. Always where family composition makes it possible, this is a female. Once the caretaker role is established, other family members are able to resume many of their precrisis outside roles. The other family members, however, must assume some of the necessary responsibilities of the precrisis roles of the disabled person and the caretaker. The disabled person and the caretaker now become the hub around which other family activities are organized.

V. 1. The family makes a partial return to the precrisis situation. The network organizational pattern returns, but there is a residual of "groupness" expressed through central purpose and direction which is transferred to other events. To illustrate, one can look at the changes in the levels of living (income) of the twelve families. Followed over time, five of the twelve families had a higher level of living at Stage V than at Stage I. Four had a similar level of living at Stage V despite the high financial cost of the disability, and only three had a lower level of living. As a result of this finding we have taken into consideration the working hypothesis that onset of disability is an event provoking family action and reaction which leads to tighter group formation, decreasing salience of individual goals, increasing salience of a group goal (rehabilitation of the disabled person), and greater planning and problem-solving ability. Once the family has had this experience as a reaction to disability, the experience may be transferred to another common goal (that is, rise in standard of living) and utilized for goal attainment.

2. The family members approximate their precrisis role functioning except that there is a tendency toward a closer integration of roles.

D. *Family Goals*

I.   Compared with the later stages there is little evidence of common goals; rather, goals are multiple and individualistic. Families honor pursuit of individuals' goals as long as these do not interfere with or jeopardize the goals of other family members.

II.   Precrisis individual goals are held in abeyance. There is a shared goal of hope for recovery of patient.

III.   The primary group goal is learning to manage the care of the disabled member.

IV.   The group goal is care of the disabled member and his/her physical and social rehabilitation.

V.   Predisability individual goals are approximated, but there is a residual competence in achieving a group goal which may be applied to new concerns.

E. *Family Entry Boundaries*

I.   Compared with later stages, there is relatively less entry of outsiders into the home.

II.   There is considerable visiting by kin and friends. The concern of visitors is focused on nondisabled family members.

III.   Friends of the disabled person visit him or her at home. Visiting usually stops within two weeks after the disabled person returns home. He/she begins to experience social isolation.

IV.   Visiting in the home is infrequent. The disabled member and the caretaker experience social isolation.

V.   Visiting patterns approximate precrisis standards.

F. *Family Exit Boundaries*

I.   Family members spend a considerable amount of time outside the home. Without too much exaggeration, one can say home is where family members are when there is no place else to go.

II.   Members leave home to visit the hospital but do not leave home for their usual leisure and social activities. Some continue to work or to go to school.

III.   Members leave home for important roles, such as worker or student, but return as quickly as possible, seldom leaving for leisure and social activities.

IV.   The disabled member and the caretaker remain at home. The caretaker frees other members to begin to resume increasingly greater outside activities. Particularly if the disabled person has a car and can drive, he/she begins to venture outside the home for short periods.

V.   Exit for all family members, including the disabled person, approximates the precrisis pattern.

Discussion

In reviewing table 3, one can read across each row and see changes in a particular property throughout the five stages. Morphogenesis occurs within families that have a newly disabled member. The impact of the crisis is sufficient to require change despite family resistance or attempts to maintain the status quo. The families' only alternative to morphogenesis is to reject the disabled member, demanding that he or she be institutionalized. Even then, the family would have to make some changes necessitated by the absence of this person. Not only does there appear to be morphogenesis during the period of adjustment to disability but most of the families evidence what might be considered residual change in role flexibility, group cohesiveness, direction, and goals, and more problem-solving and self-regulatory behavior.

By reading down each column, one can begin to posit some of the interrelationships among properties at each stage. As mentioned earlier, these interrelationships are not amenable to a cause-effect model but must be viewed from a systems perspective; that is, change in one property may result in changes in some, many, or all of the others.

Within the page limitations of this chapter it is not possible to discuss in detail tables 2 and 3, but three topics of particular importance to family adjustment will be discussed: role flexibility, permeable entry boundaries, and the exception to the statement that the study families more closely resembled the family in *Sounder* than the one in *A Delicate Balance* as both are described in table 2.

Role Flexibility

Accommodation to disability is enhanced by role flexibility in stages I through V. Families who have a history of high role flexibility or adopt this characteristic seem to adjust to disability more easily. Eleven of the twelve families exhibited considerable role flexibility by not adhering rigidly to their predisability age and sex roles. Young children and adolescents took on household tasks which otherwise they probably would not have assumed until they were several years older. Some young boys took part-time jobs earlier than might have been expected. Indeed, disability seems to accelerate the maturation process of the nonadult family members. Usually assuming greater family responsibility contributed to the positive self-image of these young people, and there was apparently little resentment about performing additional tasks.

Crossing sex boundaries seemed more problematic, particularly for families where rigid sex roles were maintained prior to the onset of the disability. Although it is seldom self-stigmatizing for a female to take on male tasks, taking on female tasks seems to lead to a negative self-image for some males. Probably overriding this stigma is the positive self-image a disabled male acquires through making a contribution to the family, regardless of whether the task is socially defined as woman's work or man's work. Some of the disabled males showed concern, too, when their wives had to take over some of their usual tasks, such as yard and repair work. For those uncomfortable about this, both husband and wife tended to maintain the fiction that, even though the wife performed the tasks, the husband supervised closely. The task remained his responsibility but her activity (performance).

Large families with fairly equal sex distributions seem to be able to handle most tasks along traditional sex lines even though one member is no longer able to perform his or her usual tasks. Sex role flexibility, however, is highly important for family maintenance in couple families and in families with only two adults and one or more small children. Perhaps out of necessity, tasks in these families are reassigned without regard for sex differences.

Permeable Entry Boundaries

Those families in which precrisis entry boundaries were very open to visitors seemed to experience social adjustment to disability more quickly and easily than those which had previously had closed entry boundaries. The Dobson family in table 1 is an excellent illustration. Their predisability boundaries were quite open to visitors. Friends, neighbors, and kin wandered in and out of their home at will. This pattern was maintained after Chester returned home, and decreased considerably the extent of social isolation. Thus, we are inclinced to think that these casual visits to the home tended to enhance social rehabilitation by reducing the social isolation of the disabled person. Interaction with visitors allows the disabled person to have considerable social contact without leaving the home. This gives him/her the opportunities to acquire techniques of stigma management in a more protected situation than public places (Cogswell, 1965, 1968*a*).

A Deviant Case

In some respects the James family in table 1 is an exception to the earlier statement that the study families can be more aptly characterized as morphogenic. In the James family the internal family dynamics approach the *Delicate Balance* end of the continuum. System regulation tends toward the morphostatic, roles are rigid, and boundaries tend to be closed to outsiders. These system properties appear to stem directly from the husband/father's refusal to acknowledge or accept either the extent or the permanence of his disability (paraplegia). He is sufficiently influential and forceful to make his family behave in terms of this delusion. Rigid sex roles are maintained, with the husband taking on as many of the traditionally masculine tasks of home and family maintenance as is physically possible despite extreme physical difficulty. In instances where the wife must perform his previous tasks, he makes all decisions and supervises his wife's performance to the last detail. For example, in redecorating their apartment the wife painted the upper portion of the walls which he could not reach from a wheelchair. However, he supervised her activity down to the last brush stroke, and both husband and wife maintain that he was responsible for the painting.

The family boundaries are essentially closed. They have re-sisted contact with other family members, neighbors, and friends. The couple seldom invites others to the home or leaves the home except for work or an occasional shopping trip. This is in direct contrast to their predisability life when their circle of friends was larger and the husband and wife went out as a couple to social and leisure activities. The husband still feels uncomfortable in the presence of others and in public places. As compensation for the deleted couple activity, the wife would like to go out with female friends, but the husband appears to resent any social contact she might have. He essentially imposes social isolation on her. Be-cause the husband cannot accept his disability, the family is pre-vented from coping with social deficits that ensue from his be-havior. In this sense the family is not self-adapting for the benefit of the group. However, from the perspective of more usual criteria of rehabilitation, the husband has adapted well. He has returned to his former job as an architectural draftsman. His physical rehabilitation has been sufficiently effective for him to be independent in self-care, to operate from a wheelchair, and to drive his own car to and from work.

In a comparison of the twelve families, the James family was different from the others in two family properties, role behavior and boundaries. Their rigid role behavior interfered with an easily workable redistribution of family responsibilities; the im-permeable boundaries of the family brought about considerable social isolation. The Jameses were also different from the other families in affective relationships between family members. The husband and wife manifested thinly veiled hostility toward each other and toward the world at large.

From the brief description of this deviant case, the reader may gain some insight into the potential analytic interrelationships between tables 2 and 3. The rigid role structure and the im-permeable entry and exit boundaries of the James family are group properties which have retarded and perhaps negated so-cial rehabilitation.

"Nothing Has Changed"

Although this chapter has dealt primarily with family change in accommodating disability, it is important to make clear that these changes have been abstracted from our data; they were not self-reported by the families themselves. A curious phenomenon, observed in previous studies by Davis (1963) and Cogswell (1965), was evident in this study. When families are asked directly about changes resulting from the disability, the consistent answer is "nothing has changed." In a study of polio children and their families, Davis originally attributed this phenomenon to the circumstance that for a child with a disability there is not that much role loss. The person continues to be a child. Davis later commented that, in view of the findings reported in this chapter about families with adult members who were disabled,[5] he was led to reassess this phenomenon. He sought ways to account for this discontinuity between what has changed and the families' peculiar inability to give the changes some kind of formulation or expression. Davis suggested that this phenomenon is a clue to the nature of the adaptive process itself, namely that it is a cumulative flow and continuous shifting of roles and identities around some core predisability-established identity. Indeed, a study of paraplegic patients (Cogswell, 1965, 1968a) has shown that one of the tasks in social rehabilitation or resocialization is for the disabled person to learn how to shift others' perceptions of him so that disability is at the periphery rather than the core of his social identity. In any case, whatever the explanation of the phenomenon, it seems unlikely that investigators will receive answers from families when they ask direct questions about general changes. It is obvious that changes do occur, but that these have to be abstracted from data on specific issues at many different points in time.

NOTES

1. Laing (1972) is one of the few exceptions, for he makes home visits to diagnose family pathology.

2. By the term "systems theory," I refer here to those systems analogous to a biological model rather than to a mechanical or thermostatic model.

3. We have reviewed the existing theories and conceptual schemes in family sociology and have listed some here. A number of emerging conceptual frameworks for family analysis are discussed in Harold T. Christensen, ed., *Handbook of Marriage and the Family* (1964); Hill and Hansen, "The Identification of Conceptual Frameworks Utilized in Family Study" (1960); and F. Ivan Nye and Felix M. Berardo, *Emerging Conceptual Frameworks in Family Analysis* (1966). The four which have gained the greatest currency are: the psycho-sociological study of family as a whole group (Handel, 1965, 1967, 1972; Hess and Handel, 1959); the developmental approach (Duvall, 1962; Glick, 1957; Lansing and Kish, 1957; Hill and Rodgers, 1964), whose theoretical properties have perhaps best been treated by Rodgers (1964), and Hill and Rodgers (1964); the interactionist approach, which has been reviewed by Eisenstein (1956) and Hoffman and Lippitt (1960); and the symbolic interactionist approach, many of whose proponents appear in Rose (1962). Other useful sources are: F. Ivan Nye and Felix M. Berardo, *The Family: Its Structure and Interaction* (1973); Wesley R. Burr, *Theory Construction and the Sociology of the Family* (1973); Roy H. Rodgers, *Family Interaction and Transaction* (1973); and Joan Aldous, "Strategies for Developing Family Theory" (1970).

4. The film (MGM, 1972) does not faithfully reflect the novel (Armstrong, 1969) which is somewhat episodic and does not portray group phenomena. Fortunately, the film is tightly structured to reveal the family as a group and therefore is used as a basis for these comments.

5. These comments are from Fred Davis' detailed response to an earlier version of this chapter.

BIBLIOGRAPHY

Albee, E.
    1966. *A Delicate Balance.* New York: Atheneum.
Aldous, J.
    1970. Strategies for developing family theory. *Journal of Marriage and the Family,* 32:250–258.
Armstrong, W.
    1969. *Sounder.* New York: Harper and Row.
Buckley, W.
    1967. *Sociology and Modern Systems Theory.* Englewood Cliffs, N.J.: Prentice-Hall.

1968. *Modern Systems Research for the Behavioral Scientist.* Chicago: Aldine.

Burr, W. R.
1973. *Theory Construction and the Sociology of the Family.* New York: John Wiley.

Christensen, H. T., ed.
1964. *Handbook of Marriage and the Family.* Chicago: Rand McNally.

Cogswell, B. E.
1965. Socialization into a role: A study of the rehabilitation of paraplegics. Unpublished Ph.D. dissertation, University of North Carolina, Chapel Hill.
1967. Rehabilitation of the paraplegic: Processes of socialization. *Sociological Inquiry,* 37:11–26.
1968*a*. Self-socialization: Readjustment of paraplegics in the community. *Journal of Rehabilitation,* 34:11–13.
1968*b*. Some structural properties influencing socialization. *Administrative Science Quarterly,* 13:417–440.

Davis, F.
1963. *Passage Through Crisis.* Indianapolis: Bobbs-Merrill.

Duvall, E. M.
1962. *Family Development.* New York: J. B. Lippincott.

Eisenstein, V. W., ed.
1956. *Neurotic Interaction in Marriage.* New York: Basic Books.

Glaser, B. G., and Strauss, A. L.
1967. *The Discovery of Grounded Theory: Strategies for Qualitative Research.* Chicago: Aldine.

Glick, P. C.
1957. *American Families.* New York: John Wiley.

Handel, G.
1965. Psychological study of whole families. *Psychological Bulletin,* 63:19–41.

Handel, G., ed.
1967. *The Psychosocial Interior of the Family.* Chicago: Aldine.
1972. *The Psychosocial Interior of the Family.* 2d ed. Chicago: Aldine.

Hess, R. D., and Handel, G.
1959. *Family Worlds: A Psychological Approach to Family Life.* Chicago: University of Chicago Press.

Hill, R.
1974. Modern systems theory and the family: A confrontation. In *Sourcebook on Marriage and the Family,* edited by M. B. Sussman, pp. 302–313. 4th ed. Boston: Houghton Mifflin.

Hill, R., and Hansen, D. A.
1960. The identification of conceptual frameworks utilized in family study. *Marriage and Family Living,* 22:299–311.

Hill, R., and Rodgers, R. H.
  1964. The developmental approach. In *Handbook of Marriage and the Family*, edited by H. T. Christensen, pp. 171–211. Chicago: Rand McNally.
Hoffman, L., and Lippitt, R.
  1960. The measurement of family life variables. In *Handbook of Research Methods in Child Development*, edited by P. H. Mussen, pp. 945–1013. New York: John Wiley.
Jackson, J. K.
  1956. The adjustment of the family to alcoholism. *Marriage and Family Living*, 18:361–369.
Laing, R. D.
  1972. *The Politics of the Family and Other Essays*. New York: Vintage Books.
Lansing, J. B., and Kish, L.
  1957. Family life cycle as an independent variable. *American Sociological Review*, 22:512–519.
Metro-Goldwyn-Mayer
  1972. *Sounder.*
Nye, F., and Berardo, F. M.
  1966. *Emerging Conceptual Frameworks in Family Analysis*. New York: Macmillan.
  1973. *The Family: Its Structure and Interaction*. New York: Macmillan.
Parsons, T.
  1951. *The Social System*. Glencoe, Ill.: Free Press.
Rodgers, R. H.
  1964. Toward a theory of family development. *Journal of Marriage and the Family*, 26:262–270.
  1973. *Family Interaction and Transaction*. Englewood Cliffs, N.J.: Prentice-Hall.
Rose, A. M.
  1962. *Human Behavior and Social Processes: An Interactionist Approach*. Boston: Houghton Mifflin.
Satir, V.
  1964. *Conjoint Family Therapy*. Palo Alto: Science and Behavior Books.
Straus, M. A.
  1968. Communication, creativity, and problem-solving ability in middle and working class families in three societies. In *Sourcebook on Marriage and the Family*, edited by M. B. Sussman, pp. 15–27. 3rd ed. Boston: Houghton Mifflin.
Strodtbeck, F. L.
  1954. The family as a three-person group. *American Sociological Review*, 19:23–29.

CHAPTER 7

Disability and Stratification Processes

Karl L. Alexander

Despite the long-standing interest of disability research in stratification-relevant variables, the interface between these two substantive domains has seldom received systematic consideration. Disagreement regarding the appropriate interpretation of stratification effects in disability research suggests, however, that such an appraisal might be of considerable utility, particularly since stratification researchers have had to cope with quite similar interpretive problems. The relationship between social status variables and various physical and psychological disorders is certainly one of the more thoroughly investigated topics in the disability literature, yet the reviews of this substantial body of material indicate little consensus regarding the interpretation or implications of these data (Kohn, 1970; Kleiner and Parker, 1963; Mishler and Scotch, 1963; Dohrenwend and Dohrenwend, 1969; Dunham, 1961).

The recent exchange between Kohn and Mechanic regarding the social status–schizophrenia relationship exemplifies this debate. Despite their other disagreements, Kohn and Mechanic concur on the need for a more adequate conceptualization of the disability process. Kohn (1972:301–302) calls for a multivariate model that explains how "social class fits into an equation that includes genetics, probably stress, and undoubtedly other, as yet

---

The author is indebted to David Featherman, Howard Kelman, and Henry Perry for extremely thoughtful and useful reactions to an earlier version of this work.

unrecognized, factors," while Mechanic (1972:309) urges "improving the conceptualization and measurement of various psychiatric conditions and . . . examining a variety of factors that may mediate their occurrence."

The life-cycle multivariate modeling framework that has proved quite useful for the study of status attainment processes may satisfy some of the conceptual needs identified by Kohn[1] and Mechanic. Indeed, it might even permit a resolution of the polemic underlying their exchange by allowing the simultaneous evaluation of various interpretations of status effects in disability research. This chapter will briefly describe the development of this conceptual-analytical strategy in stratification research and then apply the general framework to disability phenomena. While psychiatric disorders will be dealt with at some length when an example of a disability model is developed, the general framework should be equally applicable to physical impairments, and some applications of the framework to such disorders will be suggested. Finally, in view of the conceptual "parallelism" of these disability and status attainment models, the possibility of profitable "spin-off" from disability to stratification research will be considered.

Before these models are developed, certain terminological matters merit brief consideration. The empirical utility of any conceptual framework is, of course, tempered by the adequacy of the concepts which it subsumes. While it is perhaps trivial to note that the object of inquiry must be adequately specified before it can be explained, certain conceptual difficulties in the disability literature require that this be mentioned. As Featherman observes (1973), concept development and consideration of measurement strategies necessarily precede causal modeling, for without adequate treatment of the former the latter is merely an imaginative exercise. Although these matters indeed merit extensive treatment in their own right, they will not be dealt with at length here. The conceptual framework developed in this chapter will not be bound to or by any particular conceptual or operational definition of disability; hence, for present purposes these "prior" considerations may, and will, be slighted.

Suchman (1965) has stated that the disabling condition should, when feasible, be distinguished from its consequences. The question "When, how, and why does a certain physical or mental state result in interference with normal behavior so as to constitute a handicap?" then remains open (Suchman, 1965:54). If it is deemed desirable that "disability" refer to the constellation of infirmity and interfering outcomes (Nagi, 1965; Myers, 1965), then perhaps Nagi's concept of "impairment" (1965,1969) should replace disability throughout this chapter. However, because of the difficulty of applying Nagi's distinctions between pathology, impairment, and disability to the case of "personality and mental problems" (Nagi, 1969:13), which my usage of "disability" is intended to subsume, these terminological matters are not so readily resolved. In any event, when the life-cycle models to be developed are used to assess the consequences of disorders, the label used to designate such disorders should, at least in these instances, distinguish the condition from its effects.

Status Attainment and Disability Models

Status variables have had a central role in much disability research. The disproportionately high rates of various forms of psychopathology and of a wide range of physical disorders among members of the lowest social stratum are among the more robust findings in the disability literature, withstanding the vagaries of quite varied research designs and operational definitions (Kantor, 1965; Wechsler, Solomon, and Kramer, 1970; Freeman, Levine, and Reeder, 1972; various articles in Jaco, 1972). Despite this consistency, most impressive by conventional sociological standards, the appropriate explanation of these relationships remains unclear. Interpretations of the schizophrenia-social status linkage, for example, have emphasized the causal primacy of various forms of social isolation (Wechsler and Pugh, 1967;

Murphy, 1965; Schwartz and Mintz, 1963; Jaco, 1954; Faris and Dunham, 1939), frustration in goal-striving (Kleiner and Parker, 1963), stress as a consequence of socioeconomic status (Dohrenwend and Dohrenwend, 1969; Rogler and Hollingshead, 1965; Langner and Michael, 1963), and an assortment of aberrant family interaction patterns (Mishler and Waxler, 1965). Furthermore, social mobility, both upward and downward, and stress-inducing patterns of status inconsistency have similarly been linked to a variety of disability phenomena (Turner and Wagenfeld, 1967; Kasl and Cobb, 1967; Abramson, 1966; Wolf, 1963; Jackson, 1962).[2]

This proliferation of presumed explanatory mechanisms suggests the need for a more adequate conceptualization of the dynamics of "disability inducement" if the mire of endless concept-pyramiding is to be avoided. The search for such an integrative conceptual scheme might profit from a consideration of recent developments in stratification research.

The studies of status attainment processes and of disability inducement and its consequences parallel each other in a number of significant respects: both frequently assume a fundamental etiological significance of status background and status attainment variables for subsequent outcomes; both assume a dynamic process model in their causal explanations, if not in their research designs; and both assume, at least implicitly, that much of the frequently documented "status effect" is mediated by more proximate causes of the dependent variables of interest. While the distinctive characteristics of each research domain are not to be denied, these similarities in both substance (status effects) and model (dynamic process, mediation) suggest at least certain mutual problems of conceptualization.

Interest in status attainment, focusing specifically on factors affecting educational attainments and subsequent occupational outcomes, has a lengthy history.[3] It was not until 1967, however, with the publication of Blau and Duncan's *American Occupational Structure,* that a sense of coherence and cumulativeness was imposed upon this field. Blau and Duncan introduced a merged conceptual-analytical framework[4] that has exerted a profound influence on subsequent research in this area (Alexander and Eckland, 1973; 1974; 1975; Treiman and Terrell, 1973; Duncan, Featherman, and Duncan, 1972; Featherman, 1972; Hauser, 1972; Sewell, Haller, and Ohlendorf, 1970; Sewell and Hauser, 1972; Spaeth, 1970; Sewell, Haller, and Portes, 1969; Duncan, 1968; Elder, 1968; Spaeth, 1968).

Most earlier studies of mobility processes had focused on intergenerational occupational inheritance or succession, with the intent of assessing the relative "flexibility" or "rigidity" of the stratification structure. In contrast, Blau and Duncan were particularly interested in the actual processes by which youth move from a condition of more-or-less complete family dependency to their own niche in the stratification structure. This interest in "process" led to their conceptualization of status attainments as a function of various forces impinging on youth as they move through the life course.

Blau and Duncan's (1967) "basic" attainment model, presented in figure 1, documents selected aspects of the process by which parental family status variables affect the son's occupational attainments. The model includes four "waves" of variables, ordered both temporally and causally as follows: family background status (as measured by father's occupation and education), son's educational attainment, his early occupational status, and his present occupational status. The significance of the dynamic process framework lies in its simultaneous examination of multiple explanatory variables under the constraint of an explicitly formulated causal ordering, which makes possible the assessment of both direct and indirect effects implied by the model. The authors' analysis documented a largely step-wise progression of attainment influences, with most of the status background consequences for occupational sorting being mediated through educational attainment. This, of course, suggests the oversimplification of the direct status-transmission model heretofore employed.

It is not an exaggeration to consider this study a benchmark in

FIGURE 1. Blau and Duncan's "Basic Model" of the Status Attainment Process

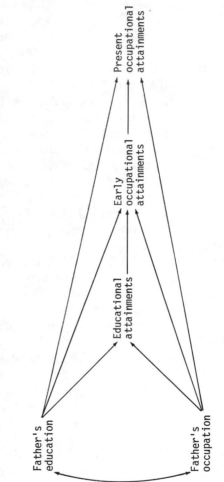

Source: Blau and Duncan (1967).

the status attainment literature. Subsequent elaborations of the Blau and Duncan structural model have included additional exogeneous variables, such as academic ability and family composition, and a multiplicity of additional intervening variables, pertaining particularly to various educational experiences and "career contingency" events, that is, age at first job, marital history, fertility, and so forth (Alexander and Eckland, 1973; 1974; Duncan, Featherman, and Duncan, 1972; Sewell, Haller, and Ohlendorf, 1970).

The specification of the more interpersonal processes by which ability and status background influences are ultimately translated into educational and occupational attainments has received particular attention. The advantages of educational institutions as the locus for such elaborations are obvious. Virtually all young people are exposed to such institutions for a considerable time at a roughly comparable period of the life cycle. Furthermore, educational experiences temporally intervene between early family dependency and establishment of adult occupational career patterns. Finally, the fundamental importance of educational certification for subsequent achievements, as documented by Blau and Duncan (1967), in conjunction with the relative malleability of various school experiences (Sewell, Haller, and Portes, 1969), has directed attention toward educational institutions in the pursuit of "equality of opportunity."

An example of such an elaborated model, with high school level intervening variables, is presented in figure 2. The school-related mediating variables include a variety of interpersonal (parents, peers, and teacher-counselors) and subjective (academic self-concept and educational expectations) influences, curriculum enrollment, and academic performance (Alexander and Eckland, 1973). It is important to note that these intervening variables are not included in the analysis solely in pursuit of additional dependent variable "explained variance." Specification of the more proximate mechanisms by which antecedent background variables actually affect later outcomes is an equally important objective. In the model presented, about half the status

FIGURE 2. A "Within-School" Elaboration of Blau and Duncan's Basic Status Attainment Model

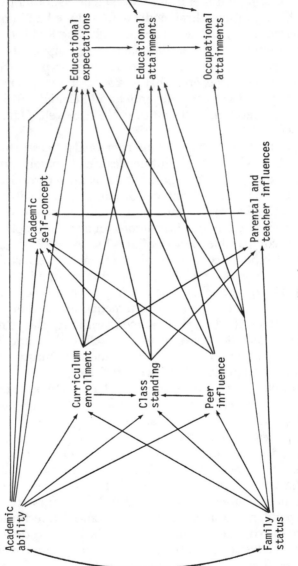

Source: Adapted from Alexander and Eckland (1973).

background and ability consequences for educational and occupational attainments were mediated by these intervening processes.

This progressive elaboration of a basic model of status effects may be appropriate for the conceptualization of at least certain disability research problems. A brief consideration of "status" as an explanatory construct will underscore the utility of such a perspective.

"Social status" is perhaps both the most frequently used and abused construct in the sociological repertoire. Recent critical assessments of commonly employed socioeconomic status (SES) indices (Haug and Sussman, 1971) and of the premature adoption of single status indicators as universally applicable to all substantive problems (Hodge, 1970) imply more fundamental questions regarding the role of status variables in our explanatory systems.

At least two, and perhaps three, often confounded usages of "social status" as an explanatory variable need to be distinguished. The first involves the assumption of status influences *sui generis*. That is, objective position in the status hierarchy in some way directly affects subsequent variables. One's occupational prestige might, for example, "directly" influence deference patterns in face to face interaction, or economic deprivation might "directly" create pressures for early employment and, hence, "cause" withdrawal from school.

In contrast to this "direct influence" usage of status indicators, it is not uncommon to find status variables employed, often unwittingly it appears, either as surrogates for more fundamental, but operationally more elusive, causal variables or as antecedent variables in incompletely specified causal models.

The surrogate function of "social status" is often encountered in socialization research, in which status background is only important insofar as it summarizes a multiplicity of particular interpersonal interactions, that is, class-related disciplinary styles, parent-child communication patterns, and so forth. Yet in the discussion of such research the notion of "status effects" frequently assumes an integrity of its own, independent of the actual causal processes for which it is but a convenient shorthand expression.

In incompletely specified causal models, on the other hand, the status variable–outcome linkage is interpreted through some unmeasured mediating mechanism. In the disability literature, for example, status effects are often interpreted in terms of various stress phenomena, presumed to be the proximate causes of disability (Cassel, 1970; Jaco, 1970; Dohrenwend and Dohrenwend, 1969).

While it is often difficult to distinguish between these two "indirect" usages of status variables, they do stand in contrast with the direct effect model.[5] Sensitivity to this heterogeneity in social status usage will likely reveal frequent discrepancies between our research designs and our actual causal thinking. The imposing interpretive superstructures so often heaped upon modest SES-dependent variable correlations are far too common in the sociological literature to require extended commentary. If status variables do often serve as imperfect surrogates for "true" explanatory variables or if their effects are mediated through unmeasured mechanisms which also contribute independently to the dependent variable of interest, then the modest magnitude of "status effects" so frequently encountered is to be anticipated. A complex phenomenon requires a complex explanation, and far too often the complexity of the explanation is revealed only in *post hoc* interpretation.

The attainment process models discussed earlier combine a conceptual and an analytical strategy appropriate for the analysis of these elaborated theories of status influence. Indeed, the "social-psychological" extensions of the Blau and Duncan "basic" model are exactly such attempts to specify the mediating mechanisms by which ability and status background actually affect adult attainments.

The most significant implication of recent developments in stratification research for the study of disability phenomena may lie in this conceptualization of research problems, rather than in any direct carry-over of profound substantive insight. While stratification variables have long played an integral role in disability research, the various rationales by which they are actually posited to affect disability conditions also merit explicit evaluation. This requires complementing macro-level models of social structure with more microsociological variables, involving, for example, family processes, peer group relations, and work experiences in the explanation of disability phenomena (Mishler and Scotch, 1963).

Thinking in terms of such elaborated causal models almost naturally inclines one to consider multiple pathways to a given outcome. The various explanations of the social status–schizophrenia relationship, for example, need not be treated as mutually exclusive. The social isolation and goal-striving frustration models, pertaining as they do to somewhat different aspects of adult life experience (paralleling Durkheim's classic distinction between causes of egoistic and anomic suicide), may both be relevant to psychological disorder.

Similarly, the various approaches dealing with intrafamilial interaction patterns and socialization experiences may complement, rather than contradict, those perspectives oriented toward either late adolescence or early adulthood. An elaborated causal process model would permit the simultaneous assessment of these various explanatory schemes.

An additional theme in the disability literature, which in some sense subsumes these particular approaches, pertains to the role of stress and stressors in the etiology of both physical and psychological disorders (Levi, 1971; Cassel, 1970; Jaco, 1970; Dohrenwend and Dohrenwend, 1969; Rogler and Hollingshead, 1965; Langner and Michael, 1963; Wolf, 1963). As Levine and Scotch (1970) point out, the analytical utility of the "stress" concept is impaired by certain unresolved issues (for example, does stress refer to some internal state or to external pressures? Can the construct be defined independently of its consequences?) However, the concept does have heuristic utility for the development of a life-cycle disability model.

In a seminal study of psychological disorder, Langner and Michael (1963) employ the concept "stress" to subsume such seemingly disparate phenomena as parents' poor physical and mental health, childhood economic deprivation, lack of family stability in childhood, family quarrels, negative evaluations of parental character, poor adult health, work and status worries, poor interpersonal relations, and various marital and family concerns. Although the authors develop a conceptual scheme quite similar to the schemes discussed here, their use of "stress" as a generic construct to subsume quite varied phenomena limits the informative value of their analysis. Their strategy both masks the unique causal efficacy of these discrete variables and slights consideration of the complex interrelationships among the explanatory mechanisms themselves.

A modest reorganization of Langner and Michael's (1963) conceptual scheme would both maintain the stress framework and, at the same time, distinguish between relatively distinct dimensions of life stress. With the appropriate mode of analysis, this framework would operationalize the life-cycle perspective that Langner and Michael develop but fail to exploit.[6] This reorganization, which is presented for its expository value and not its definitiveness, employs three types of life stress:

1. Structural stress, involving objective position in the social structure and including measures of economic deprivation and relevant ascribed statuses (race, sex, and so forth)

2. Interpersonal stress, involving impaired or distressing interactions, such as Langner and Michael's family quarrels and poor interpersonal relations

3. Personal stress or "distress," involving the concern, anxiety, or tension generated by the foregoing external stressors, such as Langner and Michael's work, status, marital, and parental "worry" variables

Such a conceptualization, imposed upon a life-cycle framework, provides a disability model conceptually quite similar to those developed in the status attainment literature. It would begin with structural or status variables and trace their effects through more interpersonal and egoistic mechanisms. Thus, the mediation of status effects would be explicitly assessed, and, as has already been noted, these mediating mechanisms may involve the presumed, but often unmeasured, "explanations" of the status-disability relationship.

Figure 3 presents diagrammatically a model constructed to reflect the causal relationships among the variables subsumed by Langner and Michael under the generic term "stress factors." It includes the three stress categories mentioned and the label "disability" for whatever physical or psychological disorders are of interest. Thus, each block-variable in the figure itself represents a cluster of variables that could be further elaborated for more detailed study.

The model presumes measurement of disability at two points in the life cycle (perhaps at early adolescence and adulthood), identifies structural, interpersonal, and subjective "stressors" as the principal determinants of disability outcomes, and distinguishes between familial and nonfamilial sources of stress. Parental structural and disability characteristics are exogenous variables in the model and are assumed to affect the quality and character of familial and extrafamilial interpersonal interaction. Individual stress (or distress), in turn, is at least in part a function of both structural placement and interpersonal stress. Finally, concluding the first stage of the model, the direct and indirect consequences of each of these antecedent factors for early disability can be evaluated. The second stage of the model replicates the first, but this time with adult measures of structural, interpersonal, and subjective stressors. Such multiple measurements would permit a relatively comprehensive analysis of disability inducement and its consequences. With the appropriate mode of analysis, the relative importance of each set of stressors would be made explicit and the dynamics of their influence documented.

The model is, intentionally, not operationally specific. The various stress blocks are themselves capable of accommodating a variety of specific research hypotheses. Indeed, each of the previously discussed interpretations of the social status–

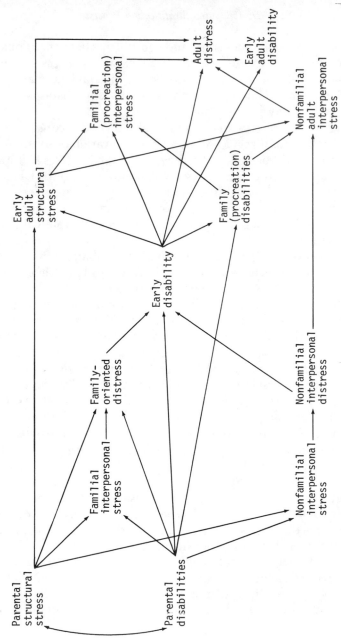

FIGURE 3. A Life-Cycle Model of Disability Inducement

schizophrenia relationship could be incorporated into such a model. The various family dynamics perspectives would be included in the "Family Interpersonal Stress" and "Family Distress" blocks. The frustrated goal-striving hypothesis would involve the "early adult structural stress" and "nonfamilial adult distress" blocks. Finally, the social isolation-integration framework could be incorporated into the two early adult interpersonal stress blocks.

Certainly this model is not presented as the definitive conceptualization of such processes. Rather, its limited intention is to suggest both the feasibility and the desirability of thinking in terms of multivariate process models in the conceptualization of disability research problems. Although, as demonstrated by Langner and Michael's (1963) approximation, this conceptualization is certainly not unprecedented, its informative value is fully realized only when it is assessed with analytical strategies that appropriately reflect such causal thinking.

Indeed, the informative value of such dynamic process frameworks can be far-reaching. With appropriate data numerous critical issues could be addressed: the downward drift versus status etiology polemic or, more generally, the direction of effect in the status-disability linkage; the relative importance of presumed etiological factors at various points in the life cycle; the cumulativeness of disability phenomena; and so forth. The ingenious researcher could probably even devise strategies by which social labeling and secondary gain (Safilios-Rothschild, 1970; Dohrenwend and Dohrenwend, 1969) phenomena could be explored in this context.

Although this example has focused on psychological disorders, similar models could be developed for the study of physical disabilities. The social readjustment framework developed by Holmes and his colleagues (Holmes and Rahe, 1967; Masuda and Holmes, 1967; Komaroff, Masuda, and Holmes, 1968) provides but one example. The frequency and severity of life changes have been related to the onset of a variety of physical illnesses,[7] including tuberculosis, cardiac disease, skin disease, and hernia (Cohen and Hajioff, 1972; Heisel, 1972; Penrose, 1972; Spilken and Jacobs, 1971; Wyler, Masuda, and Holmes, 1971; Rahe and Holmes, 1965; Rahe et al., 1964; Hawkins, Davies, and Holmes, 1957; Holmes et al., 1957). If these life changes can be subsumed under the various external stressor blocks of our disability model, and such research is obviously amenable to a stress interpretation (articles in Levi, 1971; Spilken and Jacobs, 1971; Cassel, 1970; Rahe et al., 1964; Graham and Stevenson, 1963), a formal equivalence between physical and psychological disorder-disability models might be suggested (Myers, Lindenthal, and Pepper, 1972; Paykel et al., 1969; Brown and Birley, 1968; Rogler and Hollingshead, 1965).

It may well be the case that a model including measurement of significant life events and their severity would explain much of the frequently documented social status-physical disorder linkage. Furthermore, if the parallel between these physical and psychological disability models were pursued a bit further, explicit consideration of the individual's reaction to various life changes would be a fruitful extension of Holmes' framework (Brown, 1972; Spilkin and Jacobs, 1971). Thus, a step-wise stress model, beginning with structural placement and progressing through external stressors and distress to disorder onset, may characterize a variety of disability processes, both physical and psychological.

Causal process modeling, then, is recommended as a useful strategy for the conceptualization of a variety of disability research problems. While this is not a direct substantive contribution from stratification to disability research, it is a strategy for a more informed consideration of those stratification variables that have long been employed in the disability literature. This suggestion does reflect the current "state of the arts" in stratification research; recent efforts have been directed more toward the consolidation and organization of extant themes than toward the generation of new theories.

A qualification to the utility of this general framework merits brief discussion. It was noted earlier that "with appropriate data" this strategy could be employed to address various disability issues. In this context "appropriate" may be read as "longitudinal" or "panel." Multiple measurements over time on the same sample of respondents often permit the assumption of causal asymmetry in relationships that would otherwise be treated as reciprocal.[8] With such measurements, for example, time-one status influences on time-two disabilities may be estimated without contamination from influence in the reverse direction (assuming time-one disability levels are controlled). Since an effect rarely antecedes its cause, such time-spanning data are particularly useful in unraveling patterns of mutual influence.

The informative value of longitudinal data is well recognized and need not be belabored. Despite the difficulties noted by Jaco in generating such data, there are good reasons for his observation (Jaco, 1970:219) that "longitudinal studies with adequate research controls of subjects continuing through various phases of the life cycle have often been cited as an urgent need in order to validate the etiological significance of these factors in mental health." Such urgings need to be heeded if ambiguities in the explanation of disability outcomes are to be resolved adequately.

While some previous comments regarding construct conceptualization and measurement and the desirability of longitudinal data may verge on the self-evident, they are made explicit to clarify the role of the suggested framework in the larger context of framing and pursuing the research problem. Causal modeling may contribute to clarity of thought regarding the dynamics of disability processes, but it is certainly not a panacea for all the methodological problems that beset either disability research or research in any other substantive domain. Additional matters, such as the conceptualization and measurement of disability phenomena, must be attended to before such models are taken into the field. For expository purposes, modeling strategies could be dealt with somewhat independently of other considerations. In application, however, adequate conceptualization and analysis are but two of the many components that, in conjunction, produce adequate and informative research.

Disability and Stratification Research

The foundation laid in the foregoing discussion of the conceptual carry-over from stratification to disability research allows a somewhat more concise statement regarding the possibility for reciprocity. Although the benefits accruing to disability research from this exchange involve primarily a strategy for the conceptualization of research problems, that for stratification may be more substantive in nature.

Elsewhere (Alexander and Eckland, 1973) it has been suggested that status attainment research may be close to exhausting the explanatory power of the framework that has come to circumscribe it. Extensions of the basic model to include numerous within-school social-psychological and interpersonal process indicators have been quite informative in documenting the dynamics by which antecedent influences are transmitted. However, they have produced only modest increments in attainment variable explained variance (Alexander and Eckland, 1973; Sewell, Haller, and Portes, 1969). Dramatic improvements in the overall explanatory power of such models may require, among other things, extending the bounds of the status background–academic ability–school process framework. This will be particularly important in refining understanding of the linkage between early and later occupational attainments, which remains almost entirely unspecified to date. Disability variables may be pertinent in this context, and their consequences for status outcomes have yet to be systematically assessed.

Official statistics on disability certainly suggest some implications for the occupational realm. Nagi (1969:3) summarizes some of these figures as follows:

Existing evidence . . . suggests that disability is a problem of increasing magnitude. Reports of the National Health Survey covering the period 1963–65 indicate that because of chronic ill-health, approximately 22.6 million of the non-institutionalized civilian population experienced limitations in activities they once were able to perform . . . an estimated 4.1 million were unable to carry on their major activities-employment, housework, or schoolwork. In addition, the institutionalized population in 1954 was estimated to have reached 1.2 million.

Figures from a 1966 Social Security survey indicate that fully 17 percent of the noninstitutionalized population aged eighteen to sixty-four (or 17.8 million persons) have been disabled for six months or longer, with significant variations by age, sex, and race (Safilios-Rothschild, 1970).

The prevalence of various psychological disorders appears to be sufficient that their consequences within the general population warrant consideration. Clausen (1963), for example, estimated that, if age-specific rates of illness, use of hospitalization, and average life span all were constant, 8 percent of the population living in 1963 would at some time be *hospitalized* for a mental illness.

Perhaps of even greater significance are the figures obtained by Srole and his colleagues in the Midtown Manhattan Study (1962:138). Only 18.5 percent of their sample were classified as free of psychological disorder symptoms, while fully 23 percent fell into their impaired categories. In a similar vein, 78 percent of the respondents to the 1960–62 Health Examination Survey reported at least one symptom of psychological distress, with the median number reported being 2.29. Almost 5 percent of that sample reported having had a "nervous breakdown," and an additional 13 percent indicated they had, at some point, verged on a breakdown (Dupey et al., 1970). Although these various symptom categories do not correspond to any conventional psychiatric diagnostic scheme and self-reported information of this sort must be approached with extreme caution, these data do at least suggest that psychological impairments, ranging from the mild to the relatively severe, are not uncommon.

A crude indication of the effects of disability phenomena on occupational functioning is provided by Health Survey Interview data on disability days and days of restricted activity. In 1968 the average number of disability days, or days lost from work because of injury or illness, varied from a low of 3.4 for persons earning more than $5,000 with sixteen or more years of education to a high of 7.8 for those with income less than $5,000 and fewer than nine years of schooling (Wilder, M., 1972:7). Furthermore, the average number of restricted activity days for persons normally working (if both impairments resulting in disability days and less incapacitating disorders were subsumed) was 12.7, ranging from 11.3 for the youngest age cohort to 23.0 for those seventy-five and over. Although the survey was not limited to labor force participants, persons with annual family incomes of less than $3,000 averaged 29.8 days of restricted activity in 1968 as compared to 10.7 days for individuals with family incomes of $15,000 or greater (Wilder, C., 1972:27–28).

While, again, self-reported data such as these on disability days and days of restricted activity cannot be accepted without qualification, they should be sufficiently accurate to warrant the following conclusions: Disability affects work activity, and the extent of such occupational intrusion varies somewhat with demographic and socioeconomic characteristics.

In sum, these various data suggest that significant proportions of the general population suffer from physical and psychological disorders of varying intensities and, furthermore, that such disorders may have consequences for occupational functioning. None of this necessarily implies importance of such disorders for status attainments, but their effects in this regard, though unlikely to be dramatic in studies of the general population, would seem to merit consideration.

It might be speculated that disability phenomena would be more consequential for intraoccupational career mobility than in the initial selection into broad occupational categories themselves. We suspect that such within-occupation attainments will become an increasingly important focus of attainment process research. Despite the development of occupational classification schemes considerably more refined than the simple blue collar-white collar dichotomy so characteristic of earlier research (Lipset and Bendix, 1959), these schemes are still relatively crude in many respects. All such general classification systems, for example, would include the eminent Harvard brain surgeon and the rural general practitioner in the same occupational category, masking considerable within-occupation variation. Indeed it would be meaningless to speak of career mobility for most of the free professions within such schemes.

At least partially as a consequence of obvious measurement difficulties, studies of occupational mobility are commonly restricted to movement into and out of broad occupational categories, rather than upward and downward within them. The extension of attainment process research to within-occupation variations would certainly provide a much richer account of attainment dynamics than is currently feasible (Perrucci, 1961). With more sensitive measures of occupational achievement, even the traditional status attainment framework might provide additional insights. For example, while status background is relatively inconsequential for the occupational sorting of college graduates when academic ability is controlled (Alexander and Eckland, 1975; Eckland, 1965), it may have considerable impact on within-category placement. Similarly, variables whose effects might not be reflected in gross occupational sorting may affect both placement and mobility within occupational categories.

It is at this level of analysis that disability effects would likely be most pronounced. It should be recognized, however, that only relatively high-prevalence disabilities would merit inclusion in general population studies of attainment dynamics, and even in these instances dramatic effects should not be anticipated. Nevertheless, status attainment research has been rather substantively constricted. The suggestion to explore disability effects represents but one possible extension of the framework.

A related, and perhaps more fruitful, enterprise would involve assessing the consequences of disability severity for subpopulations of the disabled. For example, the occupational recovery of stroke victims might be evaluated as a function of stroke severity, age at onset, and so forth. Labor force participation, as well as occupational attainment or mobility, could be employed as the dependent variable in such inquiries. The postdisability career attainments of disabled veterans is another area to which this framework might be applied. How, for example, do type of disability, compensation levels, and predisability career attainments affect labor force participation and occupational mobility among service-disabled youth? How do the occupational patterns of the service-disabled and non-service-disabled (perhaps those receiving disability benefits from the Social Security Administration) differ when severity of impairment is controlled?

The foregoing are but a few research questions linking disability variables with status attainment outcomes that would be amenable to causal process modeling. Whether such models pertain to the population as a whole or to specific groups of the disabled, the role of disability variables in them is readily conceptualized. If social status or occupational attainment variables were separated from the various structural strain blocks in the disability life-cycle model developed earlier, one would have a very elaborate, albeit very incomplete, model of the status attainment process, heavily weighted with disability-related explanatory variables. Disability variables, then, may have some utility as intervening variables in an elaborated status attainment model, while status variables are both antecedent and intervening in a fully elaborated disability process model. Although this represents an interesting conceptual convergence, its empirical adequacy in either research domain has yet to be assessed.

As a final note, it might be mentioned that this "convergence" may provide some limited opportunities for the generation of longitudinal disability data sets.

The status attainment literature has profited from a number of time-spanning data sets, most of which have been of relatively short duration and initiated in educational settings (Alexander and Eckland, 1973; Bachman et al., 1970; Sewell, Haller, and Portes, 1969; Elder, 1968; Flanagan and Cooley, 1966; Eckland, 1965). In view of the centrality of educational achievement for subsequent status attainments, educational institutions constitute both a convenient and a substantively significant setting for status attainment research that has no parallel in the disability area.

This absence of an institutional setting so uniquely suited for the study of disability problems affords considerable latitude in the pursuit of longitudinal disability data. Not being bound to any particular setting, research directed toward high-prevalence disabilities might be profitably pursued in conjunction with a wide variety of other substantive concerns. For example, greater disability "input" into the Oakland Growth and Guidance studies (Livson and Peskin, 1967; Kagan, 1965; Clausen, 1964; Elder, 1974), both of which span some forty years, might, in retrospect, have been desirable. Moreover, many of the questions addressed in the Midtown Manhattan Study are amenable to such "piggy-backing." Although most disability problems involve relatively low-prevalence disorders for which the general population surveys characteristic of status attainment research would not be appropriate, the merging of substantive problems merits consideration when it is feasible.

Summary and Conclusions

Researchers in disability and stratification have long shared an interest in social status as an explanatory variable. The interchange between these two research domains has seldom, however, progressed beyond this common substantive interest. In this chapter some ways have been outlined in which the two fields might profit from a more meaningful exchange.

The disability literature is replete with social stratification concepts and explanations for their importance in the disability process. It has been suggested that research in this area might benefit from recent developments in the modeling of status attainment processes. Such modeling strategies are particularly well suited for organizing a multiplicity of presumed explanatory variables into a unified framework. Life-cycle disability process models, in compelling the researcher to make explicit his causal assumptions, will encourage the analysis of mediating mechanisms in the status background-disability linkage and likely lead to an integration of extant themes in the disability literature. Such a strategy encourages the examination of multiple pathways of "disability inducement" and will thus provide a much richer empirical account of the dynamics of the disability process. An example of such a life-cycle disability model was developed to demonstrate the utility of this approach for merging extant themes, and other substantive applications were suggested.

While the carry-over from stratification to disability research primarily involves strategies for the conceptualization of research problems, the reverse exchange may be more substantive in nature. High-prevalence disability variables might be profitably incorporated into status attainment models, thereby extending the bounds of the traditional attainment framework. Such variables may be particularly useful in the examination of within-occupation attainment variations, a relatively neglected topic in the status attainment literature. The brief review of prevalence data for various disability phenomena and of their implications for occupational functioning suggested the possible relevance of disability variables for occupational attainments. While disability variables may contribute somewhat to the dynamics of status attainment for the general population, it was suggested that this framework might be particularly useful for the study of occupational recovery and mobility for particular populations of the disabled.

This exercise in "inter-domain" exchange has identified a number of fruitful avenues for further inquiry. It is hoped that it will stimulate additional efforts to bridge somewhat artificial substantive barriers. Such pursuits may uncover a wealth of untapped resources and ideas.

NOTES

1. While the model proposed by Kohn is a multiplicative one, the discussion in this chapter deals mainly with those that assume linear additivity. The intention is not to provide a detailed exposition of causal modeling *per se* but, rather, a

nontechnical discussion of the utility of causal modeling for the pursuit of disability research problems. The commonly employed linear-additive model is merely a convenient vehicle for such a presentation. As Featherman (1973) notes, however, there are statistical models that can accommodate assumptions of nonlinearity, nonadditivity, and reciprocal causation. In application, the choice of a particular statistical model is, of course, to be guided by the causal assumptions underlying the inquiry.

2. This brief listing by no means exhausts the alternative explanations of the social status–schizophrenia relationship that have appeared in the literature. In particular, the possibility that the direction of causation is actually reversed, as in the "downward drift" hypothesis, is slighted.

3. Much of the early literature in this area is summarized by Lipset and Bendix (1959).

4. Actually, Duncan and Hodge (1963) employed a quite similar conceptual-analytical strategy some years prior to the Blau and Duncan publication, but this piece does not appear to have had the same impact on subsequent work. At this point it might also be noted that, although Blau and Duncan's conceptual model is intimately related to a particular analytical strategy, this discussion does not dwell upon technical methodological issues. The assumptions, logic, and techniques of path analysis are outlined in a number of sources (Heise, 1969; Land, 1969; Duncan, 1966).

5. Upon reflection, it may be the case that instances of "pure" status effects are relatively rare. Variables such as social status are quite similar to "contextual" or "compositional" measures in many respects. While the latter aggregate people, the former often aggregate behaviors. See Alexander and Eckland (1973) and Hauser (1969) for two views on the informative value of such aggregated constructs.

6. Langner and Michael are not entirely at fault in their failure to exploit their model. It is only relatively recently that analytical strategies appropriate to such models have been extensively applied in the social sciences.

7. No rigorous attempt is being made to distinguish among such concepts as "illness," "disorder," "impairment," and "disability." In actual research enterprises, of course, considerably greater terminological precision should be maintained.

8. Such reciprocal effects can be directly estimated under some circumstances. See Hauser (1972) and Duncan, Haller, and Portes (1968) for examples from the school process–status attainment literature.

BIBLIOGRAPHY

Abramson, J. S.
  1966. Emotional disorder, status inconsistency, and migration. *Milbank Memorial Fund Quarterly,* 44:23–48.
Alexander, K. L., and Eckland, B. K.
  1973. *Effects of Education on the Social Mobility of High School Sophomores Fifteen Years Later (1955–1970).* Final Report. Washington, D.C.: U.S. Office of Education. Project No. 10202 (OEE–4–71–0037).
  1974. Sex differences in the educational attainment process. *American Sociological Review,* 39:668–682.
  1975. Basic attainment processes: A replication and extension. *Sociology of Education,* 48:457–495.
Bachman, J. G.; Kahn, R. L.; Mendick, M. T.; Davidson, T. N.; and Johnston, L. D.
  1970. *Youth in Transition.* Vol. 1. Ann Arbor, Mich.: Institute for Survey Research.
Blau, P. M., and Duncan, O. D.
  1967. *The American Occupational Structure.* New York: John Wiley.
Brown, D. C.
  1972. Stress as a precipitant factor of eczema. *Journal of Psychosomatic Research,* 16:321–327.
Brown, G. W., and Birley, J. L. T.
  1968. Crisis and life changes and the onset of schizophrenia. *Journal of Health and Social Behavior,* 9:203–214.
Cassel, J.
  1970. Physical illness in response to stress. In *Social Stress,* edited by S. Levine and N. Scotch, pp. 189–209. Chicago: Aldine.
Clausen, J. A.
  1963. Sociology of mental disease. In *Handbook of Medical Sociology,* edited by H. Freeman, S. Levine and L. Reeder, pp. 145–165. Englewood Cliffs, N.J.: Prentice-Hall.
  1964. Personality measurement in the Oakland Growth Study. In *Relations of Development and Aging,* edited by J. E. Birren, pp. 165–175. Springfield, Ill.: C. C. Thomas.
Cohen, S. I., and Hajioff, J.
  1972. Life events and the onset of acute closed-angle glaucoma. *Journal of Psychosomatic Research,* 16:335–341.
Dohrenwend, B. P., and Dohrenwend, B. S.
  1969. *Social Status and Psychological Disorder.* New York: Wiley-Interscience.
Duncan, O. D.
  1966. Path analysis: Sociological examples. *American Journal of Sociology,* 72:1–16.
  1968. Ability and achievement. *Eugenics Quarterly,* 15:1–11.

Duncan, O. D.; Featherman, D. L.; and Duncan, B.
1972. *Socioeconomic Background and Achievement.* New York: Seminar Press.
Duncan, O. D.; Haller, A. O.; and Portes, A.
1968. Peer influences on aspirations: A reinterpretation. *American Journal of Sociology,* 74:119–137.
Duncan, O. D., and Hodge, R. W.
1963. Education and occupational mobility: A regression analysis. *American Journal of Sociology,* 68:629–644.
Dunham, H. W.
1961. Social structures and mental disorders: Competing hypotheses of explanation. In *Causes of Mental Disorders: A Review of Epidemiological Knowledge, 1959,* pp. 227–265. New York: Milbank Memorial Fund.
Dupey, H. J.; Engel, A.; Devine, B.; Scanlon, J.; and Querec, L.
1970. *Selected Symptoms of Psychological Stress.* Washington, D.C.: Department of Health, Education and Welfare: Vital and Health Statistics, Ser. 11, no. 37.
Eckland, B. K.
1965. Academic ability, higher education, and occupational mobility. *American Sociological Review,* 30:735–746.
Elder, G. H.
1968. Intelligence and achievement motivation in occupational mobility. *Sociometry,* 31:327–354.
1974. *Children of the Great Depression: A Study in Social Structure and Personality.* Chicago: University of Chicago Press.
Faris, R., and Dunham, H.
1939. *Mental Disorders in Urban Areas.* Chicago: University of Chicago Press.
Featherman, D. L.
1972. Achievement orientations and socioeconomic career attainments. *American Sociological Review,* 37:131–143.
1973. Comments on Alexander's "Disability and status attainment processes." Paper presented at the Chicago Conference on Socialization and Disability, Chicago, March.
Flanagan, J. C., and Cooley, W. W.
1966. *Project Talent One-Year Follow-Up Studies.* Pittsburgh: School of Education, University of Pittsburgh. Cooperative Research Project #2333.
Freeman, H. E.; Levine, S.; and Reeder, L.
1963. *Handbook of Medical Sociology.* 1st ed. Englewood Cliffs, N.J.: Prentice-Hall.
1972. *Handbook of Medical Sociology.* 2nd ed. Englewood Cliffs, N.J.: Prentice-Hall.
Graham, D. T., and Stevenson, I.
1963. Disease as a response to life stress. In *The Psychological Basis of Medical Practice,* edited by H. I. Lief, U. F. Lief, and N. R. Lief, pp. 115–136. New York: Harper and Row.

Haug, M. R., and Sussman, M. B.
  1971. The indiscriminate state of social class measurement. *Social Forces,*
        49:549–563.
Hauser, R. M.
  1969. Context versus consex: a cautionary tale. *American Journal of Sociology,*
        75:587–611.
  1972. *Socioeconomic Background and Educational Performance.* Washington,
        D.C.: American Sociological Association, Rose Monograph Series.
Hawkins, N. G.; Davies, R., and Holmes, T. H.
  1957. Evidence of psychosocial factors in the development of pulmonary
        tuberculosis. *American Review of Tuberculosis and Pulmonary Diseases,*
        75:768–780.
Heise, D. R.
  1969. Problems in path analysis and causal inference. In *Sociological
        Methodology, 1969,* edited by E. F. Borgatta, pp. 38–73. San Francisco:
        Jossey-Bass.
Heisel, J. S.
  1972. Life changes as etiologic factors in juvenile rheumatoid arthritis.
        Journal of Psychosomatic Research, 16:411–420.
Hodge, R. W.
  1970. Social integration, psychological well-being and their SES correlates.
        In *Social Stratification: Research and Theory for the 1970's,* edited by E. O.
        Laumann, pp. 182–206. Indianapolis: Bobbs-Merrill.
Holmes, T. H.; Hawkins, N. G.; Bowerman, C. E.; Clarke, E. R.; and Joffe, J. R.
  1957. Psychosocial and psychophysiological studies of tuberculosis.
        Psychosomatic Medicine, 19:134–143.
Holmes, T. H., and Rahe, R. H.
  1967. The social readjustment rating scale. *Journal of Psychosomatic Research,*
        11:213–218.
Jackson, E. F.
  1962. Status inconsistency and symptoms of stress. *American Sociological
        Review,* 27:469–480.
Jaco, E. G.
  1954. The socialization isolation hypothesis and schizophrenia. *American
        Sociological Review,* 19:567–577.
  1970. Mental illness in response to stress. In *Social Stress,* edited by S. Levine
        and N. Scotch, pp. 210–277. Chicago: Aldine.
  1972. *Patients, Physicians and Illness.* New York: Free Press.
Kagan, J.
  1965. American longitudinal research on psychological development. *Child
        Development,* 35:1–32.
Kantor, M.
  1965. *Mobility and Mental Health.* Springfield, Ill.: C. C. Thomas.

Kasl, S., and Cobb, S.
  1967.   Effects of parental status incongruence and discrepancy on physical,
          mental health of adult offspring. *Journal of Personality and Social
          Psychology,* 7:no. 2, part 2.
Kleiner, R. J., and Parker, S.
  1963.   Goal-striving, social status, and mental disorder: A research review.
          American Sociological Review, 28:189–203.
Kohn, M. L.
  1970.   Social class and schizophrenia: A critical review. In *Social Psychology
          and Mental Health,* edited by H. Wechsler, L. Solomon, and M.
          Kramer, pp. 113–128. New York: Holt, Rinehart and Winston.
  1972.   Class, family, and schizophrenia: A reformulation. *Social Forces,*
          50:295–304.
Komaroff, A. L.; Masuda, M.; and Holmes, T. H.
  1968.   The social readjustment rating scale: A comparative study of Negro,
          Mexican, and white Americans. *Journal of Psychosomatic Research,*
          12:121–128.
Land, K. C.
  1969.   Principles of path analysis. in *Sociological Methodology, 1969,* edited by
          E. F. Borgatta, pp. 3–37. San Francisco: Jossey-Bass.
Langner, T. S., and Michael, S. T.
  1963.   *Life Stress and Mental Health: The Midtown Manhattan Study,* Vol. 2.
          London: Free Press.
Levi, L., ed.
  1971.   *Society, Stress, and Disease: The Psychosocial Environment and Psychoso-
          matic Diseases.* London: Oxford University Press.
Levine, S., and Scotch, N.
  1970.   Social stress. In *Social Stress,* edited by S. Levine and N. Scotch, pp.
          1–16. Chicago: Aldine.
Lipset, S. M., and Bendix, R.
  1959.   *Social Mobility in Industrial Society.* Berkeley: University of California
          Press.
Livson, N., and Peskin, H.
  1967.   Prediction of adult psychological health in a longitudinal study. *Jour-
          nal of Abnormal Psychology,* 72:509–518.
Masuda, M., and Holmes, T. H.
  1967.   Magnitude estimations of social readjustment. *Journal of Psychosomatic
          Research,* 11:219–226.
Mechanic, D.
  1972.   Social class and schizophrenia: Some requirements for a plausible
          theory of social influence. *Social Forces,* 50:305–309.
Mishler, E. G., and Scotch, N.
  1963.   Sociocultural factors in the epidemiology of schizophrenia. *Psychiatry,*
          26:315–343.

198 *Karl L. Alexander*

Mishler, E. G., and Waxler, N.
   1965.   Family interaction processes and schizophrenia. *Merrill-Palmer Quarterly,* 11:269–315.
Murphy, H.
   1965.   Migration and the major mental disorders. In *Mobility and Mental Health,* edited by M. Kantor, pp. 5–29. Springfield, Ill.: C. C. Thomas.
Myers, J. K.
   1965.   Consequences and prognosis of disability. In *Sociology and Rehabilitation,* edited by M. Sussman, pp. 35–51. Washington, D.C.: American Sociological Association.
Myers, J. K.; Lindenthal, J. J.; and Pepper, M. P.
   1972.   Life events and mental status: A longitudinal study. *Journal of Health and Social Behavior,* 13:398–406.
Nagi, S.
   1965.   Some conceptual issues in disability and rehabilitation. In *Sociology and Rehabilitation,* edited by M. Sussman, pp. 100–113. Washington, D. C.: American Sociological Association.
   1969.   *Disability and Rehabilitation.* Columbus, Ohio: Ohio State University Press.
Paykel, E. S.; Myers, J. K.; Dienelt, M. N.; Klerman, G. L.; Lindenthal, J. J.; and Pepper, M. P.
   1969.   Life events and depression: A controlled study. *Archives of General Psychiatry,* 21:753–760.
Penrose, R. J. J.
   1972.   Life events before subarachnoid haemorrhage. *Journal of Psychosomatic Research,* 16:329–334.
Perrucci, R.
   1961.   The significance of intraoccupational mobility. *American Sociological Review,* 26:874–883.
Rahe, R. H., and Holmes. T. H.
   1965.   Social, psychologic, and psychophysiologic aspects of inguinal hernia. *Journal of Psychosomatic Research,* 8:487–491.
Rahe, R. H.; Meyer, M.; Smith, M.; Kjaer, G.; and Holmes, T. H.
   1964.   Social stress and illness onset. *Journal of Psychosomatic Research,* 8:35–44.
Rogler, L., and Hollingshead, A. B.
   1965.   *Trapped: Families and Schizophrenia.* New York: John Wiley.
Safilios-Rothschild, C.
   1970.   *The Sociology and Social Psychology of Disability and Rehabilitation.* New York: Random House.
Schwartz, D., and Mintz, N.
   1963.   Ecology and psychosis among Italians in 27 Boston communities. *Social Problems,* 10:371–374.

Sewell, W. H.; Haller, A.; and Ohlendorf, G.
  1970. The educational and early occupational attainment process: Replication and revision. *American Sociological Review*, 35:1014–1027.
Sewell, W. H.; Haller, A.; and Portes, A.
  1969. The educational and early occupational attainment process. *American Sociological Review*, 34:82–91.
Sewell, W. H., and Hauser, R. M.
  1972. Causes and consequences of higher education: Models of the status attainment process. *American Journal of Agricultural Economics*, 54:851–861.
Spaeth, J. L.
  1968. Occupational prestige expectations among male college graduates. *American Journal of Sociology*, 73:548–558.
  1970. Occupational attainment among male college graduates. *American Journal of Sociology*, 75:632–644.
Spilken, A. Z., and Jacobs, M.A.
  1971. Prediction of illness behavior from measures of life crisis, manifest distress, and maladaptive coping. *Psychosomatic Medicine*, 33:251–264.
Srole, L.; Langner, T.; Michael, S.; Opler, M.; and Rennie, T.
  1962. *Mental Health in the Metropolis: The Midtown Manhattan Study*. Vol. 1. New York: McGraw-Hill.
Suchman, E. A.
  1965. A model for research and evaluation on rehabilitation. In *Sociology and Rehabilitation*, edited by M. Sussman, pp. 52–70. Washington, D.C.: American Sociological Association.
Treiman, D. J., and Terrell, K.
  1973. Sex differences in the process of status attainment: A comparison of working men and women. Paper presented at the American Sociological Association meetings, New York City, August.
Turner, R. J., and Wagenfeld, M. O.
  1967. Occupational mobility and schizophrenia: Assessment of the social causation and social selection hypotheses. *American Sociological Review*, 32:104–113.
Wechsler, H., and Pugh, T. F.
  1967. Fit of individual and community characteristics and rates of psychiatric hospitalization. *American Journal of Sociology*, 73:331–338.
Wechsler, H.; Solomon, L.; and Kramer, B.
  1970. *Social Psychology and Mental Health*. New York: Holt, Rinehart and Winston.
Wilder, C. S.
  1972. *Time Lost from Work Among the Currently Employed Population: United States—1968*. Washington, D.C., Department of Health, Education and Welfare: Vital and Health Statistics. Ser. 10, no. 71.

Wilder, M. H.
  1972. *Disability Days: United States—1968*. Washington, D.C.: Department of Health, Education and Welfare: Vital and Health Statistics. Ser. 10, no. 67.
Wolf, D.
  1963. Life stress and patterns of disease. In *The Psychological Basis of Medical Practice*, edited by H. I. Lief., U. F. Lief, and N. R. Lief, pp. 109–114. New York: Harper and Row.
Wyler, A. R.; Masuda, M.; and Holmes, T. H.
  1971. Magnitude of life events and seriousness of illness. *Psychosomatic Medicine*, 33:115–122.

CHAPTER 8

The Political Sociology
of Rehabilitation

Elliott A. Krause

It is the highest form of naiveté to assume that, because a researcher does not take an overt political position when he is analyzing society, he is therefore not being political. As far back as Max Weber, it was obvious that one could not do value-free sociology. Not to decide is to decide. To focus in one area is not to focus in another, and this fact has always had political implications. There is evidence, which I shall present in this chapter, that attempts are being made to sabotage the health and prevent the rehabilitation of millions of Americans. Even so, it is very important not to let emotions get in the way of the struggle to find the truth. It is necessary to look at areas that we might not want to look at, to take on even more problems when it would probably be easier to keep our focus where it has been before. There is another major reason for the broadscale political analysis of the rehabilitation field presented in this chapter. If the focus is only on activity within the field, the wider context within which all are working is ignored. The *Congressional Record* and national government studies are sources of much of the information reported. This information points up an entirely different picture from that seen in the research reports of social scientists in rehabilitation.

There are those who work to frustrate the aims of the rehabilitation process and of the handicapped because it is in their own

The author is indebted to Geoffrey Gibson and Irving Zola for their criticism of an earlier version of this work.

interest. For the rehabilitation field to ignore such forces and not to study them as a way of countering them is approximately equivalent to the conduct of the Jews in Germany, during the rise of Hitler, who persisted in saying, "But we are good Germans," almost until they were carted off to concentration camps. Perhaps the analogy is too extreme. But the political neutrality of rehabilitation professionals and rehabilitation clients at a time when forces of opposition to the aims and goals of rehabilitation are on the rise will mean the frustration of the rehabilitation task itself. We must not just study the behavior of the geese on the common while someone else steals the common away from the geese.

Power—its distribution, uses, and consequences—is the subject of this analysis. The study of power relations can begin at any point at which the lives of people are affected, but the responsibility of the analyst is to present the dynamics in a way that can be comprehended as a first step toward change, that is, to carry out an action-relevant analysis. The primary people affected are those individuals we call "the disabled." The task of this analysis is to see how the presently existing power structure in American society and the social processes which preserve it affect the fortunes of the disabled. The causes and consequences of disability, as well as the process of rehabilitation must be observed, for the forces producing disability are in large part the same as the ones preventing the successful rehabilitation of the disabled. In general, the creation and handling of disabled persons occurs only in a concrete social context.

Following Mills' prescription, this analysis is historical, does not overgeneralize, and addresses itself to the present, that is, to America in the early 1970s (Mills, 1956). It asks one thematic question: Who benefits from the existing situation? In particular, it asks how the political processes, broadly conceived, affect the situation in at least the following areas: the definition of disability, the manufacture of disability, compensation for disability, service programs for the disabled, and action by the disabled and their allies. The pattern which emerges forms the basis for a conclusion and some recommendations for the future.

The Definition of Disability

In a recent paper (Krause, 1972), a distinction was made between three kinds of definition of disability: *biopsychological* disability, *social role* disability, and *legal* disability. Biopsychological definitions are made by physicians and others qualified to judge physical and mental functioning by generally accepted standards. Social role disability is relative to the demands of the social role of the individual. For example, rheumatoid arthritis does not have quite as severe consequences for the professor as for the construction worker, in that the medical problem, though equal for both, brings more severe consequences for the latter than for the former in the social role at work. Purely social role disabilities are conceivable, too; for instance, a worker who is unable to perform at a new job because he lacks a certain skill or a school drop-out in an employment market which demands college degrees for almost everyone. Finally, there are legal definitions of disability. These are the definitions often made with relevance to medical, psychological, and social criteria which have the force of law. They may qualify an individual for payments, such as workmen's compensation, Old Age Disability Insurance (OASDI), or vocational rehabilitation services; or, in the case of an offender against the law, they may qualify him for a term in prison.

From the standpoint of political analysis, the progression from definitions of the medical/psychiatric kind to definitions of the social and, finally, legal kind is a progression from science to politics. While medical definitions primarily have "scientific" criteria, social role definitions mix values with the existing social structure and with the medical nature of the individual. For example, if a society decides that black people are unworthy of jobs or only worthy of the kind of "pickup" jobs described by Liebow (1967), then being black in that society is a form of social role disability.

The values and attitudes of others are essential components in the preservation or change of any political situation. They, as well as a lack of skills, become key ingredients in a social role definition of disability. Deviant social roles can be officially defined as disability in some political regimes. For example, in the Soviet Union the antiparty activist, critic, or author may be imprisoned in a mental hospital as "socially unstable," which, in view of the odds in the Soviet Union, perhaps he is. But no outside observer thinks that there is any reality in the definition. It is an ironic fiction and an excuse for low-visibility imprisonment of dissenters.

Legal definitions of disability clearly involve the world of politics in the direct sense of the term. Legal definitions of disability, whether definitions of criminal behavior or of incapacity to function relevant to work, are based on laws. Laws are rules constructed and passed by lawmakers, and lawmakers are elected politicians. The kind of laws they make or the changes they refuse to make in existing laws define the boundaries of criminal and civil disability. Legislators are beset by lobbyists, and, as is well known, the laws of any city, state, or nation are a monumental mixture of reason and special pleading. The laws and the politics of lawmaking in the area of disability are certainly no exception.

Only in the past few years, and only in a few states, is open homosexual behavior between consenting adults not viewed as a crime and the actors as some combination of criminal and cripple. If any state aims to revise its criminal code concerning homosexuality, the homophile associations will lobby for passage of a new law, while political conservatives will oppose them.

Women's rights are another area involving pressure groups and conflicting interests. There are those who view pregnancy as a form of medical disability, with decisions about it to be solely left up to physicians, but others affirm a woman's right to an abortion to terminate her own pregnancy. The recent Supreme Court decision on abortion shows that changes in law can affect millions of persons in social role behavior areas.

In the area of rehabilitation, the laws governing disability because of occupational disease, as contrasted with injury because of an accident at work, are a clear example of interest group lobbying. In state after state, until quite recently, slowly growing occupational *disease* (as contrasted with getting hit in the head with a fender) was not *officially* or *legally* defined as a form of work-induced disability. Thus, miners could not get workmen's compensation payments for the insidious onset of pneumoconiosis, or black lung disease (U.S., Congress, 1970). The mine owners saw to it that state laws outlining which diseases were to be excluded and how "industrial accident" was to be defined legally would get them off the hook. Years of political organizing by the miners and others were needed to modify the definitions of "disability" legally acceptable under the statutes and so to qualify individuals for compensation and possible rehabilitation at the expense of those who had disabled them.

One essential aspect of the politics of disability definition which is of primary importance to the disabled is the *consequence* of being defined as legally disabled. Under the Social Security program in the mid sixties a majority of the disabled were not receiving disability benefits (Haber, 1964). The laws made someone eligible for Social Security only if he or she worked at stable jobs in covered workplaces for a five-year period, neatly disqualified many houseworkers, farmworkers, and marginally employed people who needed the protection the most. Not accidentally, but because of lobbying by agricultural interests, the same individuals were not covered by most workmen's compensation coverage laws. In the *Congressional Record* for August 1, 1972, the summary of the final report of the National Commission on State Workmen's Compensation Laws (1972) states:

Inequity results from the wide variations among the states in the proportion of their workers protected by workmen's compensation. Inequity also results because the employees not covered usually are those most in need of protection: the low-wage workers, such as farm help, domestics, casual workers, and employees of small firms.

Being outside the laws, these individuals cannot legally get compensation when they are injured at work. For these people, there is no legal definition of disability, with accompanying rights and funds for compensation and rehabilitation.

Finally, the politics of the budgetary process (Wildavsky, 1964), play a major role in who will be the haves and who the have-nots, once a group *has* been defined legally as disabled. Political struggles in Washington and in state legislatures determine the amount of resources available for defining people with marginal medical, social, and psychological disabilities as legally disabled with rights to support and rehabilitation service, and the amount of money available for such service. The cutbacks in human service funds in the Nixon administration in Washington led local vocational rehabilitation units to hold back on any commitments to disabled clients for new artificial legs, hearing aids, and kidney dialysis or to assist only those who could be helped without extra monies being spent. There is no money from Washington, almost none at the state level, and thus none for the clients. At the very least, this immediately cuts down the willingness of compensation boards and rehabilitation agencies to define marginal cases as legally disabled in a way that will make those individuals an added drain on the disappearing money pool. Why is the money drying up? The president, against the will of Congress, is using the power inherent in the executive branch to impound funds because his own priorities do not match those of the poor, the disabled, and those working in their behalf. This is the politics of the budgetary process with a vengeance. To the handicapped, the Nixon administration proposed willpower instead of artificial limbs.

The Manufacture of Disability

Poverty is not good for one's health. Neither is most industrial work. It is not facetious to think of the ghetto and the factory as the major settings in America in which disability is manufactured. First, the correlations between poverty and disability, as a consequence of the frequency of illness in the lower socioeconomic strata, are summarized for perhaps the thousandth time by Kosa, Antonovsky, and Zola (1969). Especially in Lerner's (1969) survey on the relations between social class and physical illness and in the parallel survey by Fried (1969) on the relationship between poverty and mental illness, the issues are clear. Poor diet, severe life stress, and poor or nonexistent health care are the well-known concomitants of a poverty-level existence. Combining with these physical and mental disability-producing conditions for the poor are the conditions for the blue-collar, working class in American industry. A national study conducted for the Secretary of H.E.W. (Secretary's Committee on Work in America, 1973)had the following to say:

In 1968, 14,311 died in industrial accidents. . . . In the same year 90,000 workers suffered *permanent impairment* from industrial accidents, and a total of 2,100,000 suffered total but temporary disability. In 1969, . . . exposures to industrial pollutants in the workplace . . . caused one million new cases of occupational disease. Among the casualties were 3,600 dead and over 800,000 cases of burns, lung and eye damage, dermatitis and brain damage.

How these conditions are produced is considered, detail by detail, in Mayers' (1969) textbook on occupational health. Recent field studies on farmworkers' exposure to cancer-causing pesticides (California, Department of Public Health, 1961), on radiation poisoning in atomic power plants (Parsekian, 1958), and on the prevalence of industrial plant conditions conducive to injury in the Chicago area (U.S., Bureau of Occupational Health and Safety, 1970) indicate that the H.E.W. report's figures are, if anything, an underestimate. Yet the conditions are close to being accepted as normal by both the owners and, tragically, the workers. This aspect of industrial life in America is fatalistically described by Malone and Plant (1963) as "the unavoidable human wreckage that is involved in production."

Both the HEW report and the poverty and health reviews tend to soft-pedal the critically important issues which lie behind the century-long existence of the problems of the poor and working class in America. Who benefits from the continuation of these conditions? And who pays the bill? In the case of the poor, the extensive pathology was not really touched by programs as partial and unrealistic as the War on Poverty, which did, however, man-

age to raise the expectations of the poor to the point where they
rioted against their conditions. The riots led in turn to a backlash
and helped make possible a Nixon victory; the present punitive
action against the public social supports of the poor followed
(Moynihan, 1969). Apparently the poor are conveniently ignored
by the monied interest groups, and the middle class rejects them
in human terms.

The topic of industrial disease and injury may be considered
further under issues of compensation. Two points can be made
about these issues. First, each industry lobbies in Washington to
defeat, pervert, or weaken any occupational health and safety
legislation which is likely to cost industry more money than they
pay for occupational accident insurance. Second, the insurance
companies fight along with them to keep the eligibility limits
down. The Nixon administration severely cut the staff and funding of the Occupational Health and Safety Bureau in H.E.W., in
spite of the 1970 legislation establishing the Occupational Health
and Safety Code, and no major changes are visible under Ford.
Furthermore, the word from the field is that conditions have not
changed, new law or not (U.S., Congress, 1970). No federal help
is coming for inspection, and the states' enforcement of their
industrial safety codes is so open to political pressure that it
constitutes a national sick joke.

Most of the cost of industrial injuries is passed on to the consumer either directly through higher wholesale and retail prices
or indirectly through welfare costs when the injured workers
exhaust their disability benefits or payments from the injury
funds in Social Security. In economic terms, therefore, the cost is
externalized out of industry onto the individual private
citizen.

Galbraith's (1958) general observation on public squalor in the
midst of private affluence is particularly apposite for the social
and economic costs of disability through industrial injury. Either
the victims pay directly through their reduced life circumstances
and permanent injury, or the public at large pays directly and
individually. The political power of the eight hundred largest

corporations is such that no major legislation that would reallocate the cost share back to industry is likely to pass. The present national leadership—under Ford as well as Nixon—displays an interest in dividing the poor and the working class against each other and in reducing the financial contribution of the private citizen to the welfare and rehabilitation of those unprotected and unfortunate victims, while making very certain that the corporate share is not enlarged in any way. Thus, the overall issue of the political power of the corporate industrial interests, a main theme of social criticism and social reality in America since Veblen and the robber barons, is still directly relevant to an understanding of the specific details and the underlying forces relevant to the manufacture of disability in America.

The Struggle for Compensation

Since the turn of the century, the nations of Europe in both the capitalist and the socialist blocs have integrated their programs for Workmen's Compensation into overall schemes for social insurance. Lubove's (1968) detailed history of the movement for a Social Security system in America and Hirshfield's (1970) account of the American struggle for a national form of compulsory health insurance show a contrasting picture. Both authors stress the power of private profit-making groups, especially corporations in the manufacturing and insurance fields, and of the American medical profession, which made a series of successful stands against expanding the role of government in social insurance. The essentially private workmen's compensation programs were initiated throughout the United States in the 1920s and 1930s and are found in every state at present. In principle, the employer gives up the right to fight an employee's claim for damages in court, and the employee gives up the right to sue for large amounts. As Lubove (1968) points out, this situation was preferred by the corporations, for their costs became more predictable and lower in the long run than in the old "sue them for a fortune" system, even though the corporations might have to make payments more often. Both employer and employee submit information concerning all injuries to state boards which determine compensation for industrial injuries. In theory, Malone and Plant (1963) observe that

if the employee is no longer able to recover as much as before in the case of being injured through the employer's negligence, he is entitled to moderate compensation in all cases of injury, and has a certain and speedy remedy without the difficulty and expense of establishing negligence or proving the amount of the damages.

Corporations either pay directly into state insurance funds or buy insurance to cover the cost of administration and benefits. Because they are paying the bill, corporations fight hard and successfully to keep the amounts down by lobbying in state legislatures. Bear (1951) comments:

In short, for dependents in death cases and for seriously injured employees, the workmen's compensation acts have turned out to be a snare. The remedy, of course, is to increase compensation payments as the cost of living rises. The combined legislative-lobbying efforts of the larger employers and the insurance companies have thus far made this impossible.

Jaffe and Nathanson (1968) point out that the essential *legal* idea behind workmen's compensation is that both employer and employee are to be bound by an agreement so that the adversary process of employee suing employer is replaced, in theory, by one where no "fault" is assumed. But their case examples, and those in Malone and Plant (1963) clearly indicate that the employee must go before a board and fight against the corporation and its lawyer, with the board making the judgment. This is a *de facto* adversary situation: "In general, in a workmen's compensation case the claimant has the burden of proving that the case falls within the statutory requirements for compensability" (Malone and Plant, 1963).

In many jurisdictions, the "no fault" idea is ignored. The loophole used by the corporations and their lawyers is a clause which states that "all safety precautions were followed" or one which stipulates that the accident arose "in the course of employment," a clause that can be very strictly defined by a corporation-favoring board or court. Jaffe and Nathanson (1968) comment:

There has been complaint on the basis of delay through protracted judicial review. The question, for example, whether an accident arises "out of and in the course of the employment" is sometimes a very difficult one. Employers fight such cases through the courts, particularly if the injury is serious, entailing larger compensation. This means delayed compensation in the cases where the immediate need is greatest.

The war of the corporation against the worker in this area is summarized by a series of findings in the final report of the National Commission on State Workmen's Compensation Laws, (1972). First, the amount of benefits: "In most states, the most a beneficiary may receive, 'the maximum weekly benefit,' is less than the poverty level of income for a family of four. Moreover, many states limit the duration or the total amount of cash payments."

In fifteen states the widow of a deceased worker receives payments for only fifteen years, not for life. In eleven states, the total payment for death resulting from an employee's work is less than $25,000, about four years' full pay.

Second, in most states, though the worker needs a lawyer if the company contests the award (as is usual in cases of a serious injury), he, not the state, pays for the lawyer. Senator Javits, who wrote the legislation that established the National Commission (1972), comments on this "neutral" role of the state compensation boards. Using findings of the commission, he condemns state boards for

their failure to take the initiative in supervising and providing adequate medical care and rehabilitation, as well as technical aid and, where necessary, legal assistance. All too often workmen's compensation agencies are little more than referees in contested cases and do not conceive of themselves or function as the guardians of the welfare of injured workers.

Third, most states define eligibility by rules which deemphasize the impact of slowly growing occupational diseases such as black lung disease, asbestos poisoning, and radiation poisoning or pay lower amounts for them than for traumatic and more socially visible damage to the worker:

The traditional test for determining whether an injury or disease is compensable is that the cause must be an "accident"—sudden, unexpected and determinate as to time and place. This interpretation has served to bar compensation for most diseases and for injuries which were considered routine and usual in the place of employment. (National Commission, 1972)

Even if an occupational disease is covered in a state law, the disease often shows years after it is incurred, and most states have time limits on filing claims. If a worker quits his job at an atomic power plant, develops radiation poisoning two years later, and lives in a state with an eighteen-month time limitation on reporting, he is out of luck (St. Clair, 1958).

In general, the National Commission concluded that the workmen's compensation program should be drastically improved and that at present it was not doing its job. But from another point of view, it *was*. That is, it was unloading the human wreckage of industry at minimal cost to the corporations, paying a limited-period subsidy to the disabled worker, and then, when the money ran out, pushing him on to the welfare rolls. Attempts to rehabilitate the disabled worker are not usually mandatory, and in times of tight employment employers usually prefer not to take the extra risks of hiring the handicapped. Even if extra insurance is given to the employer for hiring handicapped persons, it is often not enough to cover their added risks. In addition, few disabled veterans of our domestic industrial Vietnam want another tour at the front line, one with lesser pay than previously at probably the same risk of injury. Thus, even in states where there is routine referral of the disabled to state vocational rehabilitation agencies, the factors resemble those in California, where Bixby (1972) observes:

If one considers that under the current system, the employee is faced with a lower permanent disability award if he rehabilitates; the possibility of not attaining employment as a rehabilitant; and the lower wages due to his status as a rehabilitant—an employee could understandably decline any proffer of rehabilitation. Certainly the fact that the employee is refused supplemental income or a maintenance allowance during rehabilitation expedites such declination. If the system of workmen's compensation and vocational rehabilitation were to be viewed from this perspective, it would certainly be no surprise to discover that the great majority of permanently handicapped employees are public charges.

To sum up, if God is a minor source of disabled individuals, the two major sources are certainly poverty and the factory. The poor are beaten before they start, by second-rate medical service, bad living conditions, and absence of preventive care. They are born on welfare, develop physical, mental, and social disabilities because they are on it, and they stay there. The power structure of the nation, operating directly out of the executive branch, fights the increase in research and services that might prevent or rehabilitate the disability of the poor. The same power structure grinds up the bodies of the working class in factories, at a rate matching that of the most active year in the Vietnam war, and then provides the trivial compensation system as a way station for unloading them onto the public rolls.

The consumer pays the bill in increasing taxes and increasing insurance costs, which are jacked up further by the costs of maintaining the growing army of disabled industrial veterans. The power structure at the same time opposes amelioration of benefits. Eventually welfare and Medicaid become the last refuge for the disabled, but these are not rehabilitation programs. Furthermore they are frequently carried out in brutally mismanaged and poorly staffed settings. In broadest terms, large segments of American society function as factories for the creation of disability, with those in power acting to prevent their profit margins from being lowered as a consequence of a more humane treatment of the wreckage which they produce.

The Delivery of Services

The same society which leaves a large segment of its people in poverty and another large segment in unrewarding and dangerous work is responsible for the delivery of rehabilitation services. There are few reliable quantitative studies which examine who is served and who is ignored or shunted away from rehabilitation services. It is for this reason that the details on the *manufacture* of disability are so important, for they point out how many persons are actively disabled and then not rehabilitated. This is the group that never gets studied by the sociology of rehabilitation.

Studies and reviews such as the one by Sussman (1969) indicate that there are special problems to rehabilitating marginal persons, both because of their high prevalence of multiple and chronic disability and because of the lack of jobs at the end of the road. Conversely, the rehabilitation system continues to be judged by congressional committees interested in saving money, as well as by the Office of Management and Budget (OMB) in the executive branch. Cost accounting means that the system, for its own self-preservation, must choose the least disabled, rather than the most disabled, and the white, middle-class trained individual with a minor problem that is inexpensive to handle rather than the poor and the disabled factory worker.

In addition to the foregoing dynamics, a policy transition has occurred that pulls the rug out from underneath responsive rehabilitation programs. While the 1960s witnessed an expansion of responsibility and funding for rehabilitation programs, the 1970s have seen a continued expansion of program responsibilities obstructed by fund cutbacks ordered by the Nixon administration and continued under Ford. There has also been an involvement of the rehabilitation field with new punitive programs. For example, the revised Work Incentive Program (WIN) was changed by the Talmadge amendments from a Johnsonian program for training some welfare mothers for employment, with some reasonable rehabilitation planning over a long period if necessary, into a crash program of forced registration of welfare mothers for job placement consideration *as a condition of receiving welfare in the first place.* While there are exceptions, the main aim is to "get those welfare mothers to work."

The primary product of the WIN program appears to be in

harassment. All welfare mothers are required to register for the WIN program; they are referred to local divisions of employment security for job placement; and they are almost always sent right back to welfare because they have no real skills and there are usually no jobs. If there are jobs, regardless of their menial nature the welfare mothers can be forced to take them, under penalty of losing benefits in the program. Meanwhile, the staffs of the vocational rehabilitation agencies are expected to stand by, to rehabilitate only those welfare mothers who can quickly be placed in jobs, and to disqualify others on the grounds of their handicaps. The WIN program does not pay for rehabilitation if handicaps are found, nor does it provide rehabilitation services. The mothers are merely sent to the local hospital or, more probably, ignored.

The cutbacks in human services funding in many areas are affecting the size and capacity of welfare and employment agency staffs and making it difficult for them to attend to their ordinary business, much less special programs like WIN. The overt political motivation behind both the unrealistic programs such as WIN II ("get them lazy mothers to work") and the cutbacks in many areas of service to the poor are essentially causing the entire rehabilitation system to become a skeleton of its former self.

At the same time, the Vietnam "benefit" is being plowed back into further military spending, for the military-industrial complex is far stronger in its political influence on the executive branch than the combined lobbies of the rehabilitation professions, the National Rehabilitation Association, and the organizations of the handicapped themselves (Krause, 1969–1970). E. B. Whitten (1973) sums up the political situation of the early 1970s and its consequences for the rehabilitation of the disabled:

These are strange days for rehabilitation, and the same might be said for other human service programs. The President of the United States pocket vetoed the Rehabilitation Act of 1972 which had been passed unanimously by both branches of Congress following lengthy hearings and tedious staff work. At the same time, he vetoed the Older Americans Act of 1972 and several other important bills. Such an act is unprecedented.

In effect, the underservice of the poor and disabled blue-collar worker of the 1940s, 1950s, and 1960s is being replaced by a literal economic war against the helpless, waged by the executive branch of government through the tactic of budgetary politics, impoundment of funds, and a series of actions which come close to provoking a constitutional crisis. Amid all of this, the major industrial corporations, and the military-industrial complex in particular, prosper while the ordinary citizen pays the bill or, if disabled, experiences harassment as well. The national political philosophy is approaching that of Ryan's (1971) critique: The victimizers are blaming the victim.

The Disabled as an Interest Group

To what extent have the disabled acted on their own behalf? To what extent is action on the behalf of the disabled the same thing as action by the disabled themselves? When these questions are addressed, the difference between ideology and reality is of critical importance.

An ideology is an explanation of a group's position which proponents use politically to influence a target group (Krause, 1968). In the area of rehabilitation, political action by the disabled and their sponsors contains a heavy baggage of ideology. First, the idea of the disabled as a potential revolutionary group, seizing control of the rehabilitation system and running it on its own behalf, seems to be either an ideology or a sophomoric fantasy. This revolt of the client, discussed as a possibility by Haug and Sussman (1969) and advocated as a strategy of sorts by some activists, is yet another example of middle-class liberals asking other people to risk their bodies and sustenance and then stepping aside when the inevitable backlash develops. It is not *their* necks which are at stake when the conservatives gain political control and use the backlash in order to cut back services. As for the disabled, the so-called revolt never got off the ground, with the possible exception of prison revolts if they are to be included in the field of analysis. In general, the disabled have *not* revolted and, indeed, with Mothers for Adequate Welfare as a possible exception, have not even organized politically.

We can contrast this overall absence of self-direction and organized action with action by the voluntary associations directly relevant to client groups of the disabled that in theory act on their behalf. The ideologies of these associations, including the mental health associations, the associations for the retarded and the cerebral palsied, and the American Heart Association, all state that they are acting on behalf of "their" group. But an objective, critical study of the fate of funds in these organizations has not been made, and neither has a study of these organizations' role in preventing the integration of service programs. Instead, these organizations push for special-interest, categorical program legislation and funding, which makes integrated and comprehensive treatment of the problems of the disabled impossible.

To what extent can we look at these organizations as being primarily interested in their own survival and only secondarily involved in the welfare of their client group? If limb manufacturers or orthopedic supply companies lobby in Washington, along with the National Rehabilitation Association, for the passage and funding of a piece of rehabilitation legislation, to what extent is this owing to pure altruism and to what extent to an interest in organizational preservation and profit-making?

In another area, organizations established during the nineteenth century, such as Goodwill industries, with its ideology of "not charity but a chance," operate large factories where donated second-hand material is rehabilitated by the handicapped, who are paid for hard work at subminimum or just over minimum wages. The whole system, which includes many sheltered workshops, provides alienating assembly work for the handicapped while psychologists and rehabilitation staff members (who do not have to assemble the widgets themselves) pride themselves on the "increase in self-esteem" that is assumed but not proved to accrue to the handicapped who do the work.[1] Certain ideologies of many rehabilitation professionals blind them to other values in life than "work." If a handicapped worker in such a setting objects to such work, his objection is written off as pathology and not as a comment on the nature of the work offered. Such work settings are part of a national organization, the National Association of Sheltered Workshops, which is not likely to take kindly to the observation of the Secretary's Committee on Work in America report (1973) namely, that *no one* should have to do that kind of work. The handicapped are *happy* in their work, the staff members in sheltered workshops reassure themselves. That assertion is, in fact, questionable.

In any case, the assumption made by service staffs, the government, and the social scientists that the rehabilitation system itself is part of the solution, instead of part of the problem, needs a far closer look. There is presently no way to be certain that organizations claiming to act on behalf of the disabled are actually doing so. The disabled themselves are rather silent on this score, or, if they do speak, they do so only after coaching and with not a little anxiety. This is the anxiety of the powerless, the dependent, and the unorganized, in short, of the colonized.

The Politics of Rehabilitation

Throughout this review of the power situation in the field of disability creation and rehabilitation, the theme of "who benefits?" comes constantly into focus. Those who have interests defend them by manipulating the definition process, by avoiding responsibility for the conditions which produce disability, by fighting the disabled in their struggle for compensation, and by either diverting money away from service programs or using the programs in a somewhat parasitical manner for organizational aggrandizement and simple profit-making. The overall social system within which this takes place is a corporate, capitalistic state, with a withered political process and a coopted executive branch working for the groups that have, in area after area, produced the conditions described in this chapter.

To talk about minor reform of this system is to be impossibly naive. The set of consequences is classic and illustrates an old lesson on the consequences of unbridled corporate power. As to whether another form of political-economic system could handle rehabilitation health care better, the answer is both obvious and irrelevant. Of course it could and does. The statistics of the World Health Organization and international authorities have been saying this for a long time. But that means political-economic change, either by revolution or by a long evolutionary political struggle. From the front lines in the area of disability and rehabilitation, it looks, at least for now, as if the people are losing. Whether they will continue to lose is up to us.

NOTE

1. The author writes from first-hand experience, having been a staff member at one of these settings for five years.

BIBLIOGRAPHY

Bear, J.
    1951. Survey of the legal profession—Workmen's Compensation and the lawyer. *Columbia Law Review,* 51:974.
Bixby, K. W.
    1972. Workmen's Compensation and vocational rehabilitation in California. *San Diego Law Review,* 9:978.
California, Department of Public Health, Bureau of Occupational Health
    1961. *Occupational Disease in California Attributed to Pesticides and Other Agricultural Chemicals,* Berkeley: Department of Public Health.
Fried, M.
    1969. Social differences in mental health. In *Poverty and Health: A Sociological Analysis,* edited by John Kosa, Aaron Antonovsky, and Irving K. Zola, pp. 113–167. Cambridge, Harvard University Press.
Galbraith, J. K.
    1958. *The Affluent Society.* Boston: Houghton Mifflin.
Haber, L. D.
    1964. *The Disabled Worker Under OASDI.* Washington, D.C.: Department of Health, Education and Welfare, Social Security Administration, Re-

search Report #6, Office of Research and Statistics, Government Printing Office.

Haug, M. R., and Sussman, M. B.
1969. Professional autonomy and the revolt of the client. *Social Problems,* 17:153–161.

Hirshfield, D. S.
1970. *The Lost Reform: The Campaign for Compulsory Health Insurance in the United States from 1932 to 1943.* Cambridge: Harvard University Press.

Jaffe, L. L., and Nathanson, N. L.
1968. *Administrative Law: Cases and Materials.* Boston: Little, Brown.

Javits, J.
1972. Summary, Final Report of the National Commission on State Workmen's Compensation Laws. *Congressional Records,* S.12336, August 1.

Kosa, J.; Antonovsky, A.; and Zola, I. K., eds.
1969. *Poverty and Health: A Sociological Analysis.* Cambridge: Harvard University Press.

Krause, E.
1968. Functions of a bureaucratic ideology: Citizen participation. *Social Problems,* 16:129–143.
1969– Poverty, human resources, and the military-industrial complex. *So-*
1970. *cial Science Quarterly,* 51:548–556.
1972. The future of rehabilitation research. *American Archives of Rehabilitation Therapy,* 20:19.

Lerner, M.
1969. Social differences in physical health. In *Poverty and Health: A Sociological Analysis,* edited by J. Kosa, A. Antonovsky, and I. K. Zola, pp. 69–112. Cambridge: Harvard University Press.

Liebow, E.
1967. *Tally's Corner.* Boston: Little, Brown.

Lubove, R.
1968. *The Struggle for Social Security 1900–1935.* Cambridge: Harvard University Press.

Malone, W. S., and Plant, M. L.
1963. *Cases and Materials on Workmen's Compensation.* St. Paul: West.

Mayers, M. R.
1969. *Occupational Health: Hazards of the Work Environment.* Baltimore: Williams and Wilkins.

Mills, C. W.
1956. *The Sociological Imagination.* New York: Oxford University Press.

Moynihan, D. P.
1969. *Maximum Feasible Misunderstanding.* New York: Free Press.

National Commission on State Workmen's Compensation Laws
    1972.   Summary, Final Report. *Congressional Record,* SS. 12332, 12333. August 1.

Parsekian, N. J.
    1958.   *Report of Atomic Energy Committee.* Proceedings, International Association of Industrial Accident Boards, Washington, D.C.: U.S. Department of Labor, Bulletin no. 201.

Ryan, W.
    1971.   *Blaming the Victim.* New York: Pantheon.

Secretary's Committee on Work in America
    1973.   Cambridge: M.I.T. Press. Published originally as *Work in America: Report to the Secretary of H.E.W.* Washington, D.C.: Department of Health, Education and Welfare, 1972.

St. Clair, A.
    1958.   What protection do present-day workmen's compensation laws afford workers and their families against wage loss from disability or death from occupational diseases? Proceedings, International Association of Industrial Accident Boards.

Sussman, M. B.
    1969.   Readjustment and rehabilitation of patients. In *Poverty and Health: A Sociological Analysis,* edited by J. Kosa, A. Antonovsky, and I. K. Zola, pp. 244–264. Cambridge: Harvard University Press.

U.S., Bureau of Occupational Health and Safety, Public Health Service, Department of Health, Education and Welfare
    1970.   *Occupational Health Survey of the Chicago Metropolitan Area.* Cincinnati, E.C.A., H.E.W.

U.S., Congress, Senate, Committee on Labor and Public Welfare, Subcommittee on Labor
    1970.   *Hearings on the Occupational Safety and Health Act of 1970.* Washington, D.C.: Government Printing Office.

Whitten, E. B.
    1973.   A crisis year? *Journal of Rehabilitation,* 39:2, 49.

Wildavsky, A.
    1964.   *The Politics of the Budgetary Process.* Boston: Little, Brown.

WIN Program
    1973.   Interview with a regional administrator, New England Regional Office (Region1), U.S. Department of Health Education and Welfare. February 26.

CHAPTER 9

The Disabled and the Rehabilitation System

Marvin B. Sussman

The notion that "making jobs" has a salutory effect upon the economy and justifies government expenditures for the training and rehabilitation of individuals has long been used by advocates of the helping professions to obtain monies to operate their programs. While the leaders of social betterment would prefer to use quality of life arguments rather than cost/benefit ones, the former do not sell legislators or managers of the public's coffers. Consequently, human service professionals and administrators expend much time and energy in providing "evidence" of economic return on investments. Often, unavoidably, the client is shortchanged in needed or desired services. The ever-growing service bureaucracy consumes many dollars in order to detail the economic gains.

However, there may be a trend away from judging value solely on economic grounds. Recently the public was asked by spokesmen for big industry to consider the social goals of economic activity. This may be a harbinger of good times to come for the humanitarians and their ideologies, but even if it is not there are points to be made in future debates. My point is that in the economic marketplace, where one expects quality products to result from an efficient approach to production and effective management and where cost/benefit analyses are worshiped on the altar of free enterprise, a Keynesian social economic philosophy has been espoused. Some of the staunchest high priests of the economic establishment made these social-oriented statements.

In the congressional debate over the one-quarter billion bail-

out loan for Lockheed Aircraft, John Connelly, then secretary of
the treasury, was questioned by Sen. William Proxmire about the
performance of Lockheed's management and the workers' low
and shoddy production. Mr. Connelly replied that the loan was
primarily intended to keep employed the 31,000 loyal Lockheed
workers throughout the country. Their loss of jobs would be an
essential loss to the well-being of the country, and this by itself was
the rationalization and justification for picking up the tab. Wit-
tingly or not, Connelly used a "theory of proximities," namely,
that what affects one person also affects those around him: family, friends, businesses, other industries, and so forth. Thirty-one
thousand times ten involves a lot of people, so what is a quarter of
a billion?

A slight variation on this theme was used in testimony by the
program chief of the ill-fated F-111 fighter bomber program.
This aircraft, produced by General Dynamics, eventually had a
500 percent overrun of its budget and still is considered highly
questionable in performance. When questioned by Congress, the
program chief said in effect that boondoggling of this order was
necessary in order to achieve desired social goals (Fitzgerald,
1973). It is very interesting that those who use "megabucks"[1] in
their jargon and are likely to toss them around in their conversations ("What do a few megabucks amount to if they are going to
help?") have accepted the philosophy of helping people by keeping them working even when their production is not up to standards and costs are fantastically high. They appear to be getting
away with it.

Keynesian economics, which for the past three decades has
provided the rationale for so many social welfare programs, is no
longer the sole possession of the human service establishment.
The big boys of economic enterprise have coopted the theory,
with one major difference. They may not believe what it says, but
they are using it for good political and economic advantage. In
contrast, human service systems such as rehabilitation have been
asked to submit themselves to costs/benefits analyses and to direct
their goals toward the rehabilitation of individuals so that they
can be restored to economic productivity if at all possible and

contribute to the national good, especially to the gross national product. As money becomes tight, the squeeze is on to evidence productivity and "tangible results" in human service programs while government subsidies, through cost overruns and tax shelters, increase in the economic sector, with cost/benefit becoming a dirty word.

It is too much to expect these happenings to catalyze a conversion to a humanitarian posture in the funding of health care and rehabilitation. While Lockheed-like events will occur in the private sector with increasing frequency in the years ahead, the acceptance of a social benefit goal and ideological stance for rehabilitation with concomitant financial support is highly unlikely. The human service system lacks the power and clout to maintain a client-oriented approach and is perceived not to have public support in relation to goals of life enhancement over economic viability. At best the human service system can use the big business defections as admonitions when it bargains for acceptance of less economic-oriented criteria.

The relevance of this ideological struggle to the care and treatment of the disabled is obvious. The resources available to the less fortunate depend in part on the resolution of the ideological take-over and the power to command and use monies for desired social ends.

The rehabilitation system has experienced cataclysmic change and growth and intensified professionalization during the last decade (Sussman and Haug, 1967). Future directions are not readily discernible. Consequently, I will analyze major streams of thought, practice, and behavior in today's rehabilitation system. The interest is in what the rehabilitation system means and does to the disabled person. How does the system affect the socialization of those who enter it?

Legislation in the 1970s

Rehabilitation legislation can trace its historic roots to the 1798 act of Congress which established a marine hospital fund to care for disabled seamen, a category of individuals who were considered at that time vital to the national economy, international trade, and empire building. (Straus, 1965). The notion of vocational rehabilitation to enable the individual to "pull his own weight" through productive labor and add an economic value to the society (first suggested in 1798) dominated the Rehabilitation Act of 1972 (H.R. 1479) and Public Law 93-112, 1973.[2]

These bills supported a policy and implementation of programs to restore the sick to health and to rehabilitate the mentally or physically disabled if these individuals could potentially contribute to the gross national product. The two bills assumed that individuals returned to gainful employment through appropriate physical and mental rehabilitation and vocational training can support themselves and add to the productive wealth of society. Their disabilities may be so severe that their employability is extremely limited. However, if they can be rehabilitated to the point where they can adequately carry out physical, social, and intellectual activities reasonably independently of others and, it is hoped, obtain full-time or part-time employment, then societal savings can accrue. Even if gainful employment is not possible, rehabilitation still is a contribution to the economic productivity of society since the disabled require less assistance. For example, if a paraplegic can be rehabilitated so as to require very few personal services this reduces the maintenance costs for him and at the same time releases individuals to work in other productive pursuits who would have had to care for him.

It is important to understand the statutory basis of the rehabilitation system if one is to comprehend what it does as a socialization system to those who are disabled. Despite many new humanistically oriented provisions, it is still a boundaried system, defining those who are deviant, who are in need of management, who are legitimate socialization agents and novices; what is to be done, by whom, and under what circumstances and for what ends (Dinitz and Beron, 1971).

The following excerpt from H.R. 1479, *Declaration of Purpose,* illustrates the traditional heritage and legal constraints under which today's rehabilitation system operates:

Sec. 2. The purpose of this Act is to provide a statutory basis for the Rehabilitation Services Administration, to establish within the Department of Health, Education, and Welfare an Office for the Handicapped, and to authorize programs to—

(1) develop and implement comprehensive and continuing State plans for meeting the current and future needs for providing vocational rehabilitation services to handicapped individuals and to provide such services for the benefit of such individuals, serving first those with the most severe handicaps, so that they may *prepare for and engage in gainful employment;*[3]

(2) evaluate the rehabilitation potential of handicapped individuals;

(3) develop, implement, and provide comprehensive rehabilitation services to meet the current and future needs of handicapped individuals for whom a vocational goal is not possible or feasible so that they may improve their ability to live with greater independence and self-sufficiency;

(4) assist in the construction and improvement of rehabilitation facilities;

(5) develop new and innovative methods of applying the most advanced medical technology, scientific achievement, and psychological and social knowledge to solve rehabilitation problems and develop new and innovative methods of providing rehabilitation services to handicapped individuals through research, special projects, and demonstrations;

(6) initiate and expand services to groups of handicapped individuals (including those who are homebound and institutionalized) who have been underserved in the past;

(7) direct the conduct of various studies and experiments to focus on long neglected problem areas;

(8) promote and expand employment opportunities in the public and private sectors for handicapped individuals and to place such individuals in employment;

(9) establish client assistance pilot projects;

(10) provide assistance for the purpose of increasing the number of rehabilitation personnel and increasing their skills through training; and

(11) evaluate existing approaches to architectural and transportation barriers confronting handicapped individuals, develop new such approaches, enforce statutory and regulatory standards and requirements regarding barrier-free construction of public facilities and study and develop solutions to existing housing and transportation barriers impeding handicapped individuals. (U.S., Congress, 1973)

Returning the disabled to gainful employment continues to be the primary intent of the Congress. The rehabilitation system still defines disability (which now includes long-term impairments as a consequence of cultural and social as well as mental and physical limitations) and potential for rehabilitation in limited vocational terms (Nagi, 1965).

One crack in the condition of economic function for entry into the rehabilitation system may result as an unintended consequence of a new provision in Public Law 93–112, section 102, "Individualized Written Rehabilitation Program," henceforth called the "contract." This is a negotiable contract between the rehabilitation agency and the client. Specifically,

each individualized written rehabilitation program shall be reviewed on an annual basis at which time each such individual (or, in appropriate cases, his parents or guardians) will be afforded an opportunity to review such program and jointly redevelop its terms. Such program shall include, but not be limited to (1) a statement of long-range rehabilitation goals for the individual and intermediate rehabilitation objectives related to the attainment of such goals, (2) a statement of the specific vocational rehabilitation services to be provided, (3) the projected date for the initiation and the anticipated duration of each such service, (4) objective criteria and an evaluation procedure and schedule for determining whether such objectives and goals are being achieved and, (5) where appropriate, a detailed explanation of the availability of a client assistance project established in such area pursuant to section 112.

This opportunity for input into the rehabilitation process may provide empirical bases for redefining current criteria of rehabilitation goals and a deemphasis on training largely for gainful employment. Potentially it can result in the kind of evaluation of and accountability for goals and procedures that both professionals and clients have long sought, ones which are honest, realistic, and within the realm of possibility. The Congress and the White House may, from such contract reviews and assessments, find fault with the revealed inadequacies of the system,[4] but more important will be the discovery of the illogicality of current ideological stances undergirding existing rehabilitation goals and the rationale for supporting a three-quarter billion-dollar government program in rehabilitation.

Emphasis on Evaluation—Cost/Benefit Model

The Rehabilitation Act of 1972 under title V proposes statutory bases for systematic evaluation of all projects and programs. Section 501 (a) (1) states:

The Secretary shall measure and evaluate the impact of all programs authorized in this Act, in order to determine their effectiveness in achieving stated goals in general, and in relation to their cost, their impact on related programs, and their structure and mechanisms for delivery of services, including, where appropriate, comparisons with appropriate control groups composed of persons who have not participated in such programs. Evaluations shall be conducted by persons not immediately involved in the administration of the program or project evaluated. (U.S., Congress, 1973)

Non-economic-based cost/effectiveness models of rehabilitation investments and outcomes may become more appropriate because of the ideological turn of big business spokesmen and new supports found in current legislation. However, it will not be easy. The unfortunate circumstance is that for years rehabilitation advocates had to employ economic arguments in order to obtain funds for their programs. The rhetoric of humanitarian concerns has elicited emotional responses but little cash from those working on Capitol Hill. Rehabilitation advocates have spent decades telling different publics what they wanted to hear and providing yardsticks of economic viability while believing that vocational placement should not be the only or even the most important measure of a rehabilitation outcome. This has precipitated the present dilemma. Can cost/effectiveness variables be other than economic ones? Socially desired goals and those concerned with the individual's well-being, comfort, and satisfaction have too long been the hidden agenda items of rehabilitation practitioners; to bring them from the inner to the outer room would be contrary to proper form.

The current strong push to establish the economic cost/effectiveness of rehabilitation investments is the result of conditions and situations both within and outside the system. High costs and doubtful quality of rehabilitation treatment and care, self-indictments, and exposes of professional incompetence and overprofessionalization of occupational roles within the system (Stroud and Sussman, 1973; Moore, 1971; Haug and Sussman, 1972; Sussman, 1965; Kellert, 1971) have provided the rationale and impetus to this thrust. The role of professionals in a number of helping fields in organizing the underclassed for community and political action is questionable and inappropriate in the view of those responsible for governing. For this reason evaluation has been extended to the sources of professional manpower itself.

In a recent longitudinal study of patients admitted to a rehabilitation hospital and followed after discharge for a period of five years, it was ascertained that approximately 50 percent of the patients "certified" as ready for admission to the rehabilitation facility by their physicians or those at the referral hospital had medical complications upon arrival. Major or minor surgery was required for 31 percent of the patients soon after their admission to a rehabilitation facility. This says something about the quality of general hospital care (Stroud and Sussman, 1973). A few other findings from the same study raise such serious questions as: How efficient and concerned are those in charge of health facilities? Do third-party payers "get their dollar's worth"? According to staff estimates, patients in all disability categories who completed a rehabilitation regimen were in both the general and the rehabilitation hospitals two to three times longer than could be considered necessary. For patients with disabilities estimated to require 6 weeks of hospitalization, the average stay was 15.6 weeks, with cost 172 percent greater than expected; 12 weeks of estimated hospital stay averaged out at 22.7 weeks and 59 percent higher cost; 26 weeks became 41 weeks, with 75 percent higher cost. Patients stayed in the hospital, on an average, 40 percent longer than predicted. Also, half of these patients made no significant improvement in their activities of daily living or mobility.

For the population covered by the study during the 1960–61 period, the average cost per patient hospitalization was approximately $4,000 for a stay just under twenty weeks at a daily bed rate of $33. Ten years later (1970–71) this daily rate had increased threefold; for a similar group then the average cost per hospitalization was $12,000.

Approximately one-third of the patients improved their activities of daily living and mobility after being discharged from the hospital.[5]

It can be expected that cost/effectiveness economic models will be ruthlessly applied to rehabilitation projects and programs in the remaining years of this decade. They will be used as a political strategy by those in government office and adversaries of the existing rehabilitation system to weaken, diffuse, and reduce the controlling power of professionals. The consequences for disabled clients are a major concern. One possibility for modifying a straight economic assessment of rehabilitation investments is for clients to have a greater input into the evaluation equation.

Within-System Innovative Care and Treatment

There is an increasing incidence of innovative research and demonstrations concerned with improving the care and treatment of the disabled. The recommended modifications range from tinkering with the system to major changes in it. Several issues obscure the meaning and significance of these undertakings and impede their implementation within current patterns of care and treatment. Most studies are undertaken by politically powerless academicians who are largely "people-oriented"; for them economic costs are low priority considerations. Milieu therapy is an exciting venture (Kutner et al., 1970; Hyde et al., 1962) and encompasses a parity socialization model, but few persons are interested because of high psychic and economic costs. Other experiments, such as using volunteers in treatment (Michener and Walzer, 1970), homebound work programs

(Towne, 1972), and group interaction, such as role playing (Green, 1970), are illustrations of what can be done, for a short time anyway.

What is most discomforting is that these often one-shot demonstrations are initiated without awareness or consideration of the legislation which controls policy and programs and which may prevent implementation of findings in the system; the constraints on innovative change characteristic of the bureaucratization of the work system and the territoriality of professionals and other occupational workers; and the heavy energy input needed to "make the demonstration work," a level of performance one usually cannot sustain or expect others to adopt without reorganization of their work roles and arrangements for suitable payoffs.

Because rehabilitation agencies have adopted so few innovative research findings or results from demonstrations, various government agencies have created dissemination and utilization units in order to link the research frontier with day-to-day practice. H.R. 1479, in fact, has a special provision which creates a Center for Technology Assessment and Application within its Division of Research, Training and Evaluation. This center "shall be responsible for developing and supporting, and stimulating the development and utilization (including production and distribution of new and existing devices) of, innovative methods of applying advanced medical technology, scientific achievement, psychological and social knowledge to solve rehabilitation problems" (U.S., Congress, 1973). Hardware utilization is stressed, with some consideration to the sociobehavioral dimensions of rehabilitation.

The prognosis regarding effectiveness of this potential venture is guarded because there does not appear to be any dramatic legislative change which can "open" the practice of rehabilitation on the local level. Program administrators are beginning to suffer from information glut and often cannot adopt a desired practice because of legislative constraints and administrative fiats.

Innovative practices can be adopted most easily if few encroachments are made on the areas of defined work responsibility, if the work load is not increased, and if the new practices are substituted for the old and some rewards are provided. Few demonstrations take these factors into account. The assumption of most researchers is that professionals and supportive staff will eagerly digest and utilize well-founded results. The reasons why this is not the case are too numerous to elaborate; only a few have been stated. Even these explanations may be too reasoned and rational, for example, that providing payoffs or incentives to potential users of innovations will promote change. Those who view work organizations as chancy arrangements of occupational holders in perpetual state of conflict, with power and control as dominant objectives, will view introduced incentives somewhat skeptically. Although we can accommodate but not prove all these hypotheses, it is apparent that eclectic and often brilliant research and demonstrations are undertaken with little forethought to the practicality and enigmas of political processes, legislative and policy constraints, and organizational power politics which pervade all large-scale service systems.

The problem is more than a communication gap between innovative researcher or demonstrator and practitioner; professional and client; socialization agent and novice. The rehabilitation system has the capacity to absorb the new learnings of research or clinical practice. However, even though information may be conveyed to participants at professional meetings such as those of the National Rehabilitation Association, this does not necessarily mean that it will be used. The heterogeneity and organizational complexity of the rehabilitation system preclude any large-scale adoption of new technologies, methods of treatment, or patient care ideologies on a voluntary basis. The communication hiatus will widen as the knowledge birthquake continues.

Client Assertiveness

The reverberations of the client rebellion in the 1960s are still being felt, and the resistance against authority and the presumptiveness of expertise continues (Haug and Sussman, 1969). This

revolt and women's lib are probably the two major social movements of the twentieth century. Assertiveness takes the form of
objecting to a care or treatment relationship (sometimes referred
to as a socialization model) which requires the disabled person to
accept the imposition of values and attitudes, assume the role of
status inferior to the professional, accept "meddling" and various
forms of behavior modification, have a minimum say in
decision-making concerning his own treatment, and make few or
no efforts to control the professional (Kendrick and Sudderth,
1970; Gersuny and Lefton, 1970).

Systemic properties of rehabilitation systems and social
psychological processes have sustained the traditional
superordinate-subordinate model of professional-client relationships. Organizational bureaucracies by their very structure have
reduced the range and possibilities of random participation and
action to a minimum. In the instance of human service systems,
socialization, education, and prescription of a therapeutic regimen have always been unidirectional. Decision-making and control rest with those who manage. These are built-in properties of
rehabilitation systems.

Related to the organizational power and status of the professional is his ability to label and stereotype his clients with different
disabilities on the bases of the clients' incompetence and to use the
label effectively in controlled treatment. Patients find it difficult
to fight the label both within and outside the system (Freidson,
1965; Sudnow, 1967; Scheff, 1965; Goffman, 1963). Which diagnostic category (label) the patient receives depends upon the
practitioner's knowledge and expertise, the patient's behavior,
the practitioner's medical research interests, and colleagues'
opinions. All diagnoses are relative with some based on scientific
and others on nonscientific criteria. Given the idiosyncratic bases
of labeling, the paucity of scientific information on etiology and
treatment of certain illnesses and diseases, and the differential
knowledge and clinical experience of professionals in diagnosis
and treatment, the "fit" of the individual's illness or disease with
the diagnosis is often a fortuitous circumstance. This condition

has led an anonymous wit to comment that the prospective patient had better arrange to have the disease or illness which fits the diagnostic interests and capabilities of the professional at that particular time and location; if he does not have the proper fit, he will be given the "right" diagnosis anyway.

Questioning the superior wisdom of the professional practitioner did not occur in a vacuum. Low rates of rehabilitation success were one important reason. Another was the policies of the Johnson presidency in the 1960s. Major efforts to reallocate resources in the War on Poverty included self-help movements on the neighborhood level using political processes for desired social change (Piven, 1966; Dubey, 1970; Shostak, 1966). Community organization, citizen participation, neighborhood control, increased pride and self-respect, and responsibility for one's affairs were the new objectives and values in that era. Soon the poor in the ghettos mastered the techniques for accommodating and confronting as well as manipulating organizational bureaucracies far beyond the expectations of their teachers, the Clowards, Ohlins, and Clarks of this new movement. A new militarism arose among the poor, disenfranchised, and neglected. The genesis of the black movement may be traced to initial efforts to provide new options for jobs, education, and power. The health care system, a major service center for the minorities in the ghetto, became an early target for testing the limits of this new power. Challenging the control and expertise of the practitioner and obtaining services at convenient times and under reasonably pleasant and personalized conditions were the major features of a new professional-client socialization model.

On the societal level client assertiveness occurred through citizen participation, especially political activity within community, state and national institutional systems. The catalyst was the "Maximum Feasibility Participation of the Poor" provision of the 1964 Economic Opportunity Act. The War on Poverty required the involvement of targeted, underprivileged, and under-classed populations. Even though this program was phased out by the Nixon Administration, the "self-help" ideology and concomitant participatory structure to reduce depersonalization (endemic to bureaucratized human service systems) have pervaded all communities and life sectors. Such involvement in the planning and implementation of services by the client patient, tenent, recipient, and others with the "do to" label is inevitable and irreversible. As the National Citizens' Conference on Rehabilitation of the Disabled and Disadvantaged in 1969 reported, "A return to the pre-1960 days is not possible. All of our institutions—whether universities or hospitals—will have to cope with this new view of the organization of our services and decision making in our various structures" (Thursz, 1970:3).

A dramatic legislative breakthrough for client advocacy almost occurred with the 1973 Public Law on Rehabilitation. The Senate passed a client advocacy provision with ombudsman overtones, earmarking about 1 percent of all expenditures for rehabilitation, estimated at $800 million for citizen participation/advocacy/ombudsman activities. The House of Representatives was adamant in its opposition, for good political reasons, and the compromise was the client contract and a specified number of demonstration programs of citizen participation and client advocacy.

A parallel development of a holistic approach to disease causality, diagnosis, and treatment began in medical schools in the early 1950s and led to basic changes in the training of health professionals. Acceptance of multicausal theories led professionals to concentrate on social and behavioral factors. "Care of the whole patient" became the clarion call. It was a well-intentioned move, but large numbers of the poor began to view this as another form of meddling and control. The search for social factors (long interviews and many questionnaires) in cause and treatment of disease led obviously into probes of life in the ghetto. In trying to understand and to be helpful, many professionals became too wrapped up in and emotionally involved with the daily activities of their patients and their patients' families. "What in hell does that nice fat cat know what it is like to live in the slum?" is the feeling not too often expressed but universally found where there are marked class and status differences. The perceived undue meddling and invasion of privacy have led to the current situation of patients insisting on participation in decisions regarding their own care, treatment, and rehabilitation.

The client's participation in a relationship is not tantamount to a takeover. What clients want are relationships that fit a reciprocal socialization model so that exchanges are made, even though one receives more than one gives (Cogswell, 1968*a*). They want more personal relationships; to teach as well as to learn; to share their lifetime of experienced frustration and sorrow and skills for survival (Cogswell, 1967; Leviton, 1967). They want to know their professional caretakers as human beings, the latter's motives, family life, hopes, and aspirations.

Client assertiveness in this period is also being expressed through various forms of self-organization and representation. Boot camp training in self-socialization began on the wards (Cogswell, 1968*a*; Keith, 1968, 1972). Patient or family clubs, welfare mothers' groups, client members on a hospital board of directors, and hired client advocates and ombudsmen are examples of current organizational forms. These developments have been abetted by the student generation of professionals-to-be, the "young Turks" who are leading their faculties in bringing medicine, health care, and rehabilitation back into the community and the home. "Family medicine," for example, is no longer a low-status field but is receiving substantial government financial aid and American Medical Association and patient acceptance.

"While the physician is functioning in a 'jack-of-all-trades' role, he is being perceived by the patient as less of a meddler and more as a collaborator-expert. These new devotees of a reciprocal model of patient-professional relationship are still too few to signify a complete remodeling of current medical care and rehabilitation delivery systems. But the handwriting is on the wall; the traditional rehabilitation and health care system no longer has the ideological supports or even political muscle to maintain its established position" (Sussman, 1972).

Advocacy and ombudsmanship as processes and structures for

representation and change in favor of the client have been suggested by a number of observers (Hansen, 1970; Margolin, 1955; Briar, 1968; Brager, 1968). Militant group organization of the disabled, with emphasis on self-approbation and the objective of creating a new image of a person so that the disabled will be accepted and treated as equal to the nondisabled, is suggested by Safilios-Rothschild (1970). Initiation of advocacy by the professionals is another tactic. The Family Service Association of America's (FSAA) publication *Family Advocacy Omnibus* outlines the philosophy, purpose, and means of advocacy in behalf of clients in the social welfare field (Blackburn, 1971). The essential message is that there is little likelihood that there will be a reversal of the current trend toward parity relationships between practitioner and client because of the insistence of so many.

Frances Brisbane, first director of advocacy of FSAA, made some poignant observations: "We must begin now to examine —not wallow in recriminations—the part we (social workers) played in creating the problems of families in economic, educational, social and political jeopardy. . . . Advocacy to change in two basic institutions—ourselves and our own agencies—is the foundation on which all other advocacy activity must be built."

New Conceptualizations: Built-in Environment

The built-in environment proposes new uses of social and physical space and a complete reorganization of human service systems so that professionals and their subalterns function as experts and consultants providing general care and treatment in the home environments of patients and their families (Sussman, 1971, 1972). The utility of this approach becomes more evident if one accepts that the family network in modern complex societies is viable as a potential therapeutic milieu and that extended kin can take care of disabled family members at costs lower than those of institutions if appropriate "incentives" and life support systems are provided (Sussman, 1973); that for political, economic, and other reasons further society-wide growth of bureaucratized and centralized health care systems will occur at a snail's pace during the remaining years of this decade; that pluralism in family forms and life styles is a reality now and that service systems must adapt their practices to single-parent, dual work, three-generation, communal, extended affiliative, and other family forms (Sussman et al., 1970; Cogswell and Sussman, 1972; Sussman and Cogswell, 1972; Sussman, 1971; Clavan and Vatter, 1972).

With these conditions, in addition to the "revolt of the client" phenomenon, continued acceptance of the notion that meaningful work for the rehabilitee is a desired goal of rehabilitation and the use of an economic evaluation model for rehabilitation investments provide both the rationales and the "critical mass" for completely reorganizing the care of the disabled.

In a recent paper I suggested the applicability of the built-in environment concept to the rehabilitation system (Sussman, 1972).

Rehabilitation services and all those that come under the rubric of human service systems should be built into the patient's environment. Families and other types of primary groups such as nursing homes and homes for the aged, relatively small units which have ultimate responsibility for the long-term care of the disabled, should be served by the health care and other service systems in their own environments.

Beyond supplying continued care, treatments, functions, and rehabilitation services, there is the further requirement of providing the family with physical space that is free of architectural barriers and that enables a number of options regarding privacy and active participation in group and community life.

In developing model towns or housing estates we would include various kinds of physical structures to match the ambulatory characteristics of family members, especially the disabled, and in consonance with the needs, desires, and aspirations of family members at different stages of the life cycle. Our environment would be for both the disabled and able-bodied and would include apartment-type units, one-family homes, dormitory or efficiency apartments for individuals or small-sized families, larger units for commune-type families, and so forth.

Optimal use of physical and social space for members of various types of family structures, at different stages of the life cycle, and with different health care and social needs, is the major objective of the built-in environment.

The major theme of the built-in environment is to provide a large number of options for variant family forms which have essentially different types of problems to solve whether or not a disabled person resides in the family. Therefore, in providing options for leisure, recreation, eating, health services, marketing, day care, and nursing care, we would then be providing for the family, especially the disabled member, an optimum environment, one that is most conducive for effective functioning with all the prospects of reducing morbidity and increasing personal satisfaction. We have in the 1970's the scientific technology and intellectual know-how to do this at no extra cost if one accounts for the massive expenditures now allocated to segmented human services. The task is to reallocate resources, reformulate current approaches that emphasize bureaucracy and mass-packaged programs, and reorganize and in some instances terminate current programs.

In this approach central medical facilities for the disabled that are now in existence would be used largely for research, consultation, and handling of extremely difficult medical and rehabilitation cases. Posthospitalization care and treatment would occur within the built-in environment. In one sense the professionals and supportive health care personnel would be coming to the patient and thereby reduce the social distance between the patient and the expert professional. By coming to the patient's home environment, and in this sense to "where the action is," the professional becomes more of an expert with autonomy to practice within the limits of his expertise and less of a controlling agent. This effects a reciprocal model of treatment, one that is a harbinger of rehabilitation practice in the 1970's and 80's.

Conclusion

The possibilities of the built-in environment as a pattern for treatment and care of the disabled in the future are enhanced by current political, economic, and social conditions that favor decentralization of power and reallocation of resources through revenue sharing, reallocation and redeployment of institutional resources, changing patterns of medical training and paraprofessional education, and social movements which provide respectability for and to some extent institutionalization of clients' rights and egalitarian relationships. It is difficult to envision an immediate society-wide transformation in ideology or action along the lines of building care and rehabilitation systems around the disabled. However, some "experiments" in new care systems may catalyze adoption of practices which are essential components of a built-in environment.

One proposed experiment would investigate the potential role of the kin family network in the care and rehabilitation of its disabled members. This is a critical issue since current support for extensive development of health care systems is problematical, in view of the current national administration's posture on expenditures for such services. Also problematical is the absorptive capacity of society if there is a continuous imbalance and conflict over the need and demand for services and the capability of the society to support them. With the further expectation that there will be insufficient manpower to meet the increasing demands for quality health care and rehabilitation, the proposed study would investigate the circumstances and conditions in which members of a family network (not necessarily members of the immediate family) would care for the disabled and also would determine how receptive those needing long-term care are to receiving it from their families.

The research would concentrate on those incentives, that is, payoffs, which would make possible a family rehabilitation milieu without diminishing the resources of the caretaking unit and which would enable the disabled person to maintain and increase his self-esteem and sustain other rehabilitation gains. This study would focus on economic and service supports and randomized feelings of filial responsibility held by the kin family member for the disabled relative. Incentives that could be used include cash payment, low-cost loan or subsidy to remodel or expand current living space in order to accommodate the disabled member; use of disabled persons' resources; rent subsidy; tax write-off or deduction; and special social and medical services such as patient-, baby- or house-sitting, transportation and shopping assistance, home medical and nursing care, vestibule training in care of the patient, and similar supports (Sussman, 1973).

Family caretaking of its disabled members is not suggested as a replacement for existing institutionalized care systems, at least

not immediately. It would be complementary to formally organized systems and could be successful only if it could develop
appropriate linkages with professionals and obtain their support,
instruction, and interest in family-oriented rehabilitation. The
objective would be to provide an environment for family members and the disabled relative which is denuded of stresses because of the economic and service burden of caring for a disabled
person, maximizes the use of available options and through
pooled resources may increase the available number, and permits
disabled and nondisabled persons to be in a parity socialization
relationship with complementary roles providing reciprocal rewards.

Research along this line, beginning with a primary socialization
group, that is, a family network, may move the rehabilitation
system back to the household, street, neighborhood, and community. If it works and stands the test of cost/benefit analysis, and
it should, then we would have an optional rehabilitative caretaking system that might be more in consonance with the wishes of
the disabled and members of their family networks.

NOTES

1. One megabuck equals one million dollars.

2. The 1972 Act, H.R. 1479 (U.S., Congress, 1973), was vetoed by President
Nixon. Public Law 93-112, 1973, is virtually the same as H.R. 1479, omitting a
number of provisions deemed "fiscally irresponsible" by the president in his veto
message. In this presentation both are discussed.

3. Italics are the author's.

4. Evaluations of any kind flush insufficiencies in structure and practice of
bureaucracies into the open. Such deficiencies are endemic to large-scale organizations and are easily detected or deduced by evaluators.

5. It is recognized that this is a single case and associating these findings with all
hospitals is a disservice to the rehabilitation field and the credulity of the reader.

BIBLIOGRAPHY

Blackburn, C., ed.
1971. *Family Advocacy Omnibus.* New York: Family Service Association of America.
Brager, G. A.
1968. Advocacy and political behavior. *Social Work,* 3:5–15.
Briar, S.
1968. The casework predicament. *Social Work,* 13:5–11.
Clavan, S., and Vatter, E.
1972. The affiliated family: A device for integrating old and young. *Family Coordinator,* 4:499–504.
Cogswell, B. E.
1967. Rehabilitation of the paraplegic: Processes of socialization. *Sociological Inquiry,* 37:11–26.
1968a. Self-socialization: Readjustment of paraplegics in the community. *Journal of Rehabilitation,* 34:3.
1968b. Socialization into the family: An essay on some structural properties of roles. In *Sourcebook in Marriage and the Family,* edited by M. B. Sussman, pp. 366–377. Boston: Houghton Mifflin.
Cogswell, B. E., and Sussman, M. B.
1972. Changing family and marriage forms: Complications for human service systems. *Family Coordinator,* 4:505–516.
Dinitz, S., and Beron, N.
1971. Community mental health as a boundaryless and boundary-busting system. *Journal of Health and Social Behavior,* 12:99–108.
Dubey, S. N.
1970. Community action programs and citizen participation: Issues and confusions. *Social Work,* 15:76–84.
Fitzgerald, E.
1973. The Pentagon as the enemy of capitalism. *World,* 2:18–21.
Freidson, E.
1965. Disability as social deviance. In *Sociology and Rehabilitation,* edited by M. B. Sussman, pp. 71–99. Washington, D.C: American Sociological Association.
Gersuny, C., and Lefton, M.
1970. Service and servitude in the sheltered workshop. *Social Work,* 15:74–81.
Goffman, E.
1963. *Stigma: Notes on the Management of Spoiled Identity.* Englewood Cliffs, N.J.: Prentice-Hall.

Green, P. S.
  1970.   Group work with welfare recipients. *Social Work,* 15:121.
Hansen, C. E.
  1970.   Rehabilitation and the ombudsman. *Journal of Rehabilitation,* 36:25–26.
Haug, M. R., and Sussman, M. B.
  1969.   Professional autonomy and the revolt of the client. *Social Problems,* 17:153–61.
  1972.   Agents of social control: Issues in rehabilitation manpower. Paper presented at the American Sociological Association meetings, New Orleans, August.
Hyde, R. W.; Bochover, J. S.; Pfautz, H. W.; and York, R. H.
  1962.   *Milieu Rehabilitation.* Providence: Butler Health Center.
Keith, R. A.
  1968.   The need for a new model in rehabilitation. *Journal of Chronic Disease,* 21:281–286.
  1972.   The effect of social control on rehabilitation treatment. Paper presented at the American Sociological Association meetings, New Orleans, August.
Kellert, S. R.
  1971.   The lost community in community psychiatry. *Psychiatry* 34:168–179.
Kendrick, J., and Sudderth, J.
  1970.   Rehabilitation in the schools. *Rehabilitation Record,* 11:10–15.
Kutner, R.; Rosenberg, P.; Berger, R.; and Abrahamson, A. A.
  1970.   *A Therapeutic Community in Rehabilitation Medicine.* New York: Albert Einstein College of Medicine of Yeshiva University.
Leviton, G. L.
  1967.   Professional and client choices in critical situations. Paper presented at the symposium on professional client relationships, American Psychological Association, Washington, D. C., September.
Margolin, R. J.
  1955.   Member-employee program: New hope for the mentally ill. *American Archives of Rehabilitation Therapy,* 3:69–81.
Michener, C., and Walzer, H.
  1970.   Developing community mental health volunteer systems. *Social Work,* 15:60–67.
Moore, W. E.
  1971.   *The Professions: Roles and Rules.* New York: Russell Sage Foundation.
Nagi, S.
  1965.   Some conceptual issues in disability and rehabilitation. In *Sociology and Rehabilitation,* edited by M. B. Sussman, pp. 100–113. Washington, D.C.: American Sociological Association.

Organization for Science and Technical Innovation
  1970. *Blindness and Services to the Blind in the United States.* Boston: OSTI
      Press.
Piven, F.
  1966. Participation of residents in neighborhood community action pro-
      grams. *Social Work*, 11:95–101.
Safilios-Rothschild, C.
  1970. *The Sociology and Social Psychology of Disability and Rehabilitation.* New
      York: Random House.
Scheff, T.
  1965. Typification in the diagnostic practices of rehabilitation. In *Sociology
      and Rehabilitation*, edited by M. B. Sussman, pp. 139–147. Washing-
      ton, D.C.: American Sociological Association.
Shostak, A. B.
  1966. Promoting participation of the poor: Philadelphia's antipoverty
      program. *Social Work*, 11:73–80.
Straus, R.
  1965. Social change and the rehabilitation concept. In *Sociology and
      Rehabilitation*, edited by M. B. Sussman, pp. 1–34. Washington, D.C.:
      American Sociological Association.
Stroud, M. W., III, and Sussman, M.B.
  1973. The patient's rehabilitation center: A longitudinal study. Mimeo-
      graphed.
Sudnow, D.
  1967. *Passing On: The Social Organization of Dying.* Englewood Cliffs, N.J.:
      Prentice-Hall.
Sussman, M. B.
  1965. Occupational sociology and rehabilitation. In *Sociology and
      Rehabilitation*, edited by M. B. Sussman, pp. 179–222. Washington,
      D.C.: American Sociological Association.
  1971. The family. In *Encyclopedia of Social Work*, pp. 329–340. New York:
      National Association of Social Workers.
  1972. A policy perspective on the United States rehabilitation system. *Jour-
      nal of Health and Social Behavior*, 12:152–196.
  1973. Family networks and care of the aged. Research project
      AOA90-A-316 under way (1974–76) in the Institute on the Family
      and the Bureaucratic Society at Case Western Reserve University,
      Cleveland, Ohio 44106.
Sussman, M. B., and Cogswell, B. E.
  1972. The meaning of variant and experimental marriage styles and family
      forms in the 1970's. *Family Coordinator*, 21:375–381.
Sussman, M. B., and Haug, M. R.
  1967. *Career Lines of Rehabilitation Professionals.* Cleveland: Institute on the

Family and the Bureaucratic Society at Case Western Reserve University.

Sussman, M. B., et al.
    1970.   Changing families in a changing society. *Report to the President, White House Conference on Children 1970*. Washington, D.C.: Government Printing Office, 227–238.

Thursz, D.
    1970.   *Consumer Involvement in Rehabilitation*. Washington, D.C.: Government Printing Office.

Towne, A.
    1972.   Homecraft, source of homebound employment. *Rehabilitation Record* 13:1–15.

U.S., Congress, House
    1973.   Rehabilitation Act of 1972, H.R. 1479. 93rd Congress, 1st sess., January 9.

CHAPTER 10

Some Notes on Rehabilitation and Models for Interdisciplinary Collaboration

Rodney M. Coe

One of the fastest developing areas of medicine nowadays is rehabilitation. In part this is the result of new knowledge and new technology in fields such as pharmaceuticals, orthotics, and psychological management and of the increasing pressure of rising numbers of patients, young and old, in need of and demanding rehabilitative services. These developments are, in turn, supported by an altered value system which promotes the goal of achieving the fullest possible physical, psychological, and social capacities of individuals. Successful evolution of new knowledge and technology in rehabilitation, however, requires the application of a variety of special skills and coordination of efforts of different people. The processes involved in meeting this requirement are of considerable sociological interest because they involve communication and integration of efforts among medical practitioners (doctors and nurses), allied health professionals, behavioral scientists, agency administrators, and third-party payers.

Rehabilitation, then, is a prototype of activity requiring interdisciplinary collaboration at almost every level and for many specific tasks. This is not to say that rehabilitation specialists always contribute equally to every situation. It is more often the case that one or another discipline will be dominant but will require the support of others. An obvious example is the joint effort of a physiatrist, a nurse, and a physical therapist working to restore use to a patient's broken limb. Each has a specific skill to bring to the problem, but no one of them alone would be sufficient.

Less obvious, but nonetheless part of the whole rehabilitation picture, is the prediction of legislative outcomes in the rehabilitation field, which is primarily the concern of political scientists but has an important message for program planners and practitioners. New emphasis on cost benefit analyses is primarily of interest to economists, but it involves setting standards and values, not to mention establishing social and technical criteria for evaluations. These examples suggest very strongly that rehabilitation is a field in which professional and occupational contacts and relationships are extremely important and in which, by necessity if not always by design, those contacts require a collaborative effort if the common objective of rehabilitation is to be achieved.

The Need for Interdisciplinary Collaboration

A number of writers have analyzed the need for and the nature of interdisciplinary and interprofessional contacts for various occupational tasks (Freidson, 1970; Vollmer and Mills, 1966; Lynn and the editors of *Daedelus,* 1965). In these studies various types of occupational relationships are delineated. At one extreme is conflict or competition for clients among professionals whose skills and knowledge overlap. (Some analysts include avoidance—a nonrelationship—at this extreme.) At the other extreme is collaboration, generally thought of as two or more professionals of more-or-less equal status and skills working together toward a common goal. In between is cooperation, which occurs when two or more representatives of different occupations work together, most often when there are clear and recognizable differences in status, level of skills, or some other hierarchical characteristic. Thus defined, interdisciplinary collaborative efforts imply a shared understanding of the common as well as separate objectives of the activities and of the values which lay behind the selection of objectives. It implies also that participating members have some knowledge of and appreciation for the methodologies of their collaborators as well as relatively equal, if interdependent, status.

Interdisciplinary collaboration is easier to define than to make operational, however. Even a casual review of research in the literature reveals examples of the barriers to collaboration that were long ago identified by Cottrell and Sheldon (1963). Their three major classes of inhibitory factors were cultural differences, which include language, definition, and perspectives; social structural and status differences; and role ambiguity and incongruent expectations. Much of the reported literature shows obvious differences in theoretical perspective between 'behaviorists and societal analysts and in choice of unit of analysis: the individual versus various social groupings. Even where there was agreement on focus on the individual, there were differences in emphasis on the importance of motivation, from great emphasis by social psychologists to very little emphasis by adherents of behavior modification techniques.

Differences in approaches to rehabilitation because of status and position in the social structure, as well as because of commitments to disciplinary views, not only produce frequent differences in outcomes but also engender continuing discussions and arguments between theorists and practitioners, between practitioners and third party payers, and between physicians and allied health personnel. Differences in power (such as between industry and government and injured people) also strongly influence the whole rehabilitation process.

Role ambiguity in the rehabilitation process is interestingly noted in terms not only of the professionals but also of the consumers. The need for and encouragement of participation of the patient and his family, the consumers, in the rehabilitation process has long been acknowledged. Yet, until recently, the professional-client relationship has functioned pretty much along the model of the doctor-patient relationship in acute, episodic care. There has always been some ambiguity in the patient's role in this process, just as lip service to "teamwork" among rehabilitative professionals has served to blur the rights and obligations of participating team members relative to the physician's role. Clearly, an interdisciplinary approach to rehabilitation would applaud the fact of increased consumer or patient participation in decision-making and cite the need for even more of it.

Trends Inhibiting Interdisciplinary Collaboration

It may be useful to identify, in addition to the broad categories of barriers to communication already noted, some specific trends more closely related to the rehabilitation process. One of the most important of these trends has been the professionalization of health care occupations. Each of the occupational groups has sought to take on the characteristics of medicine as the model for a profession by claiming certain skills or content areas as their own, developing organizations for the protection of both client and professional, and establishing and maintaining standards of performance to ensure quality. Along with this have come entry requirements, examination and licensing, development of a special language, and other restrictions. Some defensive stances and unidisciplinary perspectives which were necessary for survival in the early years of development of professional organizations tend to be continued in mature professions, thus limiting the potential for collaboration (Coe, 1970a).

One of the positive outcomes of professionalization is the rapid expansion of knowledge and the development of special skills. Specialization of function and task tends to inhibit interdisciplinary collaboration. A specialist is sometimes defined as "someone who knows more and more about less and less until he knows everything about nothing." On the contrary, specialization has made possible fantastic achievements in medical care, including rehabilitation, but at the expense of coordination and comprehensiveness of application of health care services in general, and in rehabilitation services in particular. As specialized knowledge becomes more esoteric and skills require more time to develop, communication between disciplines and, indeed, understanding of what other disciplines can do become less clear and more difficult to coordinate.

A third contributing factor, the model of professional education and training, also helps to perpetuate disciplinary specialization. Most graduate programs in health-related sciences and most professional training schools are organized along disciplinary lines, and most education is conducted along those lines. To be sure, some lip service is paid to interdisciplinary efforts, but these efforts are rarely successful or long-lived. The attractiveness of becoming "expert" and the power of highly developed technical skills foster the continuation of unidisciplinary training, which results in the kinds of problems that have been noted, that is, different theoretical perspectives, confusion in terminology, different methodological emphases, varying orientations to theory and practice, and so on.

Trends Promoting Interdisciplinary Collaboration

There are some trends toward interdisciplinary collaboration, however, and the rehabilitation process is a prime illustration. There are several factors which, taken alone, are not particularly remarkable but which, taken together, are bringing about interdisciplinary collaboration. First is that many of the health problems being presented to specialists now are the product of several causal factors, some of them of lifelong duration. Practitioners in general and rehabilitation specialists in particular are more and more often confronted with health problems that do not yield dramatically and quickly to a specific therapeutic intervention but rather require coordinated application of several modalities over a long period of time (Glazier, 1973; Coe, 1970*b*). The very nature of a multicausal chronic problem requires multiple solutions or, more directly, requires the attention of a variety of specialists: medical scientists, administrators, behavioral scientists, and engineers. Thus, analogous to Durkheim's thesis (1947), the high degree of differentiation in function leads specialists to interdependence and cooperation (if not collaboration) in working toward a common goal. Second, and related to this, is the increased sophistication of all professional groups, which means that each has more to offer the others in terms of working toward an objective. Third is the increased demand by consumers for a part in the decision-making process. Part of this demand stems from the general social movement of consumerism, but in health care it stems also from dissatisfaction with the availability and quality of services and from an increasing awareness that patients can and should be involved in the therapeutic process, whether it is for acute diseases or is part of a long-term rehabilitation process.

These factors, among others, contribute to the increase in interdisciplinary cooperation, but not necessarily collaboration, among "equals" which represents a temporary solution for providing for immediate needs. It is unrealistic to expect professionals who are products of contemporary training programs to know intuitively how to work collaboratively with other professionals. Rather, it would seem that they must train *together,* at least in part, in order for there to be shared understanding of capabilities and interests. Training together would seem to be a means for implementing activities to promote collaborative practice, including

(1) developing optimal initial orientation and level of expectation; (2) maximizing mutual assimilation of professional subcultural values, ideologies, technologies and language; (3) securing an appropriate structural position in the institutional setting . . . (4) clarification of the roles of the parties to the undertakings; (5) increasing the interpersonal skills of the participants. (Cottrell and Sheldon, 1963:126)

It is of some importance to note that, more than ten years after Cottrell and Sheldon identified some key problems and suggested ways of solving them, we are still identifying the problems and seeking solutions. To be sure there are a variety of institutes or centers where members of several disciplines, especially social sciences, come together for teaching and training. There also are some attempts at joint degree programs in professional schools such as architecture and social work or medicine and law (Norton,

1971), but these are few in number. What is badly needed are more fully developed models for interdisciplinary training on a broader basis, more students and more participating disciplines.

Developing Models for Interdisciplinary Training

Although the need for interdisciplinary training is perhaps most obvious in fields like rehabilitation, one could support the argument that a broader approach is needed for medicine in general. In this context, several models for interdisciplinary training are described. All are presently in various stages of development, and none of them has been in operation long enough for its effectiveness to be evaluated. The models are examples of ways that interdisciplinary collaboration can be facilitated at the professional level.

The Department of Community Medicine at Saint Louis University School of Medicine has developed a year-long program which is mandatory for first-year medical students but is open to graduate students in nursing and allied health professions, social work, behavioral sciences, law, and religion. About one-fourth of the course is devoted to lectures and panel presentations on basic issues in medicine and the delivery of health care services. Another fourth is spent in preceptorships with a variety of medical practitioners, mostly physicians but also osteopathic physicians, nurses, and employees of home health agencies in the community. Half the course, however, is devoted to the development, conduct, and reporting of a field-work project in neighborhoods in the urban center and suburban fringes of Saint Louis. There are eight such neighborhood training areas, each with a volunteer interdisciplinary faculty panel of a physician, a nurse, a social worker, a social scientist. and one or two residents of the neighborhood. A staff member of the Department of Community Medicine coordinates the panel's work of advising and assisting students. Beginning students in several disciplines do all parts of the course together, lectures, preceptorships and home visits, and, most importantly, work together in small groups over a long period of time on projects of mutual interest. Awareness of interdisciplinary perspectives is further reinforced by contact with the faculty panel.

A second developing model involves an "institute" which has some interdisciplinary seminars but depends on the curricular offerings of participating departments. In addition, the subject matter in this case is gerontology, which, like rehabilitation, is well suited for an interdisciplinary approach. At Saint Louis University, the Institute of Applied Gerontology involves the professional schools of social service, nursing, medicine, and health care administration, as well as the departments of psychology, sociology, and economics and the Center for Urban Programs, itself an interdisciplinary institute. Thus, students from several disciplines study together in selected seminars and, as individuals, receive instruction in multiple disciplines. Field work experiences are designed to provide opportunities for integration of interdisciplinary and multidisciplinary classroom learning.

A third approach includes combining present students in several disciplines with practitioners in the same several disciplines in a kind of advanced graduate-post-graduate continuing education course. There are several objectives in this model, including helping practitioners to keep up with new developments and teaching graduate students the realities of practice. An example of this model is the Mount St. Rose Rehabilitation Seminar held each year in Saint Louis. This seminar is a two- to three-day intensive conference involving didactic and clinical experiences for physicians, nurses, behavioral scientists, allied health personnel, administrators, and researchers. Students and practitioners in these professions learn about and discuss the medical care and social, psychological, economic, and engineering aspects of rehabilitation. Other topics include the relationships of the physical and social environments to rehabilitation and the role of rehabilitation in a comprehensive health care system. The faculty for these sessions is made up of some widely known experts in the several fields.

These models vary along almost every dimension—scope, intensity, duration, target population, mode of presentation, and so forth. However, they all share the same general objective of facilitating interdisciplinary collaboration. They also have some similar drawbacks. One of these is the lack of follow-ups of outcomes. In part such follow-ups are not feasible because none of the programs has yet been in operation long enough. Even so, there is some question about the utility of such follow-ups. There is at present no continuity in the programs. For example, once first-year medical students finish their required course, there is no program for continuing contact with students in other professions except for isolated electives for fourth-year medical students. There have been no concomitant changes in various institutional settings such as acute care general hospitals to provide for subcultural support, as in value and reward systems, for interdisciplinary collaboration.

There are difficult and high-priority problems to resolve before interdisciplinary collaboration can become widespread. Nonetheless, something of a start has been made by the models described and other similar programs. The essential features of the models include beginning with a base of common knowledge and experience and then branching off into special skill training along disciplinary lines. Part of the common base is interpersonal skills, but much more could be done in terms of combined instruction in basic sciences and in clinical training. The clarification of the student's own role and, thereby, the development of some understanding of the capabilities and the roles of others involved in health care delivery is important to this approach. The student needs to learn (not necessarily to adopt) the values and ideological tenets of other disciplines as well as to know their capabilities. Finally, training together students in various disciplines has an objective of reducing artificial barriers to communication and collaboration that are engendered and maintained by differences in status, professional rivalries, and leadership by prerogative of hierarchical rank. Professional equals, who supply the various essential skills, need to collaborate to reach a mutual goal of good patient care.

BIBLIOGRAPHY

Coe, R. M.
    1970*a*. Processes in the development of established professions. *Journal of Health and Human Behavior,* 11:59–67.
    1970*b*. *Sociology of Medicine.* New York: McGraw-Hill.
Cottrell, L., and Sheldon, E.
    1963. Problems of collaboration between social scientists and the practicing professions. *Annals of the American Academy of Political and Social Sciences,* 346:126–137.
Durkheim, E.
    1947. *The Division of Labor in Society.* Glencoe, Ill.: Free Press.
Freidson, E.
    1970. *Professional Dominance.* New York: Atherton Press.
Glazier, W. H.
    1973. The task of medicine. *Scientific American,* 228:13–17.
Lynn, K. D., and the editors of *Daedelus*
    1965. *The Professions in America.* Boston: Houghton Mifflin
Norton, M. L.
    1971. Development of an interdisciplinary program of instruction in medicine and law. *Journal of Medical Education,* 46:405–411.
Vollmer, H., and Mills, D., eds.
    1966. *Professionalization.* Englewood Cliffs, N.J.: Prentice-Hall.

CHAPTER 11

Social Policy and the Management of Human Resources

Gary L. Albrecht

The formulation and implementation of national policies and the allocation of resources are not major public issues when there is an abundance of raw materials, labor, and opportunity. However, shortages of food, housing, and jobs and the perceived inequitable allocation of resources are the bases of societal change and even revolution. In a time when limited resources are not sufficient to meet increasing demands, it is imperative to apply policies to the needs and priorities of a society. Many of the fundamental problems facing nations today revolve around the issue of life and its quality in a society.

Over much of the developing world there is a brutal battle going on between life and death. While the maintenance of life itself is not a day-to-day problem for most persons in industrialized countries, there is a struggle over the quality of life. Concerns about life and the quality of life are closely related. The tension between rapid world population growth and limited food supplies which has been accentuated by poor harvests in India and Russia and changing climatic conditions in sub-Saharan Africa is a case in point. Increased demands for food to avert starvation in many developing countries has produced a consequent rise in costs and even shortages of some items in the United States and other developed countries. Thus saving lives in one part of the world has meant more constricted life styles and inflation in other parts of the world. This dilemma raises basic questions about human life. Who shall live and who shall suffer when there are insufficient resources for all? What quality of life is acceptable to a people? What are the responsibilities of one human being to another? What sacrifices will one make to assist another? Are individuals willing to pay more for health and welfare to increase their life expectances, to give up luxuries to achieve a longer life?

National policies on resources are directed at these issues. In order for the policies to be successful, they must meet the needs of the people and have their support. Otherwise they will not be followed. In recent Swedish elections, many voters said that they would rather have more disposable personal income to use for housing, better food such as meat, and vacations than pay increased taxes for more health and welfare benefits. A unilateral decision to raise taxes under those conditions would not have been politically wise for the government.

In setting national priorities, politicians and other decision makers assess the available and projected resources and ascertain the needs and aspirations of their constituents and the other communities upon whom they are dependent. Priorities are set which fit resources to needs and expectations. This chapter is concerned with the design and implementation of social policies that affect human resources. It focuses on those social policies that affect the rehabilitation of the chronically ill and the physically disabled. Policy-setting in the rehabilitation area is examined in the light of both actual and perceived needs and expectations.

The Influence of Social Policies on Social Programs

Social policies are usually developed in relation to perceived problems. While there may be many serious existing problems, policies are generally not formulated and implemented until a problem becomes salient. The energy crisis of today is an excellent example. The world's energy use has been increasing yearly, although energy resources and output capacity are limited. Few individuals in the United States paid serious attention to this problem until the gasoline and heating-oil shortage aggravated by the 1973 Arab-Israeli war had obvious effects. Once a problem is identified and deemed salient, policies are set and then are translated into behavior through a series of specific programs designed to solve or alleviate the problem. In the case of the energy crisis, a federal energy office was established, policies were set, and energy programs were developed and implemented.

A particular social policy does not necessarily patent a unique solution to a problem. In fact, a policy may well be one of several acceptable alternate courses of action. In his analysis of Social Security benefits for injury and disability in a ten-nation study, Kaim-Caudle (1973) argues that different policies can be employed to achieve similar goals. Identifying the major possible alternative solutions to a problem, gathering and weighing relevant information about them, estimating the consequences of implementing the different courses of action, and judging how consistently one policy objective fits with others are the difficult steps confronting the policy decision maker.

One of the problems in discussing social policy is that, although many authors have written books about it (Freeman and Sherwood, 1970; Rein, 1970; Miller and Riessman, 1968; Schorr, 1968), few have carefully defined or described it. Gil (1973) reviews previous work on social policy and presents a useful definition of social policy analysis. He says:

Social policies are principles or courses of action designed to influence:
  1. the overall quality of life in a society;
  2. the circumstances of living of individuals and groups in that society; and
  3. the nature of intra-societal relationships among individuals, groups, and society as a whole. (1973:24)

Successful social policies achieve their purposes by developing new resources in areas where they are needed, allocating material and human resources to meet needs, and efficiently distributing resources to the problem areas. Frequently social policies are supported by law and enforced with legal sanctions.

Gil (1973:33–36) goes on to provide a framework for social

policy analysis that permits a comprehensive view of the process. His approach considers issues dealt with by the policy; objectives, value premises, theoretical positions, target segments, and substantive effects of the policy; implications of the policy for the key processes and common domain of social sciences; effects of interaction between the policy and forces surrounding its development and implementation; and development of alternative social policies. Utilizing this perspective, I shall examine the manner in which social policies for the rehabilitation of the chronically ill and the physically disabled are developed and implemented through social programs. It is important to remember that social policies have effect only as they are implemented through social programs designed to alleviate specific problematic conditions. The impact of the policy and related programs is dependent upon the sanctions and rewards attached to the programs and the manner in which they are accepted and valued by the target population. The success of a social policy is, then, largely dependent upon the success of the social programs generated to achieve the policy objectives.

Is Rehabilitation of the Chronically Ill and Physically Disabled a Policy Issue?

Policy issues can be viewed from both subjective and objective perspectives. While a medical, environmental, or social problem might be endemic throughout a population, it may not be perceived as a problem by the indigenous population since most individuals suffer from the malady. For instance, gastrointestinal diseases and parasites are so common in parts of East Africa that people do not perceive chronic diarrhea as being unusual (Vogel, 1968). Social psychological factors also influence the perception of a problem. In the United States gonorrhea ranks first and syphilis third among all reportable communicable diseases (U.S., Department of Health, Education and Welfare, 1973:2-3). Yet the general public seems more concerned about outbreaks of bubonic plague, smallpox, and food poisoning than it does about the major medical and social problem of venereal disease control.

Chronic illness and physical disability are objectively major problems in the United States that are beginning to receive considerable attention from the medical care community and the general public. Medical practice in the United States has traditionally been organized around prevention, acute care, and rehabilitation (Stevens, 1971). Until recently, prevention and acute care were emphasized, but little attention was given to rehabilitation. These patterns are changing as a result of changes in illness and disease distributions (Glazier, 1973) and the public visibility of disabled people.

Haber (1973*b*) reports that 17.2 percent of the noninstitutionalized population aged eighteen to sixty-four sampled in a 1966 Social Security Administration national study either were unable to work or experienced work limitations. Similar studies in Australia, Denmark, Great Britain, and Israel showed lower percentages of disabled persons, but the discrepancies could well be the result of differences in identification procedures used to locate the disabled, measurement error, and design. Even though the rates differ across countries, Haber (1973*a*:333) concludes that "there was general uniformity among the five studies in the relationship of disability to individual attributes." Wan (1974) shows that the industry in which a person works, the length of time that he is disabled, and his poverty status affect the severity of his disability. These variables could also account for some of the differences across countries. However, disability is a major problem in all the countries studied. The consequences of disability often include loss of income, reduced physical mobility, limitations in activities of daily living, decreased sexual functioning, and decreased self-expectations.

Sound empirical studies of the prevalence and incidence of disability in the United States have begun to accumulate only during the last eight years (Wan, 1974; Haber, 1971, 1973*b*). Selective perception, the social construction of reality, ideology, assumptions, and values influence the identification of a problem and the articulation of social policies to meet it. Thus, many problems are recognized and suitably addressed, but an individual's view is often affected by his position in society. Social scientists have major contributions to make in policy formulation and program development because they are trained to separate behavioral observations from ideological positions. Becker and Horowitz (1972) make the point well when they argue that neither a radical nor a conservative ideology necessarily makes a good sociologist. Description, explanation, and prediction of social structures and events are the materials that have meaning for the sociologist. Bias results when the observer continually views structures and events from one perspective. Even social scientists lapse into restricted viewpoints. Most sociology has been supported by vested interest groups and has been oriented to their interests: the problems of the teacher, the manager, the parent, and the male, middle-class, white, urban, working adult. Becker and Horowitz (1972:64) suggest that taking other viewpoints in examining any social phenomenon is likely to provide the observer with a broader and more accurate knowledge of the assumptions, ideologies, and values that color interpretations of the facts.

Even though there are many disabled people in the United States, historically there has been surprisingly little social and psychological research on physical disability and rehabilitation. Behavioral scientists are now beginning to give more attention to the antecedents, state, and consequences of disability. Furthermore, they are viewing disability and the rehabilitation process from the viewpoint of the client-consumer and others involved in and affected by the process. Scott's (1969) study of the ways in which agencies established to aid the blind actually function to keep the visually limited person dependent in order to legitimate the agencies' existence illustrates the potential conflict of interest in the rehabilitation process. Etzioni (1973) demonstrates how the process involved in deciding what to do with a potentially genetically defective human fetus is not just the concern of the physician, the woman, or the family, but impinges on the entire society and political process. Etzioni's argument suggests that disability and the rehabilitation process are major social problems in American society about which social policies are developing.

A facile solution to the disability problem is to initiate a massive program to eradicate disability by utilizing prevention techniques and curing the disabling diseases. Even if these steps were possible, there is serious question that disability would be eliminated. Gans (1972) argues that poverty will not be eliminated because it serves positive functions for some interest groups. It could be similarly argued that disability and rehabilitation serve positive functions in society and therefore will always be present. The disabled who can work perform the menial, less desirable tasks and subsidize the activities of the more affluent with their cheap labor. All of the disabled create jobs for the individuals and industries that serve them; the disabled are easily identified as deviants; they sometimes serve as scapegoats in society; and they serve as a base line in the stratification system.

Sjoquist (1973) and other economists (Becker, 1968; Fleisher, 1966) have examined the utility function of crime. They conclude that criminal delinquent behavior can be understood in terms of an economic model. Again this logic can be applied to the substantive area of disability and rehabilitation. There are strong economic reasons to suspect that disability and the rehabilitation system will not go out of existence. Many industries depend on the disabled. Disabled individuals who were poor and unskilled before the onset of disability may actually improve their standards of living by becoming functionally limited. Insurance is a stable source of income that might surpass the income they could have earned.

Thus, while disability is a national problem and social policies for rehabilitation are being developed, there are at the same time social, political, and economic reasons to suggest that disability will not be eradicated.

Goal Definition: What Is the Goal of Rehabilitation?

Before a social policy can be developed and social programs can be initiated that are aimed at the problems posed by the disabled, the goals of the American medical system and rehabilitation programs must be examined to ascertain how new policies and programs can fit in with the existing system and yet can improve upon it.

The goals of the American medical system and rehabilitation programs are based on fundamental American values. Positive value is placed on possessing an occupation, being productive at a job, and achieving in the labor force in the United States (Morgan, Sirageldin, Baerwaldt, 1966). Positive value is placed upon large amounts of social interaction with others. The diminution and disruption of this social interaction are negatively valued (Zahn, 1973). Physical and emotional independence is highly valued (Cogswell, 1967; Fink, 1967; Cohn, 1961). Great emphasis is placed upon youth and physical attractiveness (Berscheid, Walster, and Bohrnstedt, 1973; Dion, Berscheid, and Walster, 1972). Intact marriages, a cohesive family, children (Jackson and Kuvlesky, 1973; Murphy and Johnson, 1973), and active sexual lives are also valued in American society (Albrecht and Coonley, 1973). When an individual becomes sick and/or disabled, ideally efforts are made to get him back to work, to be independent, to improve his physical attractiveness, to encourage his social life, and to build upon his family ties. While these values are verbally articulated and often serve as a basis for the human service industry, they are not always the high-priority values directing behavior in the health care system.

Throughout all of the testimony before the Senate Subcommittee on Health in the Ninety-second Congress (U.S., Cong., Sen., Committee on Labor, 1971), "good" patient care, longer life expectancy, alleviation of pain, equal access to health care, and a more efficient delivery system appeared as recurrent themes. These public goals for the American health care system are translated into reduced infant and maternal mortality rates, especially in poverty areas, national health insurance plans (Glasser, 1974), more continuity in care, lower cost per illness episode, and perceived patient feelings of satisfaction with treatment. While few persons would argue with these goals, many might object to the manner in which the goals become translated into operational programs. Good patient care means different things to different people. To the patient it means prompt alleviation of symptoms at a low cost. However, to the physician, hospital administrator, medical school, and health care industry, it might mean professional treatment of diseases, illness, and symptoms at a "satisfactory" profit.

Health care is a business and in many ways it functions like a business. The patient, the family, the hospital administration, the medical school, physicians, nurses, and other health professionals are all interest groups with some unique and some overlapping goals. Even though part of the health care system is a "not for profit" business, every worker in the system is paid for his work and has some personal interest in the size of the paycheck. Also businesses do not prosper and grow unless they are solvent, expand to meet the market demands, have high staff morale, and produce a reasonable product. Ehrenreich and Ehrenreich (1971) even go so far as to argue that the three top priorities of the American health care system are to make money, to promote research and to perpetuate the system by training more doctors and other health personnel. While elements of this argument seem to be supported by evidence, the Ehrenreichs present only one viewpoint. What does become apparent is that the goals of health care undergo substantial interpretation by various political interest groups in the process of implementation. Since the professionals, major institutions, government, and large businesses have more political power than the individual patient, much of medical practice is likely to reflect this bias until the client-consumer gains an effective lobby. Therefore the study of health care goals, policies, and programs should be careful to take the viewpoints of the various interest groups into account when conclusions are drawn.

In addition to being influenced by the goals and interest groups of the larger health care system, the goals in rehabilitation are a curious mix of the utilitarian and the humanitarian. The publicly articulated goals of rehabilitation have largely reflected the values of American society. While rehabilitation agencies are very interested in assisting the disabled individual to meet his or her social, emotional, and concrete needs, the major goal of these agencies is to get the individual working on a paying job (Leary and Tseng, 1974). The dual emphasis upon humanitarian and utilitarian outcomes of rehabilitation is clearly put by George Sawyer, manager of medical services for Liberty Mutual Insurance Company (1965:11):

It is our belief that prevention or reduction of human disability is a basic responsibility of the Casualty Insurance Company. This is so, first, because of the humanitarian consideration of restoring the disabled individual, and second, because of the impact on cost control. These reasons have been sufficient to support our search for a better understanding of the use of those medical services that can assist an attending physician in accomplishing rehabilitation.

In fact, the emphasis in the insurance industry, the rehabilitation agencies, and the federal government traditionally has been more on return to work and cost efficiency than on humanitarian outcomes of preserving lives and restoring human dignity (Sawyer, 1965; U.S. Department of Health, Education, and Welfare, 1974b). This is not to say that companies, agencies, and government are callous. Both humanitarian and utilitarian goals and behavior characterize rehabilitation policies and programs. However, the utilitarian side of rehabilitation receives more attention because industries are in business to make money and government is accountable to Congress and the voting public.

The work ethic permeates American society. Government and business are operated on Weberian rational models of bureaucracies found in industrialized countries. For these reasons, cost/benefit analysis and cost effectiveness evaluations have become widely used tools in assessing policies and programs (Rossi, 1972). Because costs and outcomes must be quantified to utilize these models, numbers play an important role in making policy and program decisions (Drew, 1969). The "bottom line" and numbers of clients evaluated, served, and placed in jobs greatly influence policies in the rehabilitation field. However, dissatisfaction has arisen with the manner in which costs and benefits have been operationalized. Critics have begun to question how dollars can be assigned to human lives. What obligations does society have to a disabled Vietnam veteran who was drafted out of the ghetto and sent to fight a war that he did not understand? If a government legislates high speed limits on highways or fails to enforce pollution standards, is it responsible for the illness, mortality, and disability that result? These questions go beyond the cost/benefit and numbers approach to rehabilitation because they consider issues of responsibility.

Strong lobbies and Congress itself have stressed the humanitarian aspects of rehabilitation and the need to exercise a broader responsibility to the members of society. In 1962 the National Rehabilitation Association made a concerted effort to have as much emphasis placed on "aiding independent living" as on vocational placement in rehabilitation legislation. However, the Department of Health, Education and Welfare was opposed and the measure did not carry in Congress (U.S., Department of Health, Education, and Welfare, 1974*a*:2).

The Ninety-third Congress witnessed similar efforts to pass legislation, H.R. 8395, S. 7, and H.R. 8070, that would provide rehabilitation services to the disabled whether they had vocational potential or not. Although President Nixon vetoed that legislation, Senate Bill 1875 authorized a national study to examine how more comprehensive and extensive rehabilitation can be accomplished and what the effects of new programs would be. A policy movement toward the more humanitarian goals of rehabilitation is evidenced in the Senate report that accompanied S. 1875 (U.S., Department of Health, Education, and Welfare, 1974*a*:3):

The Committee also continues to believe that many individuals now judged unable to achieve a vocational goal can lead full and productive lives, given the full promise of technology and knowledge currently available in this Nation. Furthermore, the Committee reiterates that the goal of independent living is a legitimate one for Federal recognition and support, and one which will benefit not only the individual but his family, and society. It, therefore, urges the Secretary to explore all possible methods of providing community-based services, and stresses that such methods should include services to individuals who are currently homebound. The Committee urges the Secretary to act rapidly to set up and pursue this vital study.

This action on the part of Congress is representative of efforts in government and industry to invest more in the development and restoration of human resources than they have in the past. The inconvenience brought on by limitations in natural resources has drawn renewed attention to the value of human resources. This humanitarian movement also shows that the American people, government, and industry are in the process of accepting broader responsibilities for the members of society.

Even if new legislation is passed, policies set, and programs undertaken to provide comprehensive rehabilitation services for the disabled, there are still considerable problems in the equitable delivery of rehabilitation services. Willhelm (1971) argues that America has a racist ideology resulting from three hundred years of history that precludes equality of treatment for the black, the Chicano, or the Indian. Even if bias and prejudice are subtle, they nevertheless have their effect.

Westergaard (1972) has much the same to say about social class and stratification systems. He states that there will always be a lower class that will receive less satisfactory services than the middle and upper classes. He concludes that the dream of a classless society where every individual shares equally in the resources is an illusion. In a similar vein, Strauss (1972) reasons that the poor will never receive equitable medical care unless drastic organizational reforms occur simultaneously in all aspects of the American medical care system and unless medical techniques are developed which rely only minimally on patient judgment and motivation for utilization. In order for the poor and the racial minorities to have adequate and equitable health care, fundamental values, priorities, and even the present stratification system may well have to be changed (Mechanic, 1972).

Although these goals might be unrealistic, the implementation of a comprehensive national health insurance program would provide an effective first step toward equitable health care for all Americans (Anderson, 1972:208–209). However, even if the opportunity for health care and health service is equally offered to every citizen, there is no guarantee that everyone will utilize the services. The research on health and dental care utilization shows that there are considerable differences in utilization rates despite equal access to care. These differences in utilization rates are related to social class, race, perception of illness, values, and attitudes towards health and illness (Anderson and Andersen, 1972). Even when equal access to rehabilitation services is provided, the literature provides reason to believe that social and psychological variables will affect utilization rates.

Goal Attainment and the Achievement of Rehabilitation in the Present Medical System

The goals of rehabilitation include getting a person back to work, assisting him to achieve maximum independence, improving his self-image, and imbuing the disabled and the public with an increased respect for human life. These goals can be approached through a variety of policies and programs, but, as a matter of fact, are addressed in the United States through the American medical care system, which is oriented around physicians in private or group practice working through hospitals on a fee-for-service basis (Stevens, 1971).

Although many doctors are well trained, highly dedicated professionals discharging their essential responsibilities, their behavior is also motivated and rewarded by money. It is not by chance that the solo practice of medicine on a fee-for-service basis dominates American medical practice. Most doctors are in business for themselves in a very profitable field. Over the years physicians as an occupational group have had a remarkably high average yearly income when compared with all other occupational groups, including those requiring similar education, training and responsibility (Bogue, 1969:428–462). Their income level ranks well above that of other occupational groups, such as university presidents, airline pilots, dentists, bankers, and managers in industry. The fee-for-service method of payment has major effects on the health care delivery system of the United States (Roemer, 1971). The physician is in control of his own business. Why should he leave private practice to work similar hours for someone else for less money? The salaries of physicians employed by government, industry, group clinics, and medical schools are substantially lower than those of physicians in private practice. In order to keep physicians in institutional settings many organizations are being forced to offer the physicians incentive plans, bonuses, or free time to see private patients on a fee-for-service basis.

Because of the financial rewards of private practice, attempts to socialize medicine, encourage group practice, implement a national health insurance plan, and centralize the organization and management of the practice of medicine have met with failure. Daily hospital charges are the health care cost that has risen the most. However, physicians' fees have risen more rapidly than total medical care costs, dentists' fees, all consumer items, and prescriptions over the twenty-one-year period from 1950 to 1971 (U.S., Social Security Administration, 1972*a*:63–64). Twenty-two percent of the total amount spent on personal medical care in fiscal 1972 went to physicians' salaries (U.S., Social Security Administration, 1972*b*:3). The Committee for Economic Development, in a policy statement *Building a National Health-Care System,* commented that although the solo practice of medicine in the United States is no longer efficient and effective, it is remarkably difficult to change the system (U.S., Cong., Sen., 1973:34–36). The committee (1973:37) concludes that

paying a separate fee for each service adds considerably to the claim work involved in health insurance and has inhibited its development. This is especially true where the individual fees are not large and where the administrative cost, relative to the cost of the specific service insured, may appear to be disproportionate. In contrast, capitation (i.e., a fixed periodic payment per person) can greatly reduce the administrative cost of insurance and make possible the coverage of additional services.

Many who have studied the existing health-care system have begun to question the fundamental logic of paying separately for each service and each visit. The Ways and Means Committee of the House of Representatives, for example, found that payment for each individual service performed creates an economic incentive to furnish services that may not be essential and may even be unnecessary.

This evidence concerning the fee-for-service method of payment confirms Roemer's (1971) contention that methods of payment for medical services influence the organization of health care delivery systems and suggests that the system is inefficient and might even be detrimental to the patient-consumer. The patient-consumer might undergo unnecessary surgery, unwarranted medication, or inappropriate hospitalization in the interest of cash flow rather than in the interest of the patient's health. Much of the resistance to change in the organization of health care delivery in the United States can be attributed to the reluctance of the physician to relinquish personal control of his business, fee-for-service compensation, and high income level. This is not to argue that all physicians are self-aggrandizers; there are many idealistic, hard-working, competent, and responsible physicians. However, the data demonstrate the detrimental effects of the present medical care system which cause many consumers, physicians, politicians, and government officials to call for radical organizational changes in the system (Mechanic, 1972:80–111).

The organization of medicine in the United States is very difficult to change not only because of the established reward system but also because of the power held by the medical profession. The practice of medicine in the United States is one of the largest businesses in the world. Expenditures for health care in the medical-industrial complex totaled more than $63 billion dollars in 1973 (Meyers, 1974). In addition to the power inherent in the control over the spending of these vast monies, the medical system in the United States is essentially a self-regulated, government-controlled monopoly that has marked effects on every aspect of American life (Green, 1973). An individual cannot enter medical school unless he is screened by a selection committee composed of physicians. The student does not graduate from medical school until he is certified by the medical school. Almost every medical accrediting board, health board, medical specialty board, National Institute of Health review committee, and government health program is dominated by physicians (Stevens, 1971). Regardless of its facilities or the competency of other staff members an institution cannot be designated as and function as a hospital unless it has house staff physicians. If the institution is not designated as a hospital, it is not eligible for many types of insurance reimbursement.

The practice of medicine without a license is illegal. Indeed, the practice of medicine should be controlled for the public good, but if the "official" medical system is too expensive, distant, poorly organized, and inefficient to meet the needs of large numbers of citizens, people will go without needed medical care or alternate sources of medical care will arise and prosper. Therefore, many alternate providers of health care (such as herbalists, shamans, acupuncturists, indigenous healers, witch doctors, and medically trained nonphysicians) illegally perform services regardless of their competence or effectiveness and real community need (Torrey, 1972). This has occurred in many communities of the United States from the black and Spanish neighborhoods of the inner cities to rural Appalachia (Bazell, 1974; Torrey, 1972). Again, these results are not an indictment of individual physicians, but are the effects of an ineffective medical care system.

Rehabilitation of the disabled takes place within the organizational context of the American health care system. Therefore, rehabilitation is also greatly influenced by the private practice, fee-for-service, fragmented medical system. Rehabilitation treatment is exceedingly expensive because the disabled person typically has a series of chronic problems that are traditionally treated by multiple hospitalizations (DiAngelo et al., 1973). At the present time there are not enough rehabilitation beds in the United States to satisfy the needs of the large disabled population. One of the reasons that there are no more beds might well be that most disabled individuals cannot afford rehabilitation in the present fee-for service, expensive, hospital-based treatment system. Most disabled individuals do not have adequate insurance coverage, work potential as assessed by vocational rehabilitation agencies, youth, or the type of disability preferred for treatment. Therefore, they are not allowed to enter the rehabilitation system. Only a small percentage of the disabled receive comprehensive rehabilitation services (Nagi, 1969). Usually the disabled enter the medical system for acute care of a serious injury or disease. They receive treatment for their acute condition and perhaps some short-term rehabilitation assistance; they may even make visits to a hospital as outpatients. But, typically, they do not receive extensive, professional rehabilitation services because they cannot afford such services. Until other methods of rehabilitation are implemented, criteria for treatment are changed, delivery methods of rehabilitation services are improved, and health insurance is made available to those in need, the majority of the disabled will not receive adequate rehabilitation services.

Even when an individual passes through the extensive screening process necessary to enter the rehabilitation system and receives comprehensive services, there is frequently a lack of consensus as to what constitutes rehabilitation success. Because rehabilitation is a process that involves doctors; nurses; physical, occupational, music, recreational, and speech therapists; psychologists; social workers; vocational counselors; patients; families; friends; insurance companies; and the government, there are many different viewpoints regarding rehabilitation success. Ludwig and Adams (1968) used cooperation and completion of services as a measure of success. Vocational rehabilitation agencies consider job placement and satisfactory work performance as final measures of success (Leary and Tseng, 1974). Physical therapists view success in terms of increases in levels of physical function (Katz, 1959). Occupational therapists see success as improvements in skill levels necessary for physical independence and task performance. Government and insurance companies evaluate rehabilitation in terms of cost/effectiveness

and loss or gain in individual earnings as a result of disability and
rehabilitation (Wan, 1974; Drew, 1969). Families and friends
perceive success in terms of how much the person's disability
disrupts their lives and the amount of personal cost required of
them. If the disabled person meets the new expectations of his
family and friends, he is judged by them to have been successfully
rehabilitated (Albrecht, 1969).

A recent study (Albrecht, 1973) shows that different measures
of successful rehabilitation do not correlate highly with one another. For example, patient cooperation and completion of services as judged by the medical staff had a .04 correlation with improvement in level of physical function and a .08 correlation with
attitudinal improvement. Rehabilitation success, then, depends
in large part on the perspective of the viewer. Few researchers have examined the patient's perceptions of rehabilitation
success. The patient-consumer might be the best judge of all as to
whether his rehabilitation program is successful, but few investigators have thought to ask for his opinion. The discrepancies in
viewpoint on rehabilitation success among the experts suggest
that we take a step backwards to get a larger perspective. Since
rehabilitation actively involves the consumer and numerous professions, the outlook of each of the persons involved is likely to be
biased. The evaluation of rehabilitation success ought to include
all of the relevant viewpoints. Professionals can be evaluated by
their peers through Professional Standards Review organizations
(PSRO) (Brook, 1973). Patient-consumer progress can be
evaluated by other patient-consumers as well as by professionals.
In fact, there is sound logic in having the patient set his own goals
and evaluate his own progress in the light of his resources and
opportunities with the rehabilitation team, family, and friends
serving as consultants in this process.

Policy formulation and program evaluation would be difficult
even if the disabled did have equal and easy access to rehabilitation resources. In order for rehabilitation to be more effective,
there must be fundamental changes in the American health care
delivery system so that client-consumers and health professionals

are rewarded for achieving rehabilitation goals in an effective and cost efficient manner. Rehabilitation services should be made equally available to those disabled individuals who need them, and better measures of rehabilitation outcomes need to be developed so that policies and programs can be evaluated.

Policy Alternatives to the Present Rehabilitation System

The trend toward institutionalization in the United States has grown over the last thirty years; the results are astounding. When the populations of law enforcement, social welfare, hospital and school institutions were considered, more than seven million of the 19,834,000 residents of California were under institutional care on an average day in 1969 (Romano-V., 1974). Of those under care, 2,222,241 were wards of law enforcement or social welfare institutions, or were in hospitals. Somers (1973) predicts that the trend will be toward the increasing institutionalization of medical care. However, there is a growing impetus to reverse these trends. Illich's *Deschooling Society* (1970) has had a widespread impact on the educational world. The closing of juvenile detention facilities in Massachusetts and consequent community-based treatment for delinquents have received national attention (Bakal, 1973). The man who accomplished this reform in Massachusetts, Jerome Miller, recently attempted to do the same in Illinois (Miller, 1973).

While hospitals cannot be completely closed down, much of what occurs in the rehabilitation process can take place outside of hospitals in community settings. This type of treatment has numerous advantages: the services cost less. The disabled person can live at home, where he can begin to make the immediate physical and social adjustments that are necessary for him to function in his world; the treatment is much closer to the consumer; the family can be more easily involved in the rehabilitation process; the health professionals have to work with the patient-consumer in his environment and can better tailor a rehabilitation program to fit his needs; nonphysician health professionals can take on more responsibilities; the treatment team is better informed of patient-consumer progress and relapses since it is located in his neighborhood and can intervene quickly and effectively to arrest relapses; and the patient-consumer is compelled to take an active role in his rehabilitation program from the very onset of the program.

Many individuals who need more intensive help than can be delivered on an outpatient basis could easily be treated in a halfway house located in the community. Halfway houses for the disabled offer many of the advantages of both the hospital and the community-based outpatient clinic without the high costs of the hospital. Keith (1968; 1969; 1971) predicts that this will be the rehabilitation model of the future. Disabled persons would move from the intensive care environment of the hospital, which is needed for many seriously disabled individuals, to a community-based halfway house and then to home care. Continuity of care could be accomplished in this system in a cost efficient manner. The patient as consumer could be intimately involved in the entire process. This model of rehabilitation has added advantages in that it fits in with the concept of health maintenance organizations and community health centers (O'Donnell and Sullivan, 1969) and provides the opportunity to hire disabled individuals in the community to help other disabled persons through the rehabilitation process (Kent and Smith, 1967).

Another way to improve on the present rehabilitation system might be to introduce more competition into the industry and to provide the consumer with more options on the types, level, and location of service that he is purchasing (Somers and Somers, 1974). This could be accomplished by the government's funding more innovative rehabilitation programs which would essentially be in competition with the established system, and ensuring that basic health insurance would cover treatment in these new programs. A more effective procedure might be to give the disabled consumer more power by letting him shop around and purchase the services that he wants through a rehabilitation voucher system. The disabled person would receive from his insurers a voucher for a specified number of dollars which he could use to purchase rehabilitation services. The consumer would then be able to make the providers of services more sensitive to his needs. An open market for rehabilitation services would force both the consumer and the provider to dramatically reassess the priorities, needs, and services in the rehabilitation process. This approach to rehabilitation would also make the patient-consumer maximally independent in the decision-making process from the very beginning. Agencies, doctors, and institutions would have to compete for his business.

Another version of this model would make use of the principles of behavior modification (Bandura, 1969) through behavioral contracting. Formal contracts could be drawn up between the patient-consumer, his family, and the sources of rehabilitation help. The contributing parties could be paid for the successful meeting of performance objectives and not rewarded for failure. In this context only performance according to prearranged criteria would be rewarded. Everyone would have to produce in order to be rewarded. While these proposals have some obvious drawbacks, they would compel the rehabilitation industry to take the needs of the patient-consumer seriously and to offer good care at reasonable prices.

Whether or not the voucher or behavioral contracting systems are ever implemented, the patient-consumer is going to exert more control over his rehabilitation process and hold the system accountable for the services it renders and the prices it charges. Elling (1968) argues that the power structure in health is shifting toward a more regionalized, decentralized system with local control. In Sweden the rights of the citizen are protected by an ombudsman system (Wennergren, 1968). In the United States organizations like the American Civil Liberties Union, community health agencies, Disabled Viet Nam Veterans, and local health boards are gradually taking the role of ombudsmen in protecting the rights of the consumer of health and rehabilitation services. During these times of inflation the consumer revolution has arrived. Increasing attention is being given not only to buyers' guides to products and services but also to legal services for the consumer (Schrag, 1970). The dissatisfied consumer now has recourse through the courts, at prices that he can afford, to redress wrongs done to him. In many cases legal services are free if a consumer advocacy group or legal-aid society decides to take the case. As the price of medical care goes up and consumer satisfaction goes down, the same legal tools may be used in the purchase of medical and rehabilitation services.

Consumerism is being felt by the policy makers. Many of the professionals on presidential blue ribbon commissions are disenchanted by the government's unwillingness to accept or implement their recommendations. In fact, President Nixon disagreed with the findings of the presidential commissions both on population growth and on violence and refused to accept their suggestions (Chapman, 1973). The reaction of commission members is one of increased sympathy for and affiliation with the causes of the disenfranchised. The disabled are bound to benefit from this movement. The Committee for Economic Development was so struck by the financial reward system and inequities in American medical practice that it recommended decentralization of services, more community control, and adequate health insurance for the aged and disabled (U.S., Cong., Sen., 1973:70–71):

The insurance coverage under community trusteeships would be financed by general-revenue support for the poor and near-poor and, where appropriate, through a sliding scale of contributions according to such variables as income and family size. Persons whose income is below national poverty standards, whether or not they are receiving welfare assistance, should be relieved of both premiums and copayments; these should be financed by the federal government.

These efforts are resulting in new social policies for the delivery of health care in America that will be responsive to the resources and needs of the patient-consumer (U.S., Cong., Sen., Committee on Labor, 1971).

Conclusion

Social policies do have considerable impact on the utilization of human resources. They embody the values of a society and reflect the compromises of political interest groups. This chapter has pointed out that social policies on rehabilitation of the disabled call into question some of the basic values of American society. While our society places great value on human life and the dignity of the individual, it also supports the Protestant work ethic and the value of individual independence. In the case of the disabled these values often come into conflict, therefore rehabilitation policies and programs reflect both utilitarian and humanitarian aspects.

There is cause to doubt that the rehabilitation needs of the disabled can be met within the present health care delivery system. The system does not serve the needs of the disabled patient-consumer well. Organizational changes reflecting consumer interests are required in the health care system to make it effective. The medical profession and the entire health care system strongly resist such changes. Yet, because of the consumer revolution, political pressures are being brought to bear on Congress and the medical profession to set new policies and implement new programs that provide needed services to the disabled. Perhaps equity will never be achieved in the delivery of rehabilitation services, but a healthy balance of power between provider and consumer and a national health insurance program could bring the dream closer to the reality.

BIBLIOGRAPHY

Albrecht, G. L.
    1969.   Adult socialization: The effects of aspiration and social interaction on rehabilitation. Ph.D. dissertation, Emory University, Atlanta.

1973. Rehabilitation success: Who sets the criteria and measures the results? Paper presented at the American Academy of Rehabilitation Medicine meetings, Washington, D.C., October.

Albrecht, G. L., and Coonley, R.
1973. Sexual resocialization of the physically disabled: Constraints of time and resources on the adult socialization process. Paper presented at the American Sociological Association meetings, New York, September.

Anderson, O. W.
1972. *Health Care: Can There Be Equity?* New York: John Wiley.

Anderson, O. W., and Andersen, R. M.
1972. Patterns of use of health services. In *Handbook of Medical Sociology*, edited by H. W. Freeman, S. Levine, and L. G. Reeder, pp. 386–406. Englewood Cliffs, N.J.: Prentice-Hall.

Bakal, Y.
1973. Closing Massachusetts' institutions: A case study. In *Closing Correctional Institutions*, edited by Y. Bakal, pp. 151–180. Lexington, Mass.: Lexington Books.

Bandura, A.
1969. *Principles of Behavior Modification.* New York: Holt, Rinehart and Winston.

Bazell, R. J.
1974. Health care: What the poor people didn't get from Kentucky project. In *A Handbook of Human Service Organizations*, edited by H. D. Demone, Jr. and D. Harshbarger, pp. 178–184. New York: Behavioral Publications.

Becker, G. S.
1968. Crime and punishment: An economic approach. *Journal of Political Economics*, 76:169–217.

Becker, H. S., and Horowitz, I. L.
1972. Radical politics and sociological research: Observations on methodology and ideology. *American Journal of Sociology*, 78:48–66.

Berscheid, E.; Walster, E.; and Bohrnstedt, G.
1973. The happy American body: A survey report. *Psychology Today*, 8:119–131.

Bogue, D.
1969. *Principles of Demography.* New York: John Wiley.

Brook, R. H.
1973. *Quality of Care Assessment: A Comparison of Five Methods of Peer Review.* Washington, D.C.: Bureau of Health Services Research and Evaluation, Government Printing Office.

Chapman, W.
1973. Presidential panels are frustrated. *Philadelphia Inquirer*, September 2.

Cogswell, B.
1967. Rehabilitation of the paraplegic: Processes of socialization. *Sociological Inquiry*, 37:11–26.
Cohn, N.
1961. Understanding the process of adjustment to disability. *Journal of Rehabilitation*, 27:16–18.
DiAngelo, E.; Hamilton, B. B.; Swarts, P. S.; and Betts, H. B.
1973. *Rehabilitation Follow-up of the Accident Disabled*. Chicago: Rehabilitation Institute of Chicago.
Dion, K.; Berscheid, E.; and Walster, E.
1972. What is beautiful is good. *Journal of Personality and Social Psychology*, 24:285–290.
Drew, E. B.
1969. Cost-effectiveness in welfare: An attempt at encompassing planning. In *Societal Guidance*, edited by S. Heidt and A. Etzioni, pp. 116–142. New York: Crowell.
Ehrenreich, B., and Ehrenreich, J.
1971. *The American Health Empire*. New York: Vintage Books.
Elling, R. H.
1968. The shifting power structure in health. *The Milbank Memorial Fund Quarterly*, 46: part 2.
Etzioni, A.
1973. Doctors know more than they're telling you about genetic defects. *Psychology Today*, 7:27–36.
Fink, S. L.
1967. Crisis and motivation: A theoretical model. *Archives of Physical Medicine and Rehabilitation*, 48:592–597.
Fleisher, B.
1966. *The Economics of Delinquency*. Chicago: Quadrangle Books.
Freeman, H. E., and Sherwood, C. C.
1970. *Social Research and Social Policy*. Englewood Cliffs, N.J.: Prentice-Hall.
Gans, H.
1972. The positive functions of poverty. *American Journal of Sociology*, 78:275–289.
Gil, D. G.
1973. *Unravelling Social Policy*. Cambridge, Mass.: Schenkman.
Glasser, M. A.
1974. The approaching struggle to provide adequate health care for all Americans. In *A Handbook of Human Service Organizations*, edited by H. W. Demone, Jr., and D. Harshbarger, pp. 164–177. New York: Behavioral Publications.
Glazier, W. H.
1973. The task of medicine. *Scientific American*, 228:13–17.

Green, M. J.
  1973. Uncle Sam the monopoly man. In *The Monopoly Makers,* edited by M. J. Green, pp. 3–31. New York: Grossman.
Haber, L. D.
  1971. Disabling effects of chronic disease and impairment. *Journal of Chronic Diseases,* 24:469–487.
  1973a. Some parameters for social policy in disability: A cross national comparison. *Milbank Memorial Fund Quarterly,* 51:319–340.
  1973b. Disabling effects of chronic disease and impairment: II. Functional capacity limitation. *Journal of Chronic Diseases,* 26:127–151.
Illich, I.
  1970. *Deschooling Society.* New York: Harrow.
Jackson, S. R., and Kuvlesky, W. P.
  1973. Influence of family disability on social orientations of homemakers among different ethnic populations: Southern black, western Mexican farm migrant and eastern white rural families. Paper presented at American Home Economics Association meetings, Atlantic City, March.
Kaim-Caudle, P. R.
  1973. *Comparative Social Policy and Social Security: A Ten Country Study.* New York: Dunellen.
Katz, S.
  1959. Multidisciplinary studies of illness in aged persons: A new classification of functional status in activities of daily living. *Journal of Chronic Diseases,* 9:55–62.
Keith, R. A.
  1968. The need for a new model in rehabilitation. *Journal of Chronic Diseases,* 21:281–286.
  1969. Physical rehabilitation: Is it ready for the revolution? *Rehabilitation Literature,* 30:170–173.
  1971. The comprehensive rehabilitation center as rehabilitation model. *Inquiry,* 9:22–29.
Kent, J. A., and Smith, H.
  1967. Involving the urban poor in health services through accommodation—the employment of neighborhood representatives. *American Journal of Public Health,* 57:997–1003.
Leary, P. A., and Tseng, M. S.
  1974. The vocational rehabilitation process explained. *Journal of Rehabilitation,* 40:9, 34.
Ludwig, E. G., and Adams, S.
  1968. Patient cooperation in a rehabilitation center: Assumption of the client role. *Journal of Health and Social Behavior,* 9:328–335.

Mechanic, D.
   1972.   *Public Expectations and Health Care.* New York: John Wiley.
Meyers, H. B.
   1974.   The medical-industrial complex. In *A Handbook of Human Service Organizations,* edited by H. W. Demone, Jr., and D. Harshbarger, pp. 82–87. New York: Behavioral Publications.
Miller, J. G.
   1973.   The politics of change: Correctional reform. In *Closing Correctional Institutions,* edited by Y. Bakal, pp. 3–8. Lexington, Mass.: Lexington Books.
Miller, S. M., and Riessman, F.
   1968.   *Social Class and Social Policy.* New York: Basic Books.
Morgan, J. N.; Sirageldin, I. A.; and Baerwaldt, N.
   1966.   *Productive Americans.* Ann Arbor: Institute for Social Research.
Murphy, E., and Johnson, W. G.
   1973.   The effects of disability on the family. Paper presented at the American Sociological Association meetings, New York, September.
Nagi, S. Z.
   1969.   *Disability and Rehabilitation.* Columbus: Ohio State University Press.
O'Donnell, E. J., and Sullivan, M. M.
   1969.   Service delivery and social action through the neighborhood center: A review of research. *Welfare in Review,* 7:1–12.
Rein, J.
   1970.   *Social Policy: Issues of Choice and Change.* New York: Random House.
Roemer, M. I.
   1971.   On paying the doctor and implications of different methods. In *National Health Care,* edited by R. H. Elling, pp. 118–137. Chicago: Aldine.
Romano-V., O. I.
   1974.   Institutions in modern society: Caretakers and subjects. *Science,* 183:722–725.
Rossi, P. H.
   1972.   Testing for success and failure in social action. In *Evaluating Social Programs,* edited by P. H. Rossi and W. Williams, pp. 11–49. New York: Seminar Press.
Sawyer, G. P.
   1965.   Medical administration and rehabilitation in workmen's compensation. Paper presented at Insurance Industry Seminar, Chicago, Ill., November 30.
Schorr, A. L.
   1968.   *Explorations in Social Policy.* New York: Basic Books.
Schrag, P. G.
   1970.   Consumer rights. *Columbia Forum,* 13:4–10.

Scott, R.
  1969. *The Making of Blind Men.* New York: Russell Sage Foundation.
Sjoquist, D. L.
  1973. Property crime and economic behavior: Some empirical results. *American Economic Review,* 48:439–446.
Somers, A. R.
  1973. Some basic determinants of medical care and health policy. In *Politics and Law in Health Care Policy,* edited by J. B. McKinlay, pp. 3–21. New York: Prodist.
Somers, H. M., and Somers, A. R.
  1974. Major issues in National Health Insurance. In *Politics and Law in Health Care Policy,* edited by J. B. McKinlay, pp. 307–340. New York: Prodist.
Stevens, R.
  1971. *American Medicine and the Public Interest.* New Haven: Yale University Press.
Strauss, A. L.
  1972. Medical ghettos. In *Patients, Physicians and Illness,* edited by E. G. Jaco, pp. 381–389. New York: Free Press.
Torrey, E. F.
  1972. *The Mind Game: Witchdoctors and Psychiatrists.* New York: Bantam.
U.S., Congress, Senate, Committee for Economic Development
  1973. *Building a National Health-Care System.* New York: Committee for Economic Development.
U.S., Congress, Senate, Committee on Labor and Public Welfare
  1971. *Health Care Crisis in America, 1971.* Washington, D.C.: Government Printing Office.
U.S., Department of Health, Education, and Welfare
  1973. *VD Fact Sheet 1973.* Atlanta: Center for Disease Control.
  1974a. Comprehensive study of rehabilitation service needs of individuals most severely handicapped, RFP-SRS, 74-39. Washington, D.C.: Social and Rehabilitation Services.
  1974b. Research priorities. Mimeographed. Washington, D.C.: Social and Rehabilitation Services.
U.S., Social Security Administration
  1972a. *Social Security Bulletin,* vol. 35, no. 1. Washington, D.C.: Government Printing Office.
  1972b. *Research and Statistics Note,* no. 19. Washington, D.C.: Government Printing Office.
Vogel, L. C., ed.
  1968. *Public Health Administration: A Course for Medical Students.* Nairobi: Medical Research Centre, Department of the Royal Tropical Institute.

Wan, T. T. H.
  1974. Correlates and consequences of severe disabilities. *Journal of Occupational Medicine,* 16:234–244.
Wennergren, B.
  1968. The rise and growth of Swedish institutions for defending the citizen against official wrongs. *The Annals,* 377:1–9.
Westergaard, J. H.
  1972. Sociology: The myth of classlessness. In *Ideology in Social Science,* edited by R. Blackburn, pp. 119–163. New York: Vintage Books.
Willhelm, S. M.
  1971. Equality in America's racist ideology. In *Radical Sociology,* edited by J. D. Colfax and J. L. Roach, pp. 246–262. New York: Basic Books.
Zahn, M. A.
  1973. Incapacity, impotence and invisible impairment: Their effects upon interpersonal relations. *Journal of Health and Social Behavior,* 14:115–123.

Contributors
Index

Contributors

GARY L. ALBRECHT is Professor in the School of Public Health, University of Illinois, Chicago, Ill. 60680.

KARL L. ALEXANDER is Associate Professor in the Department of Social Relations at The Johns Hopkins University, Baltimore, Md. 21218.

RODNEY M. COE is Professor in the Department of Community Medicine at the St. Louis University School of Medicine, 1402 S. Grand, St. Louis, Mo. 63104.

BETTY E. COGSWELL is Associate Professor in the Department of Family Medicine and Director of the International Programs Office at the Carolina Population Center at the University of North Carolina School of Medicine, Box 5, Old Nurses Dorm, Chapel Hill, N.C. 27514.

WILBERT E. FORDYCE is Professor of Psychology in the Department of Rehabilitation Medicine at the University of Washington School of Medicine, Seattle, Wash. 98195.

ISRAEL GOLDIAMOND is Professor of Psychology in the Departments of Psychiatry and of Behavioral Sciences (Biopsychology) and in the College at the University of Chicago Hospitals and Clinics, 950 E. Fifty-ninth Street, Chicago, Ill. 60637.

WALTER R. GOVE is Professor of Sociology in the Department of Sociology and Anthropology at Vanderbilt University, Nashville, Tenn. 37235.

ELLIOTT A. KRAUSE is Professor in the Department of Sociology at Northeastern University, Boston, Mass. 02115.

CONSTANTINA SAFILIOS-ROTHSCHILD is Professor of Human Development at the Pennsylvania State University, University Park, Pa. 16802.

MARVIN B. SUSSMAN is Unidel Professor of Human Development at the Pennsylvania State University, University Park, Pa. 16802.

289

Name Index

Italicized page numbers indicate full references.

Abrahamson, A. A., 231, *244*
Abramson, J. S., 172, *193*
Adams, S. D., 49, *55*, 273, *282*
Akamatsu T. J., 25, *32*
Albee, E., 149, 150, *166*
Albrecht, G. L., 16, *32*, 264, 274, *279*, *280*
Aldous, J., 166, *166*
Alexander, K. L., 173, 175, 186, 189, 190, 193, *194*
Allen, J. G., 8, *33*
Altshuler, A. A., 6, *32*
Andersen, R. M., 269, *280*
Anderson, O. W., 269, *280*
Antonovsky, A., 206, *220*
Apfelbaum, E., 28, *32*
Armstrong, W., 166, *166*
Atkinson, H., 134, *137*
Averill, J. R., 14, *36*
Ayllon, T., 109, *135*
Azrin, N. H., 80, *94*, 107, 109, 115, *135*, *136*

Bachman, J. G., 190, *194*
Baer, D., 91, *94*
Baerwaldt, N. 264, *283*
Bakal, Y., 275, *280*
Bandura, A., 11, 28, *32*, 80, 82, *94*, 277, *280*
Barber, T., 99, *135*
Barrie, D., 129, *136*

Baumann, B. O., 17, *34*, 83, *94*
Bazell, R. J., 272, *280*
Bear, J., 210, *219*
Becker, G. S., 263, *280*
Becker, H. S., 57, 58, 59, 69, 70, 262, *280*
Bem, D. J., 11, 27, *32*
Bendix, R., 188, 193, *197*
Berardo, F. M., 166, *168*
Berger, R., 231, *244*
Berkson, G., 8, *32*
Beron, N., 226, *243*
Berscheid, E., 13, *33*, 264, *280*, *281*
Betts, H. B., 6, 10, 22, *33*, 272, *281*
Birley, J. L. T., 184, *194*
Bixby, K. W., 212, *219*
Blackburn, C., 238, *243*
Blanchard, E. B., 11, *32*, 82, *94*
Blau, P. M., 172, 173, 175, *194*
Bochover, J. S., 231, *244*
Bogue, D., 269, *280*
Bohrnstedt, G., 264, *280*
Bors, E., 17, *32*
Bowerman, C. E., 184, *196*
Brager, G. A., 238, *243*
Brannon, R., 11, *32*
Briar, S., 238, *243*
Brook, R. H., 274, *280*
Brown, D. C., 184, *194*
Brown, G. W., 184, *194*
Bruch, M. A., 25, *32*
Buckley, W., 153, *166*
Burr, W. R., 166, *167*
Bushell, D., 88, 91, *94*
Byrd, F. M., 26, *32*

California, Department of Public Health, 207, *219*
Carnegie-Mellon Report, 6, *33*
Caro, F. G., 130, *136*
Carr, A., 14, *37*
Cassel, J., 178, 179, 184, *194*
Chapman, W., 278, *280*
Christensen, H. T., 166, *167*
Clark, D. L., 10, *36*
Clark, R. D., III, 14, *33*
Clarke, E. R., 184, *196*
Clausen, J. A., 187, 191, *194*
Clavan, S., 239, *243*
Cobb, S., 172, *196*
Coe, R. M., 250, 251, *256*
Cogswell, B. E., 23, *33* 163, 165, *167*, 237, 239, *243, 245,* 264, *281*
Cohen, H. L., 135, *136*
Cohen, S. I., 183, *194*
Cohn, N., 23, *33*, 264, *281*
Cole, S., 16, *33*, 83, *94*
Collette, J., 7, *35*
Comarr, A. A., 17, *32*
Comer, R. J., 9, *33*
Cooley, W. W., 190, *195*
Coonley, R., 16, *32*, 264, *280*
Cottrell, L., 249, 252, *256*
Cyphers, G., 11, *32*

Davidson, T. N., 190, *194*
Davies, R., 184, *195*
Davis, E., 11, *37*
Davis, F., 8, 20, *33*, 60, 62, 67, *70*, 165, *167*
Dean, D. G., 27, *33*
DeFleur, M. L., 11, *37*
DeLateur, B., 82, 90, 91, *94*
Deutsch, C. P., 10, *33*
Devine, B., 187, *195*
DiAngelo, E., 6, 10, 22, *33*, 272, *281*
DiCara, I., 99, *135*
Dienelt, M. N., 184, *198*
Dinitz, S., 226, *243*
Dion, K., 13, *33*, 264, *281*
Dohrenwend, B. P., 169, 172, 178, 179, 183, *194*
Dohrenwend, B. S., 169, 172, 178, 179, 183, *194*

Drew, E. B., 266, 274, *281*
Dubey, S. N., 235, *243*
Duncan, B., 173, 175, *194*
Duncan, O. D., 172, 173, 175, 193, *194, 195*
Dunham, H. W., 169, 172, *195*
Dupey, H. J., 187, *195*
Durkheim, 251, *256*
Duvall, E. M., 147, 166, *167*

Eckland, B. K., 173, 175, 186, 189, 190, 193, *194, 195*
Eddy, E. M., 43, *55*
Ehrenreich, B., 265, *281*
Ehrenreich, J., 265, *281*
Eisenstein, V. W., 166, *167*
Elder, G. H., 173, 190, 191, *195*
Eliahu, Y., 129, *137*
Elling, R. H., 277, *281*
Engel, A., 187, *195*
Erikson, K., 57, 58, *70*
Etzioni, A., 262, *281*

Fain, T., 66, 67, *70*
Farina, A., 8, *33*
Faris, R., 172, *195*
Featherman, D. L., 170, 173, 175, 193, *194, 195*
Filipczak, J., 135, *136*
Fink, S. L., 10, 23, *34*, 264, *281*
Fitzgerald, E., 224, *243*
Flanagan, J. C., 190, *195*
Fleisher, B., 263, *281*
Fordyce, W., 82, 90, 91, *94*, 112, *136*
Fowler, R., 82, 90, 91, *94*
Freeman, H. E., 171, *195*, 259, *281*
French, J. R. P., Jr., 27, *34*
Fried, M., 206, *219*
Friedson, E., 59, 66, *70*, 234, *243*, 248, *256*
Friesen, E. W., 67, *70*

Galbraith, J. K., 208, *219*
Gans, H. J., 25, *34*, 263, *281*
Gaspar, E., 129, *137*
Gersuny, C., 234, *243*
Gil, D. G., 259, *281*
Glaser, B. G., 139, *167*

Glasser, M. A., 264, *281*
Glazier, W. H., 3, 29, *34*, 251, *256*, 261, *281*
Glick, P. C., 147, 166, *167*
Goffman, E., 8, *34*, 59, 60, *70*, 234, *243*
Goldiamond, I., 99, 105, 106, 115, 117, 134, *136*
Goldston, J. A., 10, *33*
Goodall, K., 99, *136*
Gottlieb, E., 129, *137*
Gove, W., 63, 66, 67, *70*
Graham, D. T., 184, *195*
Green, M. J., 271, *282*
Green, P. S., 232, *244*
Groenewald, P. T., 134, *137*
Guetta, B., 54, *54*

Haber, L. D., 4, 5, *34*, 65, *70*, 205, *219*, 261, *282*
Hajioff, J., 183, *194*
Hake, D., 80, *94*
Hallenbeck, P. N., 10, *34*
Haller, A., 173, 175, 186, 190, 193, *194, 199*
Hamilton, B. B., 6, 10, 22, *33*, 272, *281*
Handel, G., 145, 166, *167*
Hanks, J., 67, *70*
Hanks, L. M., 67, *70*
Hansen, C. E., 238, *244*
Hansen, D. A., 166, *167*
Harford, R., 106, *136*
Hastorf, A. H., 9, *35*, 67, *70*
Haug, M. R., 40, 54, *54*, 177, *195*, 216, *220*, 225, 230, 233, *244, 245*
Hauser, R. M., 173, 193, *196*
Hawkins, N. G., 184, *195, 196*
Hefferline, R. F., 106, *136*
Heise, D. R., 193, *196*
Heisel, J. S., 183, *196*
Hendershot, C. H., 99, *136*
Herbert, L., 134, *136*
Hess, R. D., 145, 166, *167*
Hesse, S., 11, *32*
Hesselbart, S., 11, *32*
Hill, R., 146, 156, 166, *167, 168*
Hirshfield, D. S., 209, *220*
Hodge, R. W., 177, 193, *196*
Hodges, H. E., 62, *71*

Hoffman, L., 166, *168*
Holland, C. H., 8, *33*
Hollingshead, A. B., 172, 179, 184, *198*
Holmes, T. H., 183, 184, *195, 196, 197, 198, 200*
Holz, W. C., 115, *136*
Horowitz, I. L., 262, *280*
Hovneh, A., 129, *137*
Howell, P., 63, *70*
Hrubec, Z., 26, *34*
Huppert, E., 129, *137*
Hutchinson, R., 80, *94*
Hyde, R. W., 231, *244*

Illich, I., 275, *282*

Jackson, E. F., 172, *196*
Jackson, J. K., 145, *168*
Jackson, S. R., 264, *282*
Jaco, E. G., 171, 172, 178, 179, 185, *196*
Jacobs, M. A., 184, *199*
Jacobson, J., 88, 91, *94*
Jaffe, L. L., 210, 211, *220*
Joffe, J. R., 184, *196*
Johnson, W. G., 10, *36*, 264, *283*
Johnston, L. D., 190, *194*
Jolly, A., 80, *94*
Jones, J. S. 47, *54*
Jordan, J., 67, *70*

Kagan, J., 191, *196*
Kahn, R. L., 190, *194*
Kaim-Caudle, P. R., 259, *282*
Kamiya, J., 99, *135*
Kantor, M., 171, *196*
Kasl, S., 172, *196*
Kassebaum, G. G., 17, *34,* 83, *94*
Katona, G., 12, *34*
Katz, S., 273, *282*
Keane, R., 11, *32*
Keenan, B., 106, *136*
Keith, R. A., 237, *244,* 276, *282*
Kellert, S. R., 230, *244*
Kendrick, J., 234, *244*
Kent, J. A., 276, *282*
Kerr, N., 42, *54,* 112, *137*
Kimmel, D. C., 13, *34*
Kish, L., 147, 166, *168*

Kjaer, G., 184, *198*
Kleck, R., 9, *35*, 67, *70*
Kleiner, R. J., 169, 172, *197*
Klerman, G. L., 184, *198*
Kohn, M. L., 169, *197*
Komaroff, A. L., 183, *197*
Kosa, J., 206, *220*
Kossowsky, R., 129, *137*
Kramer, B., 171, *199*
Krasner, L., 87, *95*
Krause, E., 43, *55*, 203, 215, 216, *220*
Kriegel, L., 46, *55*
Kubler-Ross, E., 18, 23, *34*
Kuhn, M. H., 7, *35*
Kunce, J. T., 25, *32*
Kunkel, J. H., 24, *35*
Kutner R., 231, *244*
Kutscher, A. H., 14, *37*
Kuvlesky, W. P., 26, *32*, 264, *282*

Laing, R. D., 166, *168*
Land, K. C., 193, *197*
Langner, T. S., 172, 179, 180, 183, 187, *197, 199*
Lansing, J. B., 147, 166, *168*
Lazarus, R. S., 14, *36*
Leary, P. A., 266, 273, *282*
Lefton, M., 234, *243*
Lehmann, J., 82, 90, 91, *94*
Lejeune, R., 16, *33*, 83, *94*
Lemert, E., 57, 59, *71*
Lenhausen, D., 54, *55*
Lerner, M., 206, *220*
Levi, L., 179, 184, *197*
Levine, S., 171, 179, *195, 197*
Levinson, H. S., 6, *37*
Levinson Gerontological Policy Institute, 129–130, *137*
Leviton, G. L., 47, 48, *55*, 77, *94*, 237, *244*
Lieberman, B., 19, *35*
Liebow, E., 203, *220*
Lindenthal, J. J., 184, *198*
Lippitt, R., 166, *168*
Lipset, S. M., 188, 193, *197*
Litman, T. J., 11, *35*
Livson, N., 191, *197*
Lowe, G., 62, *71*

Lowe, J. C., 13, *36*
Lubove, R., 209, *220*
Ludwig, E. G., 7, *35*, 49, *55*, 273, *282*
Lynn, K. D., 248, *256*

McDaniel, J. W., 26, 28, *35*
McHugh, P., 24, *35*
McLaughlin, B., 28, *35*
McMichael, J. K., 10, *35*
McPartland, T. S., 7, *35*
Malinowski, B., 16, *35*
Malone, W. S., 207, 210, *220*
Margolin, R. J., 238, *244*
Margulec, I., 129, *137*
Martin, J., 45, 50, *55*
Masuda, M., 183, 184, *197, 200*
Mayer, R. G., 99, *138*
Mayers, M. R., 207, *220*
Mechanic, D., 170, *197*, 268, 271, *283*
Mendick, M. T., 190, *194*
Messinger, S., 65, *71*
Metro-Goldwyn-Mayer, 149, 166, *168*
Meyer, M., 184, *198*
Meyer, R., 7, *35*
Meyers, H. B., 271, *283*
Michael, J. L., 99, 112, *137*
Michael, S. T., 172, 179, 180, 183, 187, *197, 199*
Michener, C., 231, *244*
Miller, J. G., 275, *283*
Miller, N. E., 99, *135*
Miller, S. M., 259, *283*
Mills, C. W., 202, *220*
Mills, D., 248, *256*
Mintz, N., 172, *198*
Mishler, E. G., 169, 172, 179, *197, 198*
Molinaro, L., 131, *137*
Monat, A., 14, *36*
Money, J., 19, *38*
Montgomery, P. L., 54, *55*
Moore, J. W., 13, *36*
Moore, W. E., 230, *244*
Morgan, J. N., 264, *283*
Morison, R. S., 3, *36*
Morris, R., 129, 130, *136*
Moynihan, D. P., 208, *220*
Mozden, P. J., 21, *36*
Murphy, E., 10, *36*, 264, *283*

Murphy, H., 172, *198*
Myers, J. K., 171, 184, *198*
Myerson, L., 112, *137*

Nagasawa, R. H., 24, *35*
Nagi, S. Z., 5, 10, 22, *36*, 171, 186, *198*, 228, *244*, 273, *283*
Nathanson, N. L., 210, 211, *220*
National Commission on' State Workmen's Compensation Laws, 205, 211, 212, *221*
Neugarten, B. L., 13, *36*
Neuringer, C., 99, *137*
Norton, M. L., 252, *256*
Nye, F., 166, 168

O'Brien, M., 22, *36*
O'Donnell, E. J., 276, *283*
Ohlendorf, G., 173, 175, *199*
Olson, E. V., 120, *137*
Ono, H., 9, *35*, 67, *70*
Opler, M., 187, *199*
Orne, M. T., 105, *137*
Orzack, L. H., 40, 41, *55*

Page, J. A., 22, *36*
Parker, S., 169, 172, *197*
Parsekian, N. J., 207, *221*
Parsons, T., 82, *95*, 158, *168*
Paykel, E. S., 184, *198*
Penrose, R. J. J., 183, *198*
Pepper, M. P., 184, *198*
Peretz, D., 14, *37*
Perrucci, R., 189, *198*
Peskin, H., 191, *197*
Peterson, S. G., 6, *36*
Pfautz, H. W., 231, *244*
Piliavin, J. A., 9, *33*
Pinkerfield, E., 129, *137*
Piven, F., 235, *245*
Plant, M. L., 207, 210, *220*
Portes, A., 173, 175, 186, 190, 193, 194, *199*
Premack, D., 78, *95*, 112, *137*
Psomopoulos, P., 50, *55*
Pugh, T. F., 171, *199*

Querec, L., 187, *195*

Race, W. B., 41, 43, 44, 54, *55*
Rahe, R. H., 183, 184, *196*, *198*
Raven, B., 27, *34*
Reeder, L., 171, *195*
Rein, J., 259, *283*
Reissman, F., 259, *283*
Rennie, T., 187, *199*
Ring, K., 8, *33*
Ritter, B., 11, *32*, 82, *94*
Rodgers, R. H., 156, *168*
Roemer, M. I., 270, 271, *283*
Rogler, L., 172, 179, 184, *198*
Rokeach, M., 11, *36*
Romano-V., O. I., 275, *283*
Rose, A. M., 166, *168*
Rosenberg, P., 231, *244*
Rossi, P. H., 266, *283*
Roth, J., 43, *55*
Rotter, J. B., 28, *36*
Rumbaugh, D. M., 8, *36*
Rutzen, S. R., 21, *36*
Ryan, W., 216, *221*

Safilios-Rothschild, C., 4, 10, 28, *36*, 40, 42, 43, 45, 49, 51, 53, *55*, 59, *71*, 183, 187, *198*, 238, *245*
St. Clair, A., 212, *221*
Sampson, H., 65, *71*
Satir, V., 145, *168*
Sawyer, G. P., 266, *283*
Saxon, B., 129, *137*
Scaer, R., 134, *137*
Scanlon, J., 187, *195*
Scheff, T., 234, *245*
Schneider, C., 134, *137*
Schoenberg, B., 14, *37*
Schorr, A. L., 259, *283*
Schrag, P. G., 278, *283*
Schuman, H., 11, *32*
Schuster, C. R., 99, *138*
Schwartz, D., 172, *198*
Scotch, N., 169, 179, *197*
Scott, R., 43, *56*, 59, 66, *71*, 262, *284*
Secretary's Committee on Work in America, 207, 218, *221*
Sewell, W. H., 173, 175, 186, 190, 193, *199*
Shapiro, D., 99, *135*

Sharples, N., 120–121, *137*
Sheldon, E., 249, 252, *256*
Sherman, J., 8, *33*
Sherwood, C. C., 259, *281*
Shostak, A. B., 235, *245*
Sidman, J., 112, *137*
Silberstein, J., 129, *137*
Sirageldin, I. A., 264, *283*
Sjoquist, D. L., 263, *284*
Skinner, B. F., 98, 99, 105, 135, *138*
Skipper, J. K., Jr., 10, *34*
Smith, H., 276, *282*
Smith, M., 184, *198*
Smith, R., 65, *70*
Solomon, L., 171, *199*
Somers, A. R., 275, 276, *284*
Somers, H. M., 276, *284*
Spaeth, J. L., 173, *199*
Spilken, A. Z., 183, 184, *199*
Spodick, D. H., 21, *37*
Srole, L., 187, *199*
Stevens, R., 261, 269, 272, *284*
Stevenson, I., 184, *195*
Stoddard, L. T., 112, *137*
Stoya, J., 99, *135*
Straus, M. A., 145, *168*
Straus, R., 226, *245*
Strauss, A. L., 139, *167*, 268, *284*
Strodtbeck, F. L., 145, *168*
Stroud, M. W., III, 230, *245*
Strumpel, B., 12, *34*
Stuart, R., 88, *95*
Suchman, E. A., 171, *199*
Sudderth, J., 234, *244*
Sudnow, D., 234, *245*
Sullivan, M. M., 276, *283*
Sulzer, B., 99, *138*
Sussman, M. B., 40, 54, *54*, 177, *195*,
    214, 216, *220, 221*, 225, 230, 233,
    237, 238, 239, 241, *243, 244, 245,
    246*
Swarts, P. S., 6, 10, 22, *33*, 272, *281*

Taft, E. A., 26, *32*
Terrace, H. S., 112, *138*
Terrell, K., 173, *199*
Tharp, R. G., 130, *138*

Thelen, M. H., 25, *32*
Thompson, T., 99, *138*
Thursz, D., 51, 52, *56*, 236, *246*
Torrey, E. F., 272, *284*
Towne, A., 232, *246*
Townes, R., 65, *71*
Treiman, D. J., 173, *199*
Triandis, H., 11, *37*
Truzzi, M., 41, *56*
Tseng, M. S., 266, 273, *282*
Turnbull, C., 7, *37*
Turner, R. J., 172, *199*

Ullmann, L. P., 87, *95*, 131, *138*
U.S., Bureau of Occupational Health
    and Safety, 207, *221*
U.S., Congress, 205, 208, *221*, 227,
    229, 232, 242, *246*, 264, 270, 278,
    284
U.S., Department of Health, Educa-
    tion and Welfare, 5, 6, *37*, 260, 266,
    267, *284*
U.S., Social Security Administration,
    270, *284*

Vance, E. T., 25, *37*
Vatter, E., 239, *243*
Viccaro, T., 11, *32*
Vogel, L. C., 260, *284*
Vollmer, H., 248, *256*

Wagenfeld, M. O., 172, *199*
Wahler, R., 88, *95*
Walster, E., 13, *33*, 264, *280, 281*
Walzer, H., 231, *244*
Wan, T. T. H., 261, 274, *285*
Warner, L. G., 11, *37*
Waxler, N., 172, *198*
Wechsler, H., 171, *199*
Wennergren, B., 277, *285*
Went, F., 125, *138*
Westergaard, J. H., 268, *285*
Wetzel, R. J., 130, *138*
White, K. L., 3, *37*
Whitten, E. B., 215, *221*
Wildausky, A., 205, *220*
Wilder, C. S., 188, *199*

Wilder, M. H., 188, *200*
Willhelm, S. M., 268, *285*
Williams, R., Jr., 12, *37*
Williams, T. R., 12, *37*
Wolf, D., 172, 179, *200*
Wolf, M., 91, *94*
Wolff, I. S., 42, *56*
Word, L. E., 14, *33*
Wright, D., 11, *32*
Wrong, D. H., 11, *37*

Wyler, A. R., 184, *200*
Wynn, F. H., 6, *37*

Yehia, M. A., 49, *55*
York, R. H., 231, *244*

Zahn, E., 12, *34*, 264, *285*
Zahn, M. A., 8, *38*
Zola, I. K., 206, *220*
Zubin, J., 19, *38*

Subject Index

Able-bodied
reactions to disabled, 61–64
social interaction with disabled, 7–11
Achievement: as American value, 12
Advisory boards: effectiveness of, 52
Age
adjustment to disability and, 22–23
disability related to, 5, 188
norms and, 13
Alcoholism: normalization of, 62
Alienation: of disabled, 44–45
Ambiguity
interdisciplinary collaboration and, 249–250
at onset of disability, 14–16
Aphasia: emotional effects of, 122–123
Architectural barriers: effects of removal of, 50
Artificial limbs: ranking of criteria for, 120–121
Attitudes
effect of behavior on, 11–12
behavioral approach and, 82
social role disability and, 203–204
Avoidance: of disability, 79–80

Beauty: value placed on, 13, 264
Behavior
contingencies governing, 99–100
awareness of, 106
disability-inappropriate, extinction of, 81–84
effect of attitudes on, 11–12
behavioral approach and, 82
emotion related to, 102–103

establishment of new patterns of, 114
experimental analysis of, 99
verbal versus performance, 81–82
Behavioral approach, 77–85, 87–88, 99
adjustment to disability and, 24, 74–75, 81
advantages of, 93
case illustrations of, 85–87
ethical issues in, 89–90
maintenance of performance in, 90–91
Behavioral contract, 28, 277
Behavioral disruption: stimulus change and, 107–108
Behavioral science: contributions of, to rehabilitation, 30
Behavior pharmacology, 99
Biofeedback, 99
Biopsychological disability, 203
Black lung disease: compensation for, 205
Braces
cost of, 128
failure to wear, 120

Cancer: impact on socialization, 22
Car: inability to drive, 6
Causal process modeling, 184–185, 190
Client advocacy, 237–238
legislative support for, 236
Consumerism: in rehabilitation, 277–278
Continence: social pressures for, 14–15

Contingency management. *See* Behavioral approach
Contract
  behavioral, 28, 277
  in rehabilitation legislation, 228
Corporations
  and opposition to compensation, 210–211
  political power of, 209
Cost
  of health care, 231, 270–271
  of industrial injury, 208–209
  of rehabilitation, 272–273
  of social programing, 126–131
Cost/benefit model
  economic, 229–231
  noneconomic, 229
  social policies and, 266 267
Counteraggression
  following disablement, 80
  reaction to, 80–81
Crime: utility function of, 263
Cultural differences: interdisciplinary, 249

Data analysis: in family studies, 145–146
Delicate Balance, A (Albee), 149–151
Demonstrations: implementation of, 231–233
Dependency: in severely disabled, 7
Depression: causes of, 122
Developmental stages: of adjustment to disability, 23
Deviance
  disability as, 17–20, 59–60
  establishment of, 68
  primary, 57
    disability and, 68
  secondary, 57
Disability
  acute, 20
  adjustment to, 74–75
    behavioral approach to, 24, 81–84
    pressure for, 40–43
    stages in, 23
  chronic, 21
  definition of, 171, 203

  as deviance, 17–20, 59–60
  family accommodation to, 155–165
  function served by, 263
  impact of, 3–4
    initial, 14, 16
  incidence of, 4–5, 22
  inducement of, 206–207
  lack of preparation for, 3
  legal, 203–205
  prevalence of, 4–5, 186–187, 261
  sick role acceptance and duration of, 17–20, 59–60
  social status and, 172, 178–183, 189
  unit of analysis in studies of, 26
  visibility of, 21
    interpersonal relationships and, 65–66
    prejudice of disabled and, 45–46
    treatment by able-bodied and, 8–9
Disabled persons
  as minority group, 39–43
  and participation in decision-making, 236–238
  social distance between professionals and, 47 52
  treatment by others of, 3
  as unit of analysis, 26
Disease, occupational, 204–205
Disease model, 76 77
Divorce: disability and, 10

Education: disability days and, 188
Educational institutions: in status attainment, 175
Emotion
  contingencies and, 122–124
  and relationship to behavior, 102–103
Employment. *See also* Work
  social class and, 22
Entry boundaries: permeability of, 162–163
Environment
  dependence on, 118–119
  for family research, 145
  interaction of disabled with, 25
  for rehabilitation, 48, 239–240, 275–276

and behavioral approach, 88, 91–92
Erection: psychogenic and reflexogenic, 17
Expectations: of family, 10–11

Family
    and accommodation to disability, 155–165
    art in study of, 148–155
    impact of disability on, 10–11, 21
    methodology for study of, 145–147
    social interaction with, 9
    in treatment, 238–242
    and behavioral process, 83–84, 91–92
    as unit of analysis, 26, 145
Family development framework: limitations of, 147
Family interaction: schizophrenia–social class linkage and, 171–172
Family medicine, 237
Family system, 153–154
Fee-for-service payment: impact on health care delivery, 269–271
Frustration: schizophrenia–social class linkage and, 171–172
Funding
    politics of, 205–206, 215–216
    in rehabilitation and industry, 223–225

Goals
    adjustment of, 24–25
    of family, 160
    in problem-solving approach, 24
    of rehabilitation, 263–269
Group interaction, 232

Halfway houses, 276
Homebound work programs, 231
Homosexuality: legal status of, 204
Hospitalization; length of, 230; mental, 66

Impotence: reaction to, 16–17, 19

Income
    disability days and, 187–188
    loss of, 10
Independence, 118–119
    value placed on, 264
Individualization
    in programing, 132
    of rehabilitation process, 49–50
Institutionalization
    contingencies and, 105, 131
    deviant identity and, 58–59
    impact of, on disabled, 60
    trend toward, 275
Instruction, programed, 99, 132
Interdisciplinary collaboration, 247–248
    barriers to, 249–251
    need for, 248–249
    trends toward, 251–252
Interpersonal reactions, 61–62, 65
    disengagement from, 63
    establishment of deviance by, 68
    normalization of, 62–63
Interpersonal stress, 180
Isolation
    of disabled, 63
    schizophrenia–social class linkage and, 171–172

Juvenile detention facilities: closing of, 275

Labeling theory. *See* Societal reaction theory
Learning, programed, 99
Learning model, 77–79
Legal disability, 203, 204
    politics of, 204–205
Legislation
    basis for, 225–226
    emphasis of, on evaluation, 229
    interdisciplinary collaboration and, 248
    occupational disease and, 204–205
    research implementation and, 232–233
Leisure activities: in behavioral approach, 92

Life: extension of, 3
Life changes: illness onset related to, 183–184
Lobbying: compensation and, 205, 208, 210
Longitudinal data: value of, 185

Marriage: impact of disability on, 10
Material goods: as American value, 12
Medicine
　emphases in, 29
　organization of, 269–273
Mental health: impact of disability on, 7
Mental hospitalization: redefinition of problem by, 66
Mental illness
　poverty and, 207
　prevalence of, 187
Milieu therapy: costs of, 231
Minority group(s)
　availability of rehabilitation to, 268
　disabled as, 39–43
Mobility
　limited
　　architectural barriers and, 50
　　impact of, 6–8
　occupational, 188–189
　social, 172
Monkeys: treatment of disabled, 8
Morality
　sick role acceptance and, 17–18
　values and, 12–13
Morphogenesis, 153
　in family accommodation to disability, 161
Morphostasis, 153
Motivational model, 76–77, 84
　limitations of, 92–93
　maintenance of behavior and, 90

Negotiation: in socialization process, 27–28
Neuroticism, 150
Normalization: consequences of, 62–63

Norms
　adjustment of, 20
　age-specific, 13

Occupational diseases
　compensation for, 211–212
　legislation regarding, 204–205
　prevalence of, 207
Occupational mobility, 188–189
Occupations: availability of, for disabled, 41–42
Operant approach, 77–79. *See also* Programing
Optimism: of Americans, 12

Pain: spouse's response to, 91–92
Paraprofessionals: in programing, 130
Personal stress, 180
Pesticides, cancer-causing, 207
Physical function: disability in terms of, 4
Pneumoconiosis: compensation for, 205
Political action: by disabled, 216–217
Poverty: disability and, 206–207
Power relations
　effect on disabled, 202
　interdisciplinary, 249
Pregnancy: as disability, 204
Premack principle, 78
Professionalization: inhibition of collaboration by, 250
Professional training
　inhibition of collaboration by, 251
　interdisciplinary, 253–255
　of physicians, 272
　to promote collaboration, 252
Programing, 99, 110–117
　cost of, 126–131
　targets in, 112
Public transportation: inaccessibility of, 6–7
Punishment: disability as, 79–80

Race: alcoholism and, 62
Radiation poisoning, 207

Rehabilitation
accessibility of, 63–64, 214–216, 268, 273
alternatives to present system in, 275–278
contingencies of participation in, 104
cost of, 128–129
entry into, 75
environment for, 48, 239–240, 275–276
evaluation of, 51–52, 229–231
goals of, 263–269
measures of success for, 273–274
opposition to, 201–202
responsibility for, 48, 49, 51–52
as socialization process, 20–25
as social policy issue, 261–263
utilization of, 269
Rehabilitation facilities: institutional characteristics of, 69
Rehabilitation professionals
evaluation and, 230
power of, 234–235
social distance between clients and, 47–52
reduction of, 237
stereotyping by, 40–43, 234
Reinforcement
in behavioral approach, 78–79, 81
and change in rehabilitation, 75
in natural environment, 92
in programing, 111
response to withdrawal of, 81
Renal dialysis: impact on socialization, 21
Research
areas for, 30–31
impact of, on medicine, 29
implementation of, 231–233
Resocialization: values and norms and, 14–20
Rights: acceptance of disability and, 42
Role adjustments
acceptance of sick role and, 83
mobility limitations and, 6–11
Role ambiguity: interdisciplinary collaboration and, 249–250

Role flexibility: in family accommodation to disability, 39–43, 161–162

Schizophrenia: social status related to, 169–170, 171–172
Secondary gain: of sick role, 83
Self-definitions, 46–47
implications of, for rehabilitation, 47–53
Self-esteem: negative influences on, 43–44
Self-image: impact of disability on, 7
Sex role flexibility, 162
Sexual behavior: values concerning, 19
Sexual dysfunction: relationship with spouse and, 9
Sheltered workshops: conditions in, 217–218
Sick role
acceptance of, 82–83
consequences of, 17–19
Snake phobias: reduction of, 11
Social disintegration: resocialization and, 24
Social distance
between expert and client, 47–52
reduction of, 237
Social interaction
between able-bodied and disabled, 7–11
development of skills in, 92
mobility limitations and, 7
permeability of entry boundaries and, 162–163
reciprocal nature of, 25
value placed on, 264
Socialization, 5–6
agents of, 26–28
ambiguity and, 14, 15
of congenitally and noncongenitally disabled, 42
impact of disability on, 6
modification of, by client-consumer, 26–28
rehabilitation process as, 20–25
values and norms and, 11–13
Social movement, 216–217, 233–238
development of, 45–46

facilitation of, 53
Social policies, 257–258
    application of, to rehabilitation,
        261–263
    definition of, 259
    influence of, on social programs,
        258–260
Social readjustment: disability in-
    ducement and, 183
Social role disability, 203–204
Social Security: legal disability and, 205
Social status. *See also* Status attainment
    model
    availability of services and, 268
    disability and, 22, 169–170, 171–172
    physical illness and, 206
    rehabilitation outcome and, 22, 43
    and uses of construct, 177–178
Societal reactions
    formal, 61–62
    consequences of, 64–68
Societal reaction theory, 57–59
    application of, to disability, 59–61
    inadequacies of, 68–69
Society: as unit of analysis, 26
Sounder, 149, 151–153, 154–155
Specialization, 250–251
Status. *See also* Social status
    deviant, 58
    of disabled, 42–43
    interdisciplinary differences in, 249
Status attainment model, 173–177
    disability and, 172, 178–183, 189
    explanatory power of, 186
Status inconsistency: disability and,
    172
Stereotyping
    effect on disabled, 43–45
    by professionals, 40–43, 234
Stigma
    of cancer, 22
    of disability, 8, 60
    societal reaction and, 66–67
Stimulus change: behavioral disrup-
    tion and, 107–108
Stress
    in etiology of disability, 179–183

schizophrenia–social class linkage
    and, 172
types of, 180
Structural stress, 180
Subculture, deviant, 58–59
Success: as American value, 12
Systems theory: for family studies,
    146–147

Target
    in programing, 110, 111–112, 125
    establishment of, 112
Transportation: inaccessibility of, 6–7
Treatment: impact on socialization,
    21–22

Values
    adjustment of, 20, 24–25
    in American society, 12–13
    influence on socialization, 11–13
    rehabilitation goals and, 264
    sick role acceptance and, 17–19
    social role disability and, 203–204
Voluntary organizations: motivations
    of, 217
Volunteers: in treatment, 231
Voucher system, 277

Withdrawal: from disabled, 63
Women: restriction of role of, 41–42
Work
    effects of disability on, 187–188
    as goal of rehabilitation, 266, 267
    in rehabilitation programs, 217–218
    as reinforcement, 92
    social interaction and, 9
Work Incentive Program (WIN): criti-
    cism of, 214–215
Workmen's compensation, 209–210
    amount of benefits under, 211
    eligibility for, 211–212
    legal disability and, 205
    lobbies against, 205, 208, 210
    for occupational disease, 205
    rehabilitation under, 212–213

CONTEMPORARY COMMUNITY HEALTH SERIES

CHILD CARE WORK WITH EMOTIONALLY DISTURBED CHILDREN
Genevieve W. Foster, Karen VanderVen et al.

CHILDREN IN JEOPARDY
A Study of Abused Minors and Their Families
Elizabeth Elmer

CLIFFORD W. BEERS
Advocate for the Insane
Norman Dain

CULTURE AND CURING
Anthropological Perspectives on Traditional Medical Beliefs and Practices
Peter Morley and Roy Wallis, Editors

THE DEEPENING SHADE
Psychological Aspects of Life-Threatening Illness
Barbara M. Sourkes

DISCOVERING SUICIDE
Studies in the Social Organization of Sudden Death
J. Maxwell Atkinson

THE DOCTOR TREE
Developmental Stages in the Growth of Physicians
Ralph N. Zabarenko and Lucy M. Zabarenko

FRAGILE FAMILIES, TROUBLED CHILDREN
The Aftermath of Infant Trauma
Elizabeth Elmer

A GUIDE TO MENTAL HEALTH SERVICES
Edward T. Heck, Angel G. Gomez, and George L. Adams

HANDICAP
A Study of Physically Handicapped Children and Their Families
Joan K. McMichael

HEALTH CARE IN THE EUROPEAN COMMUNITY
Alan Maynard

HOME AND HOSPITAL PSYCHIATRIC TREATMENT
An Interdisciplinary Experiment
Fred R. Fenton et al.

LITERATURE AND MEDICINE
An Annotated Bibliography
Joanne Trautmann and Carol Pollard

A MIND THAT FOUND ITSELF
Clifford W. Beers

THE PSYCHIATRIC HALFWAY HOUSE
A Handbook of Theory and Practice
Richard D. Budson

RACISM AND MENTAL HEALTH
Essays
Charles V. Willie, Bernard M. Kramer, and Bertram S. Brown, Editors

SOCIAL SKILLS AND MENTAL HEALTH
Peter Trower, Bridget Bryant, and Michael Argyle

THE SOCIOLOGY OF PHYSICAL DISABILITY
AND REHABILITATION
Gary L. Albrecht, Editor

THE STYLE AND MANAGEMENT OF A PEDIATRIC PRACTICE
Lee W. Bass and Jerome H. Wolfson

In cooperation with the Institute on Human Values in Medicine:

MEDICINE AND RELIGION
Strategies of Care
Donald W. Shriver, Editor

NOURISHING THE HUMANISTIC IN MEDICINE
Interactions with the Social Sciences
William R. Rogers and David Barnard, Editors